D1520297

Feeding Infants
in Four Societies

FEEDING INFANTS IN FOUR SOCIETIES

Causes and Consequences of Mothers' Choices

Edited by **Beverly Winikoff,
Mary Ann Castle,
and Virginia Hight Laukaran**

Under the auspices of The Population Council

Contributions in Family Studies, Number 14

GREENWOOD PRESS
New York • Westport, Connecticut • London

363.82
W 727f

Library of Congress Cataloging-in-Publication Data

Feeding infants in four societies : causes and consequences of
  mothers' choices / edited by Beverly Winikoff, Mary Ann Castle,
  Virginia Hight Laukaran under the auspices of the Population
  Council.
    p. cm. — (Contributions in family studies, ISSN 0147-1023 ;
no. 14)
    Bibliography: p.
    Includes index.
    ISBN 0-313-25798-1 (lib. bdg. : alk. paper)
    1. Infants—Developing countries—Nutrition—Cross-cultural
studies. 2. Mothers—Developing countries—Attitudes—Cross-
cultural studies. I. Winikoff, Beverly. II. Castle, Mary Ann.
III. Laukaran, V. H. (Virginia Hight) IV. Population Council.
V. Series.
RJ216.F43 1988
363.8'2—dc19   88-5672

British Library Cataloguing in Publication Data is available.

Library of Congress Catalog Card Number: 88-5672
ISBN: 0-313-25798-1
ISSN: 0147-1023

First published in 1988

Greenwood Press, Inc.
88 Post Road West, Westport, Connecticut 06881

Printed in the United States of America

The paper used in this book complies with the
Permanent Paper Standard issued by the National
Information Standards Organization (Z39.48-1984).

10 9 8 7 6 5 4 3 2 1

To Our Children,

Hilary and Lindsay,

and

Anna Magdalena,

and

Anson

Contents

viii Contents

Tables and Figures

Figures

Preface

An abundant literature on the worldwide "decline in breastfeeding" has appeared in recent years in medical, sociological and even political writings. Many authors have tried to identify the causes and possible consequences of "less breastfeeding" in poor countries. Occasionally, discussions have centered on whether any declines in breastfeeding have, in fact, occurred at all!

When the study described in this book was undertaken, the major debate was whether or not the advertising practices of infant formula manufacturers were principally responsible for less breastfeeding. The intensity of the argument succeeded in focusing worldwide attention on the potential deleterious effects of bottlefeeding in places with poor environmental conditions. Consequently, in an effort to protect breastfeeding, the World Health Organization developed an International Code of Marketing of Breastmilk Substitutes which was adopted by many countries.

The urgent nature of the discussion of breastfeeding declines also resulted in an oversimplification of the problem, and its more subtle aspects were neglected. For example, the actual meaning of a "decline" in breastfeeding was not really addressed. It is reasonable to assume that "decline" refers to fewer women beginning to breastfeed. Yet, clearly, it is possible for important changes to take place in the <u>duration</u> of breastfeeding without concomitant changes occurring in the number of mothers who initiate breastfeeding. Sensitivity has developed only lately to the particular changes in breastfeeding that may be produced by various influences, such as marketing of commercial infant foods, increased participation of women in the labor force, modern Western medical practices, and cultural predisposition to early supplementation, among others.

Much less discussion has occurred, however, about what may prove to be the crucially important issue: identification, not only of breastfeeding declines, but of changes in patterns of breastfeeding and infant feeding in general. In fact, this study was designed to describe in detail infant feeding practices in four cities of the developing world in the early 1980s. In order to achieve a richer appreciation of the meaning of infant feeding patterns in particular areas, we used several different methodologies to gain a picture of how mothers feed their infants--not simply whether or not they breastfeed them. Of course, the data represent findings from one point in time and cannot illuminate the issue of how much, if at all, feeding practices have changed. By viewing data from these urban studies in the context of information about infant feeding in rural areas, however, it is possible to get an idea of the extent to which infant feeding may have changed over time. Certainly, these surveys can be used as baselines against which other descriptive work may be compared in the years ahead.

Both breastfeeding and supplementation were of critical importance to this study, as were the factors that might influence the type and timing of feeding of young children. It was our hope that a complete picture of the details of infant feeding and the circumstances in which mothers and their children were living would give an idea of the socioeconomic correlates of different types of infant feeding patterns. For this reason, the study focuses on a broader view of women, children and their environment and suggests directions in which to look for causes of change. It also highlights potential areas for policy and program development to improve infant feeding practices and, consequently, infant health.

The work reported in this volume is the product of the labor of many individuals and the cooperation of many institutions. Parts of the endeavor were carried out at the Population Council and Columbia University in New York City, at Cornell University in Ithaca, New York, Boston University, Boston, Massachusetts, and Trost Associates, Norwalk, Connecticut. A substantial amount of work was carried out at the field sites and local institutions: Javeriana University, Bogotá, Colombia; Mahidol School of Public Health, Bangkok, Thailand; Diponegoro University, Semarang, Indonesia; Central Bureau of Statistics and African Medical and Research Foundation, Nairobi, Kenya. The overall project was managed by the Population Council.

There is no doubt that the work could not have been completed without the cooperation of all of these groups. The staff of the study are listed separately at the beginning of the volume, but thanks are due also to the secretaries, data coders, administrators, and others who made the study, data analysis, and report writing possible. Funding was provided by the Office of Nutrition of the U.S. Agency for International Development; the International Development Research Centre, Canada; the Rockefeller Foundation; and UNICEF.

We hope that, by sharing this information, we will clarify some issues regarding infant feeding in the developing world and also stimulate discussion of ways to increase women's opportunities for providing their children with an improved health environment. In a way, the entire effort has been one of consciousness raising, not only about the issues involved, but also about their complexity. It is our hope that this will be as true for the readers of this report as it has been for those of us who have worked on the project.

Beverly Winikoff

Personnel

PRINCIPAL INVESTIGATORS
   Beverly Winikoff, M.D., M.P.H.
   Michael C. Latham, O.B.E., M.B., M.P.H,
    D.T.M. and H., F.F.C.M.
   Giorgio Solimano, M.D.

CONSORTIUM STAFF
   Virginia Hight Laukaran, Dr.P.H.
   James E. Post, J.D., Ph.D.
   Penelope Van Esterik, Ph.D.
   Mary Ann Castle, Ph.D.
   Barry J. Cerf, Ph.D.
   Lily W. Lee, Ph.D.
   Robert A. Smith, Ph.D.
   Joanne Spicehandler, M.S.
   Yvette Bayoumy, B.A.
   Jane A. Campbell, B.F.A.
   Christina M. Dunstan
   Robert E. Sendek, B.A.
   David Trail, M.A.
   Trost Associates, Inc.

BANGKOK STAFF
   Debhanom Muangman, M.D., Dr.P.H.,
    Principal Investigator
   Somchai Durongdej, Dr.P.H., Project Director
   Thavisak Svetsreni, Ph.D.
   Thonglaw Dejthai, Ph.D
   Deemar, Inc.

BOGOTA STAFF
   Belen Samper de Paredes, M.A.,
    Principal Investigator
   Maria Eugenia Romero, M.A.
   Adela Morales de Look, M.S.

NAIROBI STAFF
   K. Okoth Agunda, Ph.D.,
    Principal Investigator
   Terry Elliott, M.S.
   John Kekovole, Ph.D.
   John Kigondu, M.D.
   Norman Scotney, Ph.D.
   Wambui Kogi
   Wamucii Njogu
   Margaret Okello
   Research Bureau (E.A.), Ltd.

SEMARANG STAFF
   Moeljono S. Trastotenojo, M.D.,
    Principal Investigator
   Fatimah Muis, M.D., M.Sc, Project Director
   Hariyono, Ph.D.
   Ag. Sumantri, Ph.D.
   Budioro, M.P.H.
   Nico Kana, Ph.D.
   Sahid Wiratno, Ph.D.
   P.T. In-Search Data

Feeding Infants
in Four Societies

1 Introduction

Virginia H. Laukaran, James E. Post,
Penny Van Esterik, and Beverly Winikoff

The recognition that breastfeeding has declined in many developing countries and the increased awareness of the importance of appropriate nutrition for child survival led to an interest in the factors that determine infant feeding practices. Better knowledge of the factors that influence feeding patterns under different social and economic conditions can guide the development and improvement of nutrition policies and programs to create circumstances more favorable to breastfeeding. Because of the increasing number of alternatives for infant feeding available in modernizing societies, mothers need culturally appropriate information to enable them to make better feeding choices. Clearer understanding of the forces that influence mothers is needed to begin to design such information.

The research that is described here was begun in 1979 and was designed to examine the determinants of infant feeding practices in cities in four developing countries. The study specifically focused on the role of health care systems, infant food marketing and distribution strategies, and women's labor force participation and the nature and magnitude of their contributions to infant feeding patterns. Information was also collected on a broad range of biological, cultural, social, and economic factors.

A research consortium, which included investigators at the Population Council, Columbia University, and Cornell University was formed to carry out the work. Studies were undertaken in collaboration with investigators in Bangkok, Thailand; Bogotà, Colombia; Nairobi, Kenya; and Semarang, Indonesia. An interdisciplinary research team was formed in each site to address each of three selected study components.[1] The first component was ethnographic field work, consisting of participant observation of infant feeding practices in the home and similar observation in health service settings. A second component was a cross-sectional household survey of mothers of infants, focused on infant feeding practices and their determinants. Finally, a market research component on the infant food market for each country included the analysis of the development and state of the infant food industry and the structure of the market. As part of the market research, a cross-sectional survey in each site included a module of questions designed to provide data on consumer behavior with regard to acquisition and use of infant food products. In each site, the study components were timed to ensure that the first phase of the study, the ethnographic field work, could be used as a basis for the development of the survey questionnaire for mothers and the research design for studies of the infant formula market.

STUDY TEAMS AND COLLABORATING INSTITUTIONS

As with any project of this magnitude, many individuals and organizations participated in the effort both in the United States and abroad. The principal investigators at the U.S.-based institutions were Beverly Winikoff of the Population Council, Michael Latham of Cornell University, and Giorgio Solimano of Columbia University. Senior staff and consultants to the consortium during the planning and data collection and preparation consisted of Virginia Hight Laukaran, an epidemiologist; Penny Van Esterik, an anthropologist; and James Post, an expert in marketing. In addition to these principal investigators and original staff, Mary Ann Castle, Barry Cerf, Lily Lee, Robert Smith, and David Trail participated in various aspects of the analysis and report preparation.

Under the direction of James Post, Trost Associates, Inc., of Norwalk, Connecticut, was responsible for collection and analysis of the marketing data. Trost Associates also established subcontracts with firms and individuals in each site to carry out the market audits and surveys. These firms and individuals are described in the discussion of the methods for the market research.

In each site, a principal investigator, together with senior staff and others took major responsibility for data collection, editing, and analysis. In Bangkok, the study was conducted at Mahidol University School of Public Health with Debhanom Muangman as the principal investigator. The study director was Somchai Durongdej. The ethnographic team in Bangkok was under the direction of Thavisak Svetsreni. Thonglaw Dejthai assisted with the research.

In Bogotá, the field work was conducted by Javeriana University under the leadership of Belen Samper de Paredes. The ethnographic studies were directed by Maria Eugenia Romero and the market research was done by Adela Morales de Look.

In Nairobi, the lead institution for the study was the Central Bureau of Statistics (CBS), a government organization responsible for multi-sectoral survey research. The principal investigator at CBS was K. Okoth Agunda with John Kekovole as project director. The ethnographic studies were conducted by the African Medical and Research Foundation (AMREF) under the direction of Norman Scotney with the assistance of Wimbui Kogi, Wamucii Njogu, and Margaret Okello. Terry Elliott of Cornell University, the field coordinator for the Nairobi study, was in residence in Nairobi working at CBS. He took the lead role in instrument development, staff training and supervision, and data entry and preparation.

In Semarang, the study was conducted by Diponegoro University. Moeljono S. Trastotenojo was the principal investigator. Fatimah Muis was the project director. The study team consisted of Hariyono, Ag. Sumantri, Sahid Wiratno, and Budioro. The ethnographic research was under the direction of Nico Kana.

ETHNOGRAPHIC RESEARCH

The ethnographic study teams consisted of senior staff members in the social sciences and field workers who were selected and trained using manuals developed by consortium staff and modified for each country. The first phase of the ethnographic field work consisted of participant observation and informal household interviews designed to explore a broad range of information including the physical setting, family and household composition, mothers' activities, the community context, and infant feeding practices. The methods and results of these ethnographic studies have been reported in more detail elsewhere.[2] Throughout the data collection stage the senior ethnographic staff visited the workers in the field sites and met with them to supervise the data collection process. During the first phase, each ethnographic team conducted in-depth studies of approximately forty families.

The second phase of the ethnographic research, which

was carried out concurrently with the survey research, emphasized the interactions of mothers with their local communities. In Bangkok, the ethnographers visited government and private hospitals, health centers, stores, and homes to examine the policies and procedures of these institutions and to determine their influence on mothers. In Bogotá, participant observation studies were undertaken in the communities to investigate social institutions and their impact on infant feeding. This included interviews with grandmothers, local merchants, and traditional healers. The second phase of the ethnography in Nairobi was designed to follow mothers of clinically diagnosed malnourished children in rehabilitation programs. The purpose was to explore further infant feeding practices and the role of the health care system in treating some of the most seriously affected malnutrition cases. In Semarang, additional ethnographic work was done in retail outlets and pharmacies selling infant foods and related products and in a community health center.

SITE DESCRIPTIONS

Bangkok, the largest city in Thailand, is a crowded metropolis with many educational and cultural facilities as well as the usual range of urban problems, including pollution, overcrowding, traffic congestion, crime, prostitution, and unemployment. Rapid population growth and rising gasoline and food prices in the 1970's led to increased subsistence problems for all residents. Bangkok is home to temporary and permanent migrants from all parts of the country. More recent migrants are employed in the informal sector of the economy and produce goods for a small-scale "bazaar-type" economy. Four communities were studied by the ethnographers in Bangkok: (1) Phasicharoen, a self-contained community with residents working primarily in the community or in surrounding government institutions; (2) the Central Plaza construction site, an enclave of short-term migrants who lived in temporary housing consisting of rows of single rooms with communal washing and toilet facilities; (3) Senanikhom, a suburban community where most men and women were employed in shift work at a nearby blanket factory or in heavy industrial factories; and (4) the Din Dang flats, a neighborhood with temporary squatter settlements and public housing.

Bogotá, Colombia, has also faced rapid population expansion and a continuous influx of rural migrants. At the time of the survey, a severe recession had increased prices of basic commodities and thereby lowered the already poor standard of living for low-income families. There were three communities included in the ethnography. One was a neighborhood in southeast Bogotá with few services, high unemployment, and irregular opportunities in the informal labor force. There, women were employed as domestic servants, in very small businesses, or at home. The second area was in west Bogotá in a middle- and low/middle- income community with access to a full range of public services. The third sector, in the northwest part of the city, was smaller than the other two communities. Settled by recent migrants, it had no paved streets and insufficient public services.

Nairobi, Kenya's capital, is made up almost entirely of recent migrants with strong ties to rural areas. Household amenities and community services are limited in many areas. Although all of the tribal groups of Kenya have settled in Nairobi, for logistic reasons, Luo, Kikuyu, and Luhya, the largest population groups, were the main groups represented in the ethnographic sample. The ethnographic field work in Nairobi focused on Kibera, a community of mixed living standards close to the industrial section of the city.

Semarang, located on the north coast of central Java, is the fifth largest city in Indonesia. Most of the population is Javanese with a substantial minority of people of Chinese-Indonesian origin. There are large differences, however, within the Javanese population which consists of several social groups: the peasant farmers (called abangan) who adhere to Javanese rituals; the santri who are followers of strictly Moslem practices and are generally richer peasants and merchants; and the prijaji, government workers and members of the more educated class, who are descendants of the hereditary aristocracy and who maintain, to some extent, Hindu-Javanese court traditions.

Three communities were chosen as ethnographic sites here. Kranggan Dalam is a heavily populated urban district with fairly well-to-do Chinese and low-income Javanese. Most families had electricity and water from municipal water pipes or wells, but sanitary facilities were poor. Krobokan, in the suburbs in west Semarang, is a recently developed area with a population of educated middle-class families with regular incomes as well as poorer families employed as day laborers. Mangkang Kulon is a peri-urban area where educated middle-class government workers reside in proximity to farmers and unskilled workers with low incomes and insecure employment.

SURVEY OF INFANT FEEDING PRACTICES

The survey component of the study was designed to describe infant feeding practices in each city and to quantify the relative importance of demographic, socio-economic, women's employment, and health service variables as determinants of infant feeding behavior. The survey also incorporated a consumer behavior module that was designed as part of the market research.

Several hypotheses were formulated to structure the survey design and subsequent data analysis. Among the more important were:

o   Women who receive prenatal care from physicians and nurses or experience labor and delivery in a hospital are less likely to initiate breastfeeding, more likely to terminate breast-feeding early and to use breastmilk substitutes and introduce semi-solids during the first four months.

o   Mothers who are exposed to health facility practices that separate mothers and infants or promote or distribute breastmilk substitutes will be less likely to initiate breastfeeding and more likely to terminate breastfeeding early and introduce breastmilk substitutes.

o   Women with higher social mobility aspirations will be less likely to initiate breastfeeding and more likely to breastfeed for a shorter time and to introduce supplementary feeding earlier.

o   Mothers who believe they have or have had insufficient milk are likely to introduce breastmilk substitutes early.

o   Paid labor force participation outside the home increases the probability of early use of breastmilk substitutes, early supplementary foods, and substitution of convenient but nutritionally inappropriate foods.

o   Among women who do work for wages outside the home, specific attributes of labor force participation are important determinants of infant feeding practices.

INSTRUMENT DEVELOPMENT

The research consortium developed a model instrument
for all study sites which included information on households, index mothers, and index children. The basis for
the selection of variables for inclusion was described
in a 1981 working paper by the consortium.3 Key variables
were to be included in each instrument. Basic household
information consisted of income, water supply, electricity, sanitation, refrigeration, numbers of persons in
the household, and recency of urban migration. Information
on the index mothers included age, number of live births,
number of years of education, and employment of the male
head of the household. For each child, the sex, date
of birth, age, birth order, place of birth, name of
mother, previous hospitalizations and morbidity in the
last two weeks were recorded and height and weight were
measured using standard techniques. The following infant
feeding variables were included:

    o   ever breastfed
    o   currently receiving breastmilk
    o   currently receiving non-human milk
    o   currently receiving other foods
    o   duration of exclusive breastfeeding
    o   age at first breastfeeding
    o   age at cessation of human milk
    o   age at introduction of non-human milk
    o   age at introduction of infant formula
    o   age at introduction of other foods
    o   type of other foods given

Other information included in the survey covered
utilization of prenatal care and health services, characteristics of mother's employment before and after the
birth of the index child, knowledge and attitudes about
breastfeeding, bottle feeding, and weaning and consumer
behavior and attitudes toward infant feeding products.

In each site a draft instrument was prepared based
on the core instrument developed by the consortium util-
izing the results of the local ethnographic field work.
The consortium staff provided technical assistance for
the revision of these instruments, which were pretested,
reviewed with the ethnographic teams, revised, and finally
approved by the consortium prior to use in the field.

SAMPLING

Sampling frames for the four sites were developed
using established sampling frames for each urban area:

The National Institute of Development Administration (NIDA) sampling frame in Bangkok, the National Statistics Department (DANE) in Bogotá, the Central Bureau of Statistics (CBS) in Nairobi, and the sampling frame of the Provincial Office of Census and Statistics for Central Java in Semarang. Representative samples were chosen to fulfill the primary objective of the study: to describe infant feeding practices in each site as a basis for the improvement of programs and policies.

The sampling plan designs for the four sites are shown in Table 1.1. In order to ensure that each site sample would cover the weaning period, the samples included older infants in places where the mean duration of breastfeeding was longer. In Semarang, all children in the selected households under 24 months of age were included; in Nairobi, all those under 18 months were included, and in Bangkok and Bogotá, the sample encompassed only those under 12 months of age. In Semarang, the sample was expanded to include a newly annexed section of the city, Tugu, which was essentially rural in character.

The final sample sizes were 1,422 in Bangkok, 980 in Nairobi, 711 in Bogotá, and 1,356 in Semarang. All of the sampling frames (with the exception of the CBS frame in Nairobi) used equal probability, multistage cluster samples. In the CBS frame, however, individuals were assigned case weights proportional to the probability of selection for each cluster (Chapter 4 and Table 4.1).

Table 1.1   SAMPLING FRAMES FOR INFANT FEEDING STUDY

	BANGKOK	BOGOTÁ	NAIROBI	SEMARANG
Approximate Population (in millions)	6*	4.5	.7	.75
Exclusions	None	High Income Tracts	High Income Tracts	None
Age Range of Infants (months)	0-11	0-11	0-17	0-23
Final Sample Size	1,422	711	980	1,356

*1975 boundaries

There were several significant differences in the methodologies used by the study teams. The study teams in Bogotá and Nairobi elected to modify their sampling procedures to exclude upper-income strata. In Bogotá, this was done to focus study resources on the poorer population of the city, and in Nairobi upper-income res-pondents were excluded because these groups included a large number of non-Kenyans. This was done in Bogotá by excluding upper and upper-middle social sectors from the sampling frame. In Nairobi, the twelve clusters of the sampling frame with the highest income were excluded. These clusters were estimated to account for 10 percent of the population in each city.

The Semarang protocol also differed significantly in the manner in which the age of each index child was recorded by field workers. As in the other sites, each child's age was recorded in months. The monthly inter-vals, however, were <u>centered</u> on the month "birthday" of each child, rather than <u>ending</u> with the completion of each month of life, as is usual. This procedure facili-tates analysis of anthropometric data by age, but the recorded age of each child is no longer directly com-parable to that of children in the other sites. Thus, in Semarang, the age for children 0-1 completed weeks of age was recorded as 0 months; the age for infants 2-5 completed weeks of age was recorded as 1 month, that for infants of 6-9 completed weeks was recorded as 2 months, and so forth. In other sites, children 0-3 com-pleted weeks of age were recorded as 0 months old, 4-7 completed weeks were recorded as 1 month of age, 8-11 completed weeks were counted as 2 months of age, and so forth.

DATA COLLECTION

Survey field work was carried out by interviewers chosen and supervised by the study directors and senior staff in each site. Specific field procedures varied for the different sites and have been described in more detail elsewhere.[4]

DATA ANALYSIS

Data analysis for the surveys of infant feeding practices was preceded by editing and verification of the data in each country. Further editing and preparation of combined data tapes was carried out by staff of the New York-based consortium. To the extent possible, these

combined tapes consisted of recorded data that were standardized to facilitate comparisons among the sites. Frequencies and cross-tabulations were first examined to
determine the relationships of demographic characteristics, women's employment, and health services to infant
feeding practices. In the course of examinations of bivariate and multivariate contingency tables, the most
salient attributes with respect to infant feeding practices were selected from the many variables describing
women's employment, health services, and consumer behavior.

In order to utilize both the current status data
collected on infant feeding and the histories mothers
gave of prior feeding for each index child, categorical
variables were constructed to classify each child by
feeding mode up to the age at the time of the interview.
For example, a child who was thirteen months old at the
time of the interview and who was breastfed until the
tenth month would have been coded one (or "yes") for
the variables: breastfed two months, three months, six
months, nine months. The case would be coded zero (or
"no") for breastfed twelve months and "missing" for variables beyond that age. Similar variables were constructed
for time of first introduction of infant formula or other
non-human milks, again combining current status and retrospective reporting for each index child. These categorical
variables were used as the dependent variables for subsequent multivariate analysis of the determinants of feeding
practices.

Multiple logistic regression was chosen the most
appropriate linear model, multivariable technique for
use with dichotomous dependent variables. It permitted
the evaluation of the predictive power of entire models
and allowed the assessment of the effects of individual
predictor variables (i.e., background, maternal employment, health services) while simultaneously controlling
for the effects of the other independent variables. Thus,
a first analysis used only background variables as predictors. A second analysis, building on the first, added
maternal employment variables to the background variables.
In Nairobi, Bogotá, and Semarang a separate analysis
was performed adding health services variables to the
background variables, but without using maternal employment as a predictor in the model. A final analysis in
all sites included background, maternal employment, and
health services variables and served as an "Overall
Model." The beta coefficients and associated chi-square
values provide an indication of which of the predictors
exert a significant effect on the probability of the
infant feeding outcome under consideration. Since the

interpretation of the magnitude of effect represented by the beta coefficients is not readily apparent, the adjusted risk odds ratio (RÔR) was used to quantify and compare the different predictors. For each variable, this ratio represents the probability of a given outcome divided by the probability of the alternative.

The SAS programs used for this analysis came from the Supplemental Library Procedure, LOGIST, by Frank E. Harrell, Jr., Duke University Medical Center.

Other analyses were performed in each site focusing on a concept termed the "weaning interval." This idea was developed by the consortium to represent the time from first introduction of infant formula or other milk to the cessation of breastfeeding. Interest in a "weaning interval" emerged from the fact that the transition from breast to bottle feeding is virtually never abrupt and the widespread belief that early initiation of bottle feeding is itself an important determinant of cessation of breastfeeding.

MARKET RESEARCH

The marketing studies were designed to examine the influence of infant food marketing and distribution strategies on infant feeding behavior. Because commercial marketing strategies and practices are developed, or refined, on a country by country basis, and because no prior studies of infant food marketing had been undertaken in the participating countries, much of the marketing research was descriptive and exploratory in nature. Five questions guided the market research.

  o   What current practices and strategies characterize the infant food marketing in each nation?
  o   What factors account for the current marketing environment?
  o   What is the intensity of promotional activities of infant food sellers directed at mothers, health care providers, and others who make infant feeding choices?
  o   What effects, if any, do these marketing practices and policies have on mothers?
  o   What, if any, effects do the marketing practices and strategies of the infant food sellers have on health care providers?

Studies of the retail market, the state of the industry, and consumer behavior were used to answer these questions.

The retail market substudy explored the distribution of breastmilk substitutes by examining the number, variety, and prices of products in a sample of sales outlets (food stores, shops, pharmacies). Preliminary market investigations and ethnographic field research focusing on commonly sold foods and related infant products were conducted to develop a list of products in current use in each country. A retail audit provided baseline information about commercial infant food marketing by collecting and analyzing data on pricing, products, and promotion practices. These data were collected through visits to retail shops and outlets in each field site by local subcontractors, who were trained and supervised by Trost Associates. Retail audit reports were tabulated and analyzed by Trost Associates prior to submission to the consortium.

In each site, an overview of the state of the infant food industry was developed. This included a descriptive picture of the development and current size of the industry. Trade policies and regulations of national governments were analyzed to determine their influence on the production, distribution, and advertising practices of producers and sellers of infant foods. Secondary data analysis as well as interviews with appropriate industry, government, and health personnel were also used to collect information. Interviews were conducted with infant food company executives and employees, other businessmen directly involved with the industry, and health providers possessing firsthand information about industry actions. Direct observations of industry activity were made by consortium staff, consultants, or subcontractors.

A consumer behavior questionnaire was administered as a segment of the cross-sectional survey of infant feeding practices. It was designed to provide data on the demand for breastmilk substitutes. Questions focusing on product and brand awareness, past feeding behavior, and hospital practices (such as receipt of an infant formula sample or feeding bottle) were also included. The decisions to purchase a commercial breastmilk substitute and then to feed such a product to an infant were explored through survey questions on the use of commercial products as well as through observations of retail practices.

Specific practices such as the distribution of free samples of infant food products and promotional activities directed toward the medical profession were also included in the database for marketing. Interviews were conducted with health care personnel and infant food company representatives. In order to determine the effects of marketing practices on health professionals, consortium staff, consultants, or subcontractors also directly observed the contacts between health personnel and marketing agents.

Local firms and personnel in each city were employed to conduct aspects of the market research. In Indonesia, the marketing studies were conducted by P.T. In-Search Data of Jakarta and by Sahid Wiratno of the Faculty of Economics at Diponegoro University. The retail market and state of the industry substudies in Bangkok were conducted by Deemar Company, Ltd. Thonglaw Dejthai of Mahidol University provided information on government regulations concerning infant foods, conducted interviews with health care personnel, and reported on his observations at health facilities. In Bogotá, the retail market studies and analysis of the state of the infant food industry were carried out by Adela Morales de Look of Javeriana University under the direction of the staff of Trost Associates. In Nairobi, the retail market and state of the industry studies were conducted by RBL, Ltd.

The questionnaire items to elicit consumer behavior information were designed by the staff of Trost Associates in consultation with consortium staff members who had overall responsibility for the surveys of infant feeding practices.

OVERALL STUDY

The combined studies, including ethnographic field work, survey research, and market research, were designed to produce a multi-disciplinary analysis of infant feeding and its determinants in each city and to serve as a guide for policy interventions for the improvement of infant nutrition and health.

The ethnographic studies provided rich contextual data on infant feeding that was used in questionnaire development as well as to elucidate the cultural context of infant feeding in the sample communities. The market research contributed descriptive information on the state of the infant food industry, the extent and nature of marketing to health professionals, and the knowledge and behavior of consumers. This study component was designed to allow examination of the influence of various marketing practices. The consumer behavior component of the market research was closely linked to the survey of infant feeding practices since the questions were administered as part of the survey. Particularly in Bangkok, where the second phase of the ethnographic research examined the marketing practices in hospitals, the marketing and ethnographic components were also closely linked.

All of the components of the study made unique contributions to the whole, and the multidisciplinary nature of the research was designed to permit a broad view of infant feeding patterns, their determinants, and policies useful for their improvement.

NOTES

1. The selection of the cities to be included in the study was made in cooperation with the sponsor for the study, The Agency for International Development (AID) of the United States Department of State.

2. Penny Van Esterik, Integrating Ethnographic and Survey Research. Working Paper No. 17 The Population Council, International Programs, January 1983. Beverly Winikoff, et al. The Infant Feeding Study: Bangkok Site Report; The Infant Feeding Study: Bogotá Site Report; The Infant Feeding Study: Nairobi Site Report; The Infant Feeding Study: Semarang Site Report. (Reports submitted to AID by the Population Council in fulfillment of Contract No. AID/DSAN-C-0211.) In addition, the following donors provided support for portions of data analysis: UNICEF, the Rockefeller Foundation, and International Development and Research Centre (Centre File: 3-p-83-0061) January 31, 1986.

3. V. H. Laukaran et al., Research on Determinants of Infant Feeding Practices: A Conceptual Framework. Working Paper No. 15. The Population Council, International Programs, November 1981.

4. Winikoff et al., The Infant Feeding Study reports.

2 Infant Feeding in Bangkok, Thailand

Beverly Winikoff, Somchai Durongdej, and Barry J. Cerf

Bangkok is the vital, teeming, noisy urban center of Thai national life. It is over 40 times larger than the next largest city in Thailand and contains the major political, economic, religious, educational, and health care institutions in the country. Bangkok attracts migrants from all over Thailand and sets values and standards for the entire country. As a sprawling urban and industrial center, it is not surprising that Bangkok shares many problems with other large developing country cities, including pollution, overcrowding, congestion, crime, unemployment, and difficulties in maintaining public services.

Like the city, its inhabitants are vibrant, energetic, and sophisticated. There is a long tradition of concern with education and provision of health care to the populace. In fact, Bangkok has been a center of medical education and has seen the creation of substantial numbers of well-trained health workers, innovative public health programs, and superior medical institutions based on the Western medical model.

For both historical and cultural reasons, it appears that Thailand and the Thai people have been particularly receptive to the incorporation of new forms and new approaches to solving problems of daily living. Thai mothers are no exception, and the feeding of young children has been profoundly influenced by new customs imported from abroad. For example, new ways of feeding infants were common in Bangkok as early as the 1920s, and the government felt it necessary by 1929 to pass a "Skimmed Milk Act" to control the quality of milk manufactured for infant feeding, in order to promote better health and nourishment of Thai children.[1]

Although breastfeeding has been a cultural norm and continues to be widely practiced, Thai mothers have been ready to adapt to new circumstances and to try new ways to feed their children if they appear promising and seem to have worked for others. There is a clear independence of spirit manifest among the Thai mothers, who are, on the whole, a well-educated, literate group. Their economic aspirations often lead them to enter the cash economy and to make decisions about the allocation of cash resources for the family. In addition, many mothers have a positive orientation to Western medical traditions and Western-style medical institutions. In this context, it is not surprising that the use of bottle milk is widespread in Bangkok and has become an easily available option for many Thai women.

HOUSEHOLD AND DEMOGRAPHIC CHARACTERISTICS

A total of 1,422 mothers and their youngest child comprise the cross-sectional survey sample of the Infant Feeding Study in Bangkok. Almost half of the sample mothers live in nuclear families, and the rest live in extended families or with non-relatives. Eighty percent of the sample have monthly family incomes lower than 6,000 Bhat (about US $260) and only 6 percent have incomes higher than 10,000 Bhat (US $435).

Almost every household was reported to have electricity, an indoor flush toilet, and access to piped water. The ethnographers, however, found the Central Plaza construction area and the Din Dang slum community to have notably poor sanitary conditions and poor quality housing. Almost all respondents (92%) reported that they boil drinking water; however, 35 percent said that they did so only for young infants. Fewer than half of the mothers reported living in households owning either refrigerators or gas or electric stoves (Table 2.1).

Almost two-thirds of the mothers were between 20-29 years old, with a sample median of 26 years. The large majority reported having had at least some formal education, with a bare 5 percent reporting no schooling. Most of the mothers have had between one and four years of education (Table 2.1). This reflects Thailand's compulsory education law, which mandates a minimum of formal schooling for all citizens. The sample is almost evenly divided between those mothers who were born in Bangkok and those who were born elsewhere and later migrated to the capital (Table 2.1). Thirty-six percent of the mothers were engaged in some form of wage earning activity with daily wage laborer, merchant, and civil servant the most frequently cited occupations.

Table 2.1   SAMPLE CHARACTERISTICS

Mother's Age	n	%
14-17	26	2.0
18-19	78	6.0
20-24	417	30.0
25-29	467	34.0
30-34	263	19.0
35-39	108	8.0
>40	32	2.0
Total	1,391	101.0

Mother's Schooling	n	%
none	68	5.0
1-4 yrs	835	60.0
5-7 yrs	190	14.0
8-10 yrs	139	10.0
>10 yrs	157	11.0
Total	1,389	100.0

Parity	n	%
1	603	43.0
2-3	629	45.0
4-5	124	9.0
6-7	24	2.0
8-9	11	1.0
Total	1,391	100.0

Place of Infant's Birth	n	%
Public Hospital	1,133	80.0
Private Hospital	253	18.0
Home	32	2.0
Total	1,418	100.0

Mother's Place of Birth	n	%
Bangkok	593	43.0
Other	788	57.0
Total	1,381	100.0

Socioeconomic Indicators	n	%
Electricity	1,394	98.0
Indoor Toilet	1,409	99.0
Refrigerator	572	40.0
Gas/Electric Stove	584	41.0

Maternal Employment	n	%
Yes	502	35.6
No	902	64.2
Total	1,404	99.0

Parity of the sample mothers was low: 43 percent had had only one live birth (the index child) and 45 percent had had two or three. Since the study sample is a random sample of all mothers of infants, the observation that almost half are primiparous suggests a pattern of current low fertility in Bangkok. Almost all births took place in hospitals, and 101 (7%) of the children were reported to have been rehospitalized since birth. The mothers of 44 percent of the children stated that they had been ill sometime during the two weeks prior to the survey.

Given the low fertility of mothers and the low age of the children in this sample, it is not surprising that only 2 percent of the sample mothers had become pregnant again by the time of the survey. This may be explained by postpartum lactational infertility and by extensive use of contraception. One-third of the mothers reported current amenorrhea and 60 percent reported that they or their partners used some form of contraception. The most common methods used were pills (27 percent of the entire sample) and female sterilization (15 percent of the sample). Ten percent of the sample reported the use of contraceptive injections which may have increased the number of women who reported a current state of amenorrhea.

INFANT FEEDING PRACTICES
Breastfeeding

The vast majority (90%) of the sample mothers reported initiating breastfeeding. The number who report current breastfeeding quickly and steadily declines very soon after birth, however. This is reflected in a relatively short median duration of lactation of six months. The most precipitous decline apparently occurs in the immediate postpartum period: while 90 percent of the sample reported having breastfed at some time, only 76 percent of all children aged 0-29 days were being breastfed at the time of the survey! From four months of age on, slightly less than half the infants (40-45%) are still breastfeeding. This remains stable until the twelfth month when there is another large decline. Exclusive breastfeeding is rare except during the first month, when 60 percent of all breastfed infants receive nothing else. By the end of five months, there are virtually no exclusively breastfed children. A graphic display of the percentages of children who never breastfed, those who breastfed at some time but stopped, those who are currently breastfeeding, and those who are exclusively breastfeeding with no supplements, according to the age of the child at the time of the survey, is presented in Figure 2.1.

Despite the short duration of lactation, early breastfeeding among these Thai mothers appears to follow the advice offered for successful lactation: 82 percent of mothers reported use of colostrum and 93 percent reported feeding on demand. The average number of feedings per day does not differ by the age of the child. The mean frequency of breastfeeding is 8.3 times per day for children age 0-2 months and only slightly lower for all other children 3-5, 6-8, and 9-12 months old.

Over 95 percent of all breastfed infants are offered the breast during the night. The practice of night feeding does not appear to decline with age. This is consistent with the stability in reported breastfeeding episodes per day. Higher income is associated with a slightly lower probability of breastfeeding at night, but the overwhelming majority of all breastfeeding mothers (over 90 percent of every income group) practice night feeding.

The survey suggests that the 10 percent of women who never breastfed differed from other women with respect to a number of characteristics. Mothers who were aged 40 or more, with parity of 4 or above, born in Bangkok and with deliveries at public hospitals were much more likely (approximately twofold) never to initiate breastfeeding. In addition, a more discrete group can be defined as particularly at risk of never breastfeeding. This group includes women who had caesarean deliveries and those whose babies had health problems at birth or had to stay extra days in the hospital.

There are a number of attitudes about breastfeeding on which there is near unanimous agreement among the mothers, regardless of breastfeeding history. Almost all agree that breastfeeding allows more intimacy, that it provides an adequate and valuable food for the child, that it is of higher nutritional value than formula, and that it gives more immunity. Exposure to information about the beneficial aspects of breastfeeding, therefore, appears to be widespread. On the other hand, a majority of both women who had and those who had not breastfed felt that using formula milk is "modern." Women who never breastfed seem to view breastfeeding as slightly more burdensome and inconvenient for the mother.

Figure 2.1   BREASTFEEDING PATTERNS IN BANGKOK

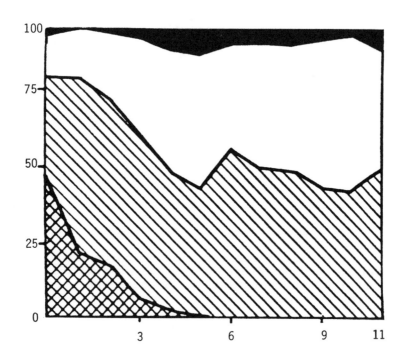

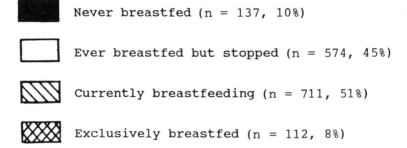

Never breastfed (n = 137, 10%)

Ever breastfed but stopped (n = 574, 45%)

Currently breastfeeding (n = 711, 51%)

Exclusively breastfed (n = 112, 8%)

Weaning

Insufficient milk was the most frequently cited breastfeeding problem. When mothers were asked how they knew they had insufficient milk, 54 percent simply reiterated the problem, citing either a complete cessation of output or a reduction in quantity. Most of the others (43%) cited crying of the baby. None cited medical diagnosis or failure of the baby to gain weight. Because estrogen-containing oral contraceptives have been shown to reduce milk production, the data were examined for evidence of such an effect. Pill users report insufficient milk (65%) at about the same rate as users of all other forms of contraception (69%), providing no evidence of a specific relationship between pill use and insufficient milk. Nevertheless, pill users appear to have particular concern about the effect of their chosen contraceptive on breastmilk, as confirmed by ethnographic reports.

When mothers were asked what course of action they took in response to insufficient milk, most responded that they changed the child's diet (70%). Sixty-two percent of the mothers reported giving formula to the child, by far the most common "treatment" for the problem. Twenty-six percent of the mothers treated themselves. Treatments included dietary change (15%), local treatment of the breast (8%), and use of drugs (3%). No mother mentioned increasing the frequency of breastfeeding, the recommended response. A majority of the mothers (66%) did not discuss this problem with anyone else. Only 16 percent sought advice from physicians or other health personnel.

Some breastfeeding problems were attributed to the infant. The most common problem was the infant refusing breastmilk. Two-thirds of mothers of infants who refused to breastfeed had given supplements to their children before the problem arose. The most common response to this problem, once again, was to give formula (88%). Most mothers did not consult anyone for advice on this problem either.

Return to work (35%) was the single most frequently cited reason for complete weaning, with insufficient milk almost as common (29%). The frequency of responses such as "insufficient milk" and "child refused breast" (13%) suggests that involuntary weaning was quite common and probably associated with lack of good advice on how to avoid and/or solve common problems of breastfeeding. Less than 10% of the mothers reported that they received the suggestion to wean from anyone else, and Bangkok women seem to take pride in the fact that weaning decisions rest almost exclusively with themselves. This is in accord with the clear disinclination of mothers to seek advice about breastfeeding problems.

The ethnographic data reveal that the decision to stop breastfeeding may involve a series of interacting factors and events. For example, one twenty-year-old mother gave the following description of what led her to stop breastfeeding:

> When I was in the hospital after child delivery, I had no milk so the nurse used bottle milk......When I came back home, [my] husband bought Nan Brand [formula]......I used that to alternate with breastmilk for three days when the baby developed diarrhea. I didn't know whether it was because of the formula or my milk. [I] decided to stop breastfeeding and continue Nan.

Another young woman essentially "weaned" before she began to nurse:

> Vasna was born in Bangkok......she lived at home with her parents in a construction site......and got a Japanese husband [not a legal marriage]. When she became pregnant, the husband left her. She returned to stay with her parents again. Initially, breastfeeding was intended, but Vasna's nipples were too short and [were] refused by the baby. The hospital staff suggested formula milk to her. S-26 brand was started according to her mother's advice. After 20 days, Meiji Brand [was substituted] because during the previous three weeks there was no sign of the baby's growth

Here, difficult social circumstances, physical problems with breastfeeding, and inappropriate medical advice, combined to undermine breastfeeding where there were no true contraindications or absolute barriers. It is probable that breastfeeding failure is often due to such unfortunate coincidences of discouraging events, each of which makes breastfeeding marginally more difficult. This, plus readily available alternatives to breastmilk, influence certain women to end--or never really start--breastfeeding.

The weaning interval in these infants clearly varies with the age at which bottles are introduced into the diet. Among those babies who receive a bottle in the first two months, more than half are totally weaned from the breast in less than one month. Among those receiving their first bottle at age four months or older, the majority experience weaning intervals of two months or longer.

Details of Supplementation

Most supplementation occurs very early in Bangkok. Two-thirds of one-month-old children were receiving food, and 45 percent received bottle milk. Among children aged five months and older, the percentages of children that bottlefed or consumed other foods remained fairly stable at about 60 percent and 95 percent, respectively.

Feeding patterns can be broken down into several discrete categories (Table 2.2) in order to give additional detail about the pattern of supplements consumed by the sample children at different ages. The use of foods alone with no milk, for example, almost never occurs, regardless of the age of the child. Likewise, the use of bottle feeding as the sole source of nutrition is uncommon: with the exception of the 0-2 month cohort (where about 8 percent use bottle milk alone), only a very small minority of children depend on this pattern. Even less common is a milk diet consisting of a combination of breast and bottle milk. In the 0-2 month group, only about 8 percent of children are fed this way. The most frequent pattern at all ages is milk (either breastmilk or from a bottle) along with other foods. Even in the earliest period of infancy (0-2 months), 57 percent of the children were receiving non-milk foods. Introduction of other foods is thus early and widespread in Bangkok, regardless of whether breastmilk or substitutes are the source of milk in the diet.

The introduction of breastmilk substitutes is associated with relatively rapid cessation of breastfeeding in Bangkok. Thus, for most children, milk feeding involves either breastmilk or breastmilk substitutes, but rarely breastmilk and breastmilk substitutes together. When mixed milk feeding is seen, it is likely part of a transitional phase leading to the cessation of breastfeeding.

Regardless of the current age of the child, the use of bottle feeding is close to or equals 100 percent throughout the first year among those children no longer breastfeeding. Reasons given by mothers for introducing formula milk are essentially the same as reasons given for weaning. A majority of the women gave one of two responses: they had to return to work (37%) or they had a problem with insufficient milk (31%). An additional 8 percent of the women also reported that they began to give formula milk because the child refused to breastfeed.

Supplementation of breastfeeding may have a very different outcome depending on whether the supplements are breastmilk substitutes or other foods. Unlike breast-

Table 2.2 FEEDING PATTERN BY AGE OF CHILD (PERCENT)

	Age in Months			
	0-2 (n=292)	3-5 (n=380)	6-8 (n=372)	9-12 (n=336)
Breast Only	27	5	4	1
Breast & Bottle	8	2	1	1
Bottle Only	8	5	4	1
Breast & Food	26	29	31	30
Bottle & Food	18	48	50	57
Breast, Bottle & Food	12	13	12	9
Food Only	0	0	0	2

milk substitutes, supplementation with other foods seems quite compatible with continued breastfeeding. Introduction to a variety of foods is often viewed as essential to proper integration of the young child into society in Thailand, as in other Southeast Asian cultures. The ethnographers observed that the great majority of mothers introduced early supplementation with non-milk products in Bangkok. Most mothers gave either mashed banana or banana and rice within the first month of the infant's life. Reasons for introducing such supplements at an early age range from doing so on the advice of neighbors or relatives to the belief that these foods will "fill up" the baby, increase strength, and decrease fussiness. Nangsorawang, aged 24, tells us "Now I am feeding [the baby] by....... chewing white rice mashed with banana to add sweet flavor......I began this [when] the baby was seven days old. The people next door told me to do so, and I followed [their advice]......"

The pattern of consumption of foods differs markedly between the older and younger children. For example, in the 0-2 month group the most widely consumed food is fruit, followed by grains, fruit juice and sugar. Almost none of the children received vegetables or animal protein supplements. After six months of age, a majority eat animal protein, but only a minority are reported to consume sugar.

DETERMINANTS OF INFANT FEEDING PRACTICES
Influence of Background Factors

Prior research shows clearly that infant feeding patterns vary with different demographic and socioeconomic attributes. In Bangkok, there appears to be a lower like-lihood of breastfeeding initiation as the age of the mother increases. Among mothers who do initiate breast-feeding, duration is longest among the very oldest (older than 40 years) mothers. Yet, bottle feeding by two months of age is slightly more common among mothers older than 30 years. Initiation of breastfeeding is somewhat lower in the very highest parity group, perhaps corresponding with the older age group, above. Breastfeeding duration is shorter among women having their first birth, and early introduction of bottle feeding is more common among these women (Table 2.3).

Rural-born women initiate breastfeeding slightly more often and breastfeed substantially longer than those born in Bangkok. Only 58 percent of Bangkok-born mothers breastfeed for three months versus 71 percent of rural born women, and the Bangkok-born women are more likely (53% versus 43%) to introduce early bottle feeding. While initiation of breastfeeding shows no trend by educational level of mother, shorter duration seems to be associated consistently with more educational attainment. In addi-tion, there is more early introduction of bottle feeding among the more educated mothers.

Finally, family income is associated strikingly and consistently with infant feeding patterns. The per-centage of women reporting initiation of breastfeeding declines with increasing family income. This same inverse relationship is clearer and more pronounced for breast-feeding duration, with likelihood of breastfeeding for six months declining from 65 percent to 27 percent from the highest to the lowest income groups (Table 2.3). Consistent with these findings is the fact that early introduction of bottle feeding increases directly with level of family income: the highest income group is almost twice as likely as the lowest to have introduced bottle feeding by two months. Thus, breastfeeding duration and early bottle feeding co-vary with demographic-socioecon-omic indices to a much greater extent than does breast-feeding initiation.

Table 2.3   BREASTFEEDING AND BOTTLE FEEDING PRACTICES
             BY SELECTED VARIABLES

	Ever Breastfed		Breastfed 3 Months		Breastfed 6 Months		Bottle by 2 Months	
	n	%	n	%	n	%	n	%
Mother's Age								
<20 years	104	94.2	69	60.9	34	44.1	77	44.2
20-29	882	92.0	628	65.0	408	55.9	751	43.5
30-39	370	85.0	257	63.0	178	50.6	331	55.9
$\geq$40	32	75.0	20	75.0	16	88.7	29	51.7
Education								
None	68	82.4	46	67.4	33	60.6	59	42.4
1-4 years	834	92.1	593	70.2	379	61.7	712	41.0
5-7 years	190	90.0	134	62.7	94	50.0	167	46.7
8-10 years	139	83.5	94	55.3	60	36.7	120	65.8
>10 years	155	89.0	107	46.7	70	30.0	129	67.4
Parity								
1	801	89.4	419	58.2	262	44.7	515	52.6
2-3	624	92.9	450	70.0	301	59.8	533	42.2
4-5	124	85.5	84	71.4	57	63.2	111	47.7
6-7	34	70.6	18	66.7	13	69.2	29	44.8
Mother's Origin								
Bangkok	590	86.1	414	57.7	267	44.6	560	52.5
Other (rural)	787	93.5	552	70.5	364	61.3	657	42.5
Family Income*								
500-3,000	550	92.2	387	74.9	245	64.5	473	36.6
3,001-6,000	537	98.8	383	63.7	263	54.4	484	50.2
6,001-10,000	190	86.3	137	47.4	86	36.0	171	67.8
>10,000	72	86.1	42	45.2	30	26.7	59	67.8

*Bhat

Table 2.3   BREASTFEEDING AND BOTTLE FEEDING PRACTICES
(Cont'd)   BY SELECTED VARIABLES

	Ever Breastfed		Breastfed 3 Months		Breastfed 6 Months		Bottle by 2 Months	
	n	%	n	%	n	%	n	%
Maternal Employment								
No	--	--	606	76.4	390	65.4	735	36.1
Yes:								
Work in home	--	--	90	70.0	61	60.7	111	43.2
Work out	--	--	273	37.4	181	27.1	332	73.8
Place of Infant Birth								
Private hospital	1113	91.3	780	65.6	509	56.0	954	46.4
Public hospital	243	84.0	171	60.2	112	40.2	229	58.1
Home	28	96.4	19	78.9	12	91.7	28	28.6
Rooming-In								
Yes	705	93.5	512	65.8	342	57.0	602	41.7
No	680	86.8	461	64.0	293	50.5	583	53.0
Formula Sample								
Yes	171	88.9	125	57.6	76	43.4	150	58.0
No	1216	90.3	849	66.1	560	56.6	1037	45.7

In order to evaluate the effect of each of these background variables on infant feeding choices while controlling for the effects of the other predictors, multiple logistic regression was carried out (statistics not given). Increasing age and urban birthplace are, independently, significantly associated with lower likelihood of initiation of breastfeeding. For age, however, this relationship is not linear, and, the cross-tabulations show that much of the effect may be due to the fact that younger mothers are least likely to initiate breastfeeding--and not that oldest mothers are most likely to do so (Table 2.3).

Parity, mother's birthplace, and family income are significant variables for breastfeeding duration. Among Bangkok-born mothers, low parity women, and high-income families, the probability is reduced that the index child will be breastfed for longer durations. The effects of mother's age and mother's education are not significant. A Bangkok-born mother is only about half as likely to breastfeed for three or more months as a rural-born mother; upper income group mothers are only about one-fourth as likely to do so as mothers from the lowest income group.

Each of the background variables examined exerts a significant effect on the probability of early bottle feeding. Low-parity mothers, Bangkok-born mothers, high-income mothers, and older mothers all have an increased probability of using bottles by two months. A mother born in Bangkok is 1.5 times as likely to introduce an early bottle as a mother born elsewhere, and upper-income mothers are three times as likely as lower-income mothers to introduce early bottles.

Overall, high income and very high parity seem to exert some of the strongest effects in the model. The influence of urban versus rural birth is also substantial and very pervasive. Interestingly, after controlling for other variables, education of the mother has no independent effect on likelihood of initiating or continuing breastfeeding.

Since cessation of breastfeeding follows rapidly after first initiation of bottle feeding, an additional logistic model was tested, using early bottles as one of the variables predicting the probability of breastfeeding duration (results not shown). In this further analysis, early bottle feeding has a dramatic negative association with duration of breastfeeding: it reduces by 25-fold the odds that a child will breastfeed for as long as three months and by elevenfold the odds of breastfeeding for six months. The magnitude and significance of the coefficients for mother's birthplace, mother's age, and family income are reduced by the addition of early bottle feeding as a predictor. This suggests that a good part of the effect seen for the above background variables is actually due to the influence of use of bottles.

If early introduction of the bottle were part of a deliberate weaning strategy, it would be, by definition, associated with shorter breastfeeding. It is thus impossible to say how much of the apparent impact of early bottle feeding on shortened duration of breastfeeding is due to the mother's intention to wean her child rapidly and how much is due to unintentional weaning caused by disruption of lactation. It should be noted, however, that in the companion studies for Nairobi and Semarang,

introduction of early bottle feeding by two months <u>did</u>
have a significant, independent effect on the probability
of breastfeeding for six months and longer, even when
children weaned by three months were excluded from the
analysis. Support for the existence of a sequence of
events beginning with early bottles and ending with unintentional weaning was provided by the ethnographers who
noted cases where introduction of bottle feeding was
associated with subsequent undesired termination of
breastfeeding.

> Samlee was married at the age of 20...... she
> and her husband moved to work in Bangkok. After
> the first baby was born she stopped working
> ......She believes that mother's milk is good
> and it helps the baby to grow fat, to be strong
> and to love its' parents. The baby was breastfed
> from the second day until the twentieth day
> when the husband said that the baby is not
> fleshy (<u>mai rud nua</u>). Her mother-in-law suggest-
> ed that powder milk should be additionally
> given. Her husband bought a tin of Meiji. The
> baby would be breastfed before he was bottle
> fed. Once the baby reached one month old he
> gave up mother's breast and only continued
> taking powder milk

Early use of bottles is, thus, both an outcome and a
possible determinant of feeding practices. Other background variables influence breastfeeding duration either
directly or through the decision to introduce bottle
milks early in infancy.

Influence of Maternal Employment

Maternal employment has been linked to infant feeding
behavior in various studies, and the association is one
of the central concerns of the current study as well.
Yet, most of the women interviewed did not earn income.
At the time of the cross-sectional survey, almost two-
thirds did not report any form of income-generating activity. Only about 7 percent of mothers earned money in
the first postpartum month. In all, about 9 percent of
the total sample were engaged in income generation <u>at
home</u>. Employment <u>outside</u> the home rose steadily with
the age of the child through the first four months and
then leveled off between 25 percent and 30 percent.
Through the end of the first year, women who worked outside the home remained a distinct minority.

Breastfeeding initiation was substantially the same
among women who did not work, those who worked at home,

and those who worked away from home. Work appeared to affect duration of breastfeeding much more strongly than it affected initiation. Without controlling for other background or health services factors, women who worked at home were only slightly less likely to breastfeed for three or six months than those who did not work for pay, but women who worked away from home had only about one-half the probability of breastfeeding for three or six months (Table 2.3). Similarly, women who worked outside their homes were twice as likely as non-workers to introduce bottles by two months whereas women who worked at home are only slightly more likely to do so. These differences become even larger in logistic regression which controls for background and health services variables. The fact that women who earn income at home display infant feeding patterns similar to those who do not earn income suggests that income generation, as such, is not the critical factor in determining feeding patterns (Chapter 6).

Employment might affect infant feeding most strongly if the mother spent a considerable portion of the day away from the infant. Child care arrangements and length of the workday were therefore examined specifically. Most infants of mothers who work outside the home remain in the home (76%) or at a relative's home (13%) and only 2 percent were brought to the workplace. Thus, separation from children during working hours is the norm. Over three-quarters of mothers who earned income worked at least eight to nine hours per day, not including travel time to and from the job (Chapter 6). The number of hours worked per day appears not to be associated with breastfeeding initiation. Breastfeeding duration, however, is longer among the small group of mothers who work only one to three hours per day. Generally, greater percentages of women report early introduction of bottle feeding as the length of the workday increases.

Many more mothers worked prior to the birth of the index child than reported employment postnatally. About one-third of women employed before the birth of the child were no longer working at the time of the survey. Nonetheless, women who worked prenatally constitute almost all of those who work during the early postnatal months (87%). Only 30 percent of women who worked prior to their child's birth reported receiving the benefit of any maternity leave. In most cases (60%), mothers received 30 days of leave. A far larger proportion of mothers who received maternity leave reported current employment than those who did not receive leave (87.1% versus 45.3%). For women with occupations where leave was generally not available, a large portion suspended work temporarily.

    Because of the occupational differences among the
women who are likely and not likely to receive maternity
leave--and since receipt of maternity leave is highly
correlated with current work--women with the highest
incomes (and most education) are also most likely to
be working outside the home during early infancy. Mothers
in the highest income group are more than three times
as likely to be working outside the home as mothers in
the lowest income group. Similarly, women with the highest
educational attainment were about four times as likely
to engage in early outside work as women with no education. Clearly, then, women who work outside the home
during the early infancy of their children are a minority
of the sample who tend to come from higher than average
income families. Thus, it should not be surprising if
women who have maternity leave share the feeding patterns
of other women like themselves: those from higher income
and educational groups.

    In fact, women who report having received mater-
nity leave are slightly <u>less</u> likely to initiate breastfeeding, more likely to have weaned by three or six
months, and to have introduced bottles by two months
as women with no leave. On the other hand, among women
who have leave, longer leave time is associated with
longer breastfeeding. Chapter 6 provides a detailed discussion of these issues.

    The full impact of working outside the home on infant
feeding outcomes can be seen in Tables 2.4 and 2.5. This
logistic regression model indicates that working outside
the home has no significant effect on the probability
that breastfeeding will be initiated. Working outside
the home, other predictors controlled, does have a very
strong association with shortened duration of breastfeeding and earlier use of bottles. Mother's age and level
of education do not seem to exert a significant effect
on breastfeeding duration in Bangkok once employment
and other factors are controlled. Increasing maternal
age, low parity, high family income, and being a Bangkok-
born mother increase the odds that bottle feeding will
be introduced by two months.

    Although maternal employment outside the home emerges
as a significant predictor of infant feeding behavior
in Bangkok, it is important to bear in mind that, at
the present time, relatively few Bangkok women work outside their homes during the immediate postnatal period.
Consequently, the potential population-wide impact of
such work is limited. To the degree that greater numbers
of Bangkok women begin to hold outside jobs in the future,
the effects may become more common. Among those who do
work away from home, the impact on infant feeding patterns

is primarily that of earlier use of bottles and shorter breastfeeding. The impact on breastfeeding initiation is negligible, in part because employed women either receive maternity leave or quit their jobs. In either case, this permits enough time at least to initiate breastfeeding.

Influence of Health Services Factors

A distinctive feature of medical care in Bangkok is the pervasiveness of modern maternity practices. More than 99 percent of the sample reported receiving some form of prenatal care, and almost all births (98%) took place in hospitals. Eighty percent occurred in public hospitals and 18 percent in private institutions.

Just over half the infants roomed with the mother during the hospital stay, while 47 percent were kept in the nursery. Some infants who were kept in a nursery spent all their time there and were not brought to mothers even for breastfeeding. In other cases, although the baby did not stay with the mother, it was brought by a nurse to the mother's room. The most prevalent reason given (32%) for not bringing infants to mothers for breastfeeding was a hospital rule against this practice. Other common reasons were maternal (25%) or infant (22%) illness.

The median postnatal hospital stay was 3.4 days, but a surprising 20 percent of mothers reported staying in the hospital longer than one week. Advice on breast-feeding was reported by about 12 percent of mothers as part of prenatal care and one-half of the mothers reported such advice during the hospital maternity stay. Nine percent of the respondents stated they received pamphlets that dealt specifically with infant feeding. Overall, only a small proportion of women (12%) recalled receiving infant formula samples during their hospital stay. This proportion was far higher in some hospitals than in others. For example, receipt of samples was reported by over 40 percent of mothers who gave birth in Huacheay Hospital.

Infant feeding practices seemed to vary by location of birth (Table 2.3). The prevalence of initiation of breastfeeding was highest among the very few mothers who had home births (96%). Initiation was somewhat lower among mothers who gave birth in public hospitals (91%), and lowest (84%) among those who delivered in private

Table 2.4   OVERALL LOGISTIC REGRESSION MODELS
             (BETA STATISTICS)

	Breastfed 3 Months	Breastfed 6 Months	Bottle by 2 Months
Parity	0.307*	0.463**	-0.289**
Urban Mother	-0.469**	-0.510	0.261
Family Income	-0.184***	-0.175**	0.182***
Mother's Age	0.023	-0.084	0.188**
Education	-0.004	-0.105	0.107
Mother-Infant Contact in Hospital	0.040	0.092	-0.153***
Hospital Sample	-0.237	-0.435	0.249
Work Out	-1.444***	-1.339***	1.377***
Model Chi^2	(156.40)***	(112.20)***	(193.12)***

Statistical significance: *p $\leq$ .05,   **p $\leq$ .01,
                             ***p $\leq$ .001

hospitals. The same trend is evident with respect to breastfeeding duration. There is an opposite trend for introduction of bottle feeding by two months, with twice as many private hospital-born children receiving early bottles as those born at home. These differences may be due to specific attributes of the health care institutions or to confounding with other attributes of the women likely to give birth in each place.

Initiation of breastfeeding is somewhat higher (94% versus 87%) among infants who room with the mother than among those who are kept in the nursery. Life table analysis demonstrates that mothers who roomed-in had about a 10 percent greater chance of still breastfeeding at all ages of the child. More children who are kept in the nursery (53%) initiate bottle feeding by two months than children who roomed with the mother (42%).

Table 2.5   ADJUSTED RISK ODDS RATIOS AND 95% CONFIDENCE
            INTERVALS FOR PREDICTOR VARIABLES WITH
            SIGNIFICANT P VALUES

	Breastfed 3 Months	Breastfed 6 Months	Bottle By 2 Months
Parity			
6-7 vs. 2-3	1.85	2.52	0.56
	(1.43, 2.38)	(1.87, 3.41)	(0.46, 0.69)
Urban Mother	0.63	0.60	NS
	(0.46, 85.0)	(0.42, 0.87)	
Family Income*			
10,000-15,000	0.40	0.42	2.48
vs. 2,000-3,000	(0.36, 0.44)	(0.37, 0.47)	(2.28, 2.70)
Mother's Age			
35-39 vs.	NS	NS	1.45
25-29			(1.2, 1.65)
Mother-Infant Contact in Hospital			
Most vs.	NS	NS	0.54
Least			(0.50, 0.58)
Work Out	0.24	0.26	3.98
	(0.17, 0.32)	(0.17, 0.39)	(2.94, 5.38)

*Bhat

Because of the great variation in extent of mother-infant contact in the hospital, an attempt was made to combine the information available on rooming-in and breastfeeding in the hospital to grade the intensity of mother-infant contact. The sample was divided into five groups: (1) no rooming-in, child never brought to mother; (2) no rooming-in, child brought but no breastfeeding; (3) no rooming-in, child brought and breastfed; (4) rooming-in but no breastfeeding; (5) rooming-in and breastfeeding.

The results of life table analysis show clearly that the group which both roomed-in and breastfed had the highest proportion breastfeeding at each age interval. Groups who experienced any breastfeeding (whether rooming-in or not) had the highest likelihood of continued breast-feeding in every monthly interval until six months of age. Beyond age six months, those mothers who roomed-in, whether breastfeeding took place or not, have consistently higher proportions breastfeeding. Among those who did not room-in, having the child brought to the mother for breastfeeding in the hospital (Group 3) is associated consistently with longer duration of breastfeeding.

Influence of Infant Foods Marketing

Bangkok is a consumer-oriented cultural center with a population very familiar with commercial infant foods. Mothers are knowledgeable about such foods, including specific brands. Breastmilk substitutes, particularly infant formulas, are widely available. A high degree of competition among manufacturers is manifest by the number of brands, sizes, competitive pricing, and promotional activities of the sellers. Although only 12 percent of the mothers reported receiving a free sample of infant formula, this was the highest percentage of all the study cities. The primary source was the hospital where the baby was born. Fewer than one in ten women who had their baby in a public hospital left with a sample of infant formula, whereas nearly one in three who delivered in a private hospital reported receiving a sample. Higher income and education, as well as labor force participation prior to having the baby, were all significantly associated with receiving a sample of infant formula (Chapter 8).

Although the overall rate of sampling, or placement of supplies into the hands of new mothers, is relatively low, the promotional activity appears to have had an effect. Women who received samples were able to recall the brand, knew where it could be bought, and, in fact, many had purchased the sample brand at least once (Chapter 8). Fewer mothers who received formula samples continued to breastfeed their children for at least three months or six months, and more of these women (58%) initiated early bottle feeding than did mothers who did not receive a sample during the hospital stay (46%).

The special relationship between health service personnel and sales representatives (detailers) from the formula companies in Bangkok appeared to create an institutional atmosphere conducive to use of bottles in the maternity hospitals.

Provision of free samples, product placement in retail outlets, product visibility, courting health care workers and encouraging them to advise mothers to use a particular brand, and distribution of supplies to hospitals, many of which eventually become free samples for mothers, form a total marketing approach. The emphasis on promotion within the health care system, together with the underlying consumerist culture, pose a powerful stimulus for the use of breastmilk substitutes among Bangkok mothers.

Overall Model

Logistic regression analysis was expanded by including variables to represent the extent of mother-infant contact and receipt of formula sample (Tables 2.4, 2.5 and 2.6). Both mother-infant contact and mother's birth outside Bangkok were highly significantly associated with increased probability of initiating breastfeeding. Mother's age is significant as well. Mothers with the most contact with their infants had 3 1/2 times the probability of initiating breastfeeding as mothers with the least contact, other factors controlled. High income, low parity, urban birth of the mother, and, most especially, working outside the home for income appeared to shorten duration in these models. Neither of the new variables was significantly related to breastfeeding duration when other factors were controlled.

More intense contact with the mother strongly decreased the odds of early bottle feeding (as did rooming-in alone, in a separate analysis not shown). Infants who had more contact with their mothers in the hospital had only two-thirds the chance of other infants of early bottle feeding. Lower parity, higher age, education, income, and working outside the home all act to increase the probability of early bottle feeding. Working outside the home exerts perhaps the strongest effect, with mothers who work outside the home almost four times as likely to introduce early bottle feeding as those mothers who do not engage in such work, even controlling for family income and mother's education.

Given the extreme magnitude of the effect of working outside the home in these models, it appears that women who do and do not have outside employment may be so different that models should be constructed separately for each of the two groups. Results of the segregated models present striking contrasts (Table 2.6). Many fewer explanatory variables are related to the behavior of women who work outside the home than those who do not, suggesting that work itself is overriding in its importance. Nonetheless, even for these women, increased in-hospital contact remains an important predictor of initiation of breastfeeding. The odds are two and one-half times as great that a child will be breastfed if it has more contact with its mother in the hospital.

Table 2.6   DETERMINANTS OF BREASTFEEDING INITIATION, DURATION AND USE OF
             SUPPLEMENTARY BOTTLES FOR ALL WOMEN AND BY WORK STATUS

	All Women	Women Who Work Out	Women Who Do Not Work Out
Parity	Duration(++) Bottles(--)	Duration(+)	Duration(+)
Mother's Age	Initiation(--)	-0-	Bottles(+)
Family Income	Duration(---) Bottles(+++)	-0-	Duration(---) Bottles(+++)
Education	-0-	Bottles(++)	
Bangkok- Born Mother	Initiation(---)	Initiation(-)	Initiation(--) Duration(-) Bottles(++)
Mother-Infant Contact in Hospital	Bottles(---)	Initiation(+++) Bottles(---)	Initiation(+++) Bottles(---)
Formula Sample	-0-	-0-	-0-

Sign indicates direction of association

(+) (-)   p≤ .05
(++) (--)   p≤ .01
(+++) (---)   p≤ .001

For breastfeeding duration among women who work away from home, there are strikingly few significant associations: only parity is significantly associated, and only for the three-month interval. Higher education is associated with early bottle feeding while both lower income and increased early contact predict less early bottle feeding for this group of working mothers. Mothers with the most in-hospital contact are about half as likely to introduce bottles by two months as mothers with the least contact.

For mothers who do not work outside the home, there are many more variables significantly associated with feeding outcomes. Again, contact is extremely significantly associated with the probability of initiation of breastfeeding. Mothers with the most contact are three times more likely to initiate breastfeeding than those with the least contact. Shorter duration of breastfeeding is associated with receipt of formula samples, lower parity, urban birth, and, especially, higher income. Women who receive a free formula sample are only 60 percent as likely to breastfeed for at least three months as those who do not receive such samples. Four predictors (urban birth, higher family income, older age, and lack of contact with infants in the hospital) are identified as significantly related to the probability of early bottle feeding.

Rooming-in appears to be of potential importance for all women, but generally health service practices have a stronger impact among women who do not work outside the home. Since most women do not work outside the home, especially in the first half-year of an infant's life, these effects deserve careful consideration. For the smaller subgroup of women working outside the home, infant feeding decisions appear to be tied closely to the fact of their employment. Nonetheless, increased mother/infant contact is significant for the decision to initiate breastfeeding and not to use early bottles. Since women who work outside the home tend, as a group, to have a lower rate of breastfeeding initiation and more frequent early supplementation, the strong positive effect is noteworthy.

CONCLUSION

Despite the rapid modernization and shifts in life-style of the past decades, Bangkok mothers maintain a high rate of initiation of breastfeeding. Nonetheless, breastmilk substitutes are introduced early, with most children receiving some form of milk supplementation by the fourth month. Food supplements are introduced even earlier, with almost all children receiving foods

by three months of age. Those children who are offered
breastmilk with other foods but no bottle feeding tend
to breastfeed longer. In this regard, it is not surprising
that early bottle feeding appears independently associated
with truncated breastfeeding, both in the survey results
and in the ethnographic observations. Interestingly,
regression analysis demonstrates that maternal education
is not independently related to breastfeeding initiation
or duration.

Maternal income generation, when it takes place
in the home, does not appear to influence infant feeding
behavior. Work outside the home, however, has a very
important influence on infant feeding practices. The
overall effect is to increase the probability of introduction of early bottle feeding and decrease the duration
of breastfeeding. Probability of initiation of breastfeeding is little affected. Most mothers of infants in Bangkok
do not work, however, and most babies who are weaned
early and supplemented early do not have working mothers.

Logistic regression analysis shows clearly that
women who do not work outside the home respond to influences that do not affect women who work out. The strongest, most consistent relationships for the women who
do not work out are with Bangkok birth of the mother
and higher income, both of which depress the duration
of breastfeeding. Higher parity is associated with breastfeeding for at least six months (but not three months).
For working women, virtually none of the standard set
of factors explain differentials in duration of breastfeeding. If a woman works outside the home, her feeding
patterns are so influenced by that fact that virtually
nothing else matters.

A number of health care practices were found to
be associated with infant feeding behavior in Bangkok.
Contact between mother and infant during the hospital
stay appears to have a positive effect on breastfeeding
initiation and a negative effect on the probability of
early supplementation for all women, but the association
is stronger for women who do not work away from home.
Contact does not appear to affect breastfeeding duration.
Receipt of free formula samples appears associated with
shorter breastfeeding duration, but only among women
who do not work away from home.

When early bottle feeding is added to the regressions
as an independent variable, the independent effects of
income, Bangkok birth, and receipt of formula samples
in the hospital all disappear. This suggests that these
factors may affect breastfeeding duration largely through
their tendency to increase early bottle feeding.

Many of the factors associated with early supplementation and shortened breastfeeding appear to be immutable--or at least difficult to modify by nutrition or health policy. Urban birth, family income, and whether mothers work for income are unlikely to be changed by those interested in improving early infant nutrition.

On the other hand, a sensitive and much more easily accessible avenue for influence may be available in Bangkok: the health care system itself. Health care practices surrounding birth do appear to affect feeding practices among the majority of Bangkok mothers. In addition, the current practices in health care institutions seem inconsistent and ready for thoughtful reexamination. Certainly, the promotion of early contact, early exclusive breastfeeding, rooming-in, and discontinuation of formula samples on discharge are neither radical nor difficult recommendations. Fortunately, the very professionals who are most concerned about maternal and child health do have some ability to influence hospital and health care service policy.

The information gathered by this study suggests that, of all interventions, those which change hospital practices may also have the greatest potential for affecting the practices of women who do work outside the home. While almost no factors can be identified which affect the feeding practices of these women, certain hospital policies which promote early contact appear to have some effect. Because the women who receive maternity leave are also women with the background characteristics associated with earlier supplementation and shorter duration of breastfeeding, the effect of leave policy in promoting breastfeeding cannot be assessed by this study. This is an area which surely merits further investigation. Nonetheless, it is clear that maternity leave as used by Bangkok mothers is not sufficient to ensure better feeding patterns. Bangkok mothers begin supplementation before the end of maternity leave, and some mothers who do receive maternity leave never breastfeed at all.

In fact, it appears that the benefits and the possibility of exclusive breastfeeding during maternity leave are not clear enough in this population. As in many other places, mothers and their medical advisers seem to discount the importance of, for example, one month of exclusive breastfeeding if supplements will need to be given in the second month. Similarly, the idea and techniques of maintenance of mixed feeding (breast and bottle milks) for mothers who must be away from home do not appear to be part of the common wisdom available to mothers or medical professionals. Opportunities to educate or re-educate all levels of health care workers on these points, including pharmacists, midwives, nurses, and physicians, should be sought actively.

Further assessment is needed of labor policies which would facilitate improved infant feeding practices among mothers who work. Certain policies might be more appropriate and effective for some groups of working mothers than for others. Options which need exploration for their potential feasibility and impact include:

1. more flexible leave policies, including the possibility of part-time work
2. leave policy for classes of workers not covered
3. nursing breaks during the day
4. day care near worksites
5. child care information through the workplace

The positive aspects of Bangkok mothers' attitudes toward breastfeeding should be cultivated. These attitudes, along with the clearly independent spirit of Bangkok women, suggest that, when given appropriate information and the opportunity to act upon it, they will be able to choose a reasonable pattern of infant feeding, with longer durations of breastfeeding and less discretionary use of early supplementation.

NOTE

1.   Infant Feeding in Bangkok, Thailand, Vol. II Ethnographic Study: Phase One. (final report), ed. Somchai Durongdej. The Faculty of Public Health, the Faculty of Social Sciences and Humanities and the Institute for Population and Social Research, Mahidol University, Bangkok.

3 Infant Feeding in Bogotá, Colombia

Mary Ann Castle, Giorgio Solimano,
Beverly Winikoff, Belen Samper de Paredes,
Maria Eugenia Romero, and
Adela Morales de Look

> At three months of age it is good to begin
> to feed children other things besides breast-
> milk. Before that time they should only breast-
> feed, otherwise they catch cold and become
> potbellied. (Sector I mother)

> During the first month I breastfed only, but
> my milk wasn't good, it was too watery......and
> a doctor told me to stop breastfeeding. My
> father said the same thing, and he assured
> me that it was because I have a very ill temper
> and this affected the baby and also because
> I was very skinny......then one day I took
> off my blouse, wet with milk and put it in
> the sun to dry. That's why my milk dried off
> (Sector II mother)

All societies have cultural norms for dealing
with reproductive processes, including pregnancy,
childbirth, and lactation. Practices and rituals also
exist to prevent or reverse impairment of these vital
functions. In Bogotá, there appears to be widespread
knowledge of the role of breastmilk in infant survival as illustrated by the first quotation, above.
There is also, however, a not so subtle form of control over women's feeding decisions by both physicians and dominant male family members. This has
importance, since it appears that beliefs which can
interfere with breastfeeding are being fused with new
consumer practices and values. For example, there is
penetration of the belief that bottle milks are superior nutritionally to breastmilk. At the same time,
commercial marketers of infant formula utilize health
institutions and medical personnel to promote their

products. The outcome may be less than optimal infant feeding decisions, especially in households with a low standard of living and accompanying health and nutritional problems.

HOUSEHOLD AND DEMOGRAPHIC CHARACTERISTICS

The three communities from which the sample of 711 study mothers was selected represent low-and middle-income families in Bogotá. Chapter 1 briefly describes the three sectors and their salient social and economic characteristics. The Colombian investigators' primary concern with the health and nutritional problems of less advantaged families led them to exclude upper-income households from the sample. The impact of changing feeding practices, it was assumed, would be most dramatic on babies in poorer households.

The median aggregate family monthly income in this sample was 10,000 pesos (US $185 at the time of the study). When food expenses are deducted from monthly income, 54 percent of the households in the sample have less than 5,000 pesos per month available for other necessities. In general, since poorer people spend a greater proportion of their income on food purchases, there are some families who have just a few pesos remaining after buying food.

The majority of the households reported access to electricity, running water, and toilets (Table 3.1). Almost one-half of the families live in boarding house-type dwellings, however, and share both toilets and running water with other families. Five percent have no facilities whatsoever. At least 20 percent of the families stated that they store water in buckets, pots, pails, large cans, or drums--containers that are easily contaminated. Less than one-third of the sample owns a refrigerator. Variations exist in cooking facilities, with 45 percent using a gas or electric oven or stove.

Sample mothers are young, half younger than 25. Over 60 percent completed less than eight years of education. One-third of the women were born in Bogotá, the other two-thirds are migrants from other parts of the country. Over 80 percent of the women have three children or fewer (Table 3.1). Almost 90 percent of the index children were born in a hospital. The remainder were born either at home or at the home of a midwife.

Table 3.1   SAMPLE CHARACTERISTICS

Socioeconomic Indicators	n	%
Running Water	630	96.0
Electricity	683	97.0
Toilet	645	92.0
Refrigerator	211	31.0

Mother's Schooling	n	%
0	16	2.3
1-4	148	21.2
5-7	264	37.7
8-10	161	23.0
11-12	87	12.5
13+	23	3.3
Total	699	100.0

Mother's Age	n	%
12-17	27	3.9
18-19	74	10.6
20-24	253	36.1
25-29	173	24.7
30-34	111	15.9
35-39	43	6.1
40+ 19	19	2.7
Total	700	100.0

Origins of Mother	n	%
Bogotá Born	247	36.0
Migrant to Bogotá	439	64.0
Total	686	100.0

Parity	n	%
1	265	38.1
2-3	321	46.1
4-5	89	12.8
6-9	21	3.0
Total	696	100.0

Place of Infant Birth	n	%
Public hospital	332	47.7
S.S.hospital	163	23.4
Private hospital	128	18.4
Home	73	10.5
Total	696	100.0

A little over 5 percent of the infants were hospitalized sometime in the first year following birth, and 37.4 percent were reported to be ill in the two weeks previous to the survey.

Fifty-eight percent of the mothers were not using any contraceptive technique at the time of the interview. Many women in the ethnographic study indicated a desire to limit the number of children in their families but noted their husbands' opposition to the use of contraceptives. Women appear not to control such decisions. Ethnographic evidence does suggest, however, that employed women control their own income. They generally use it to supplement food purchases either because their husbands' incomes are inadequate or because they receive only a small portion of it to buy food. Twenty-five percent of the sample mothers were working for income outside of the home at the time of the survey. The most common occupations were domestic service (31%), followed by factory work (15%), secretarial work (9%), and teaching (8%).

INFANT FEEDING PRACTICES
Breastfeeding

Although 97 percent of the sample mothers initiated breastfeeding, there was a rapid introduction of a wide variety of supplements very early in infancy. Less than 10 percent of the infants were exclusively breastfed at the time of the interview. Forty-nine percent were partially breastfed, and 42 percent were completely weaned (Figure 3.1). Forty-six percent of the children are exclusively breastfed in the first month of life. This declines to 10 percent by the end of the second and 2 percent by the end of the third month of life, as food supplements and breastmilk substitutes are added to the diet. Aside from the low incidence of exclusive breastfeeding, there is also a rather short duration for any breastfeeding. By three months of age, one-third of the babies are given nonhuman milk as the only source of milk. After 3 months, the single most common feeding pattern is food plus nonhuman milk (Table 3.2).

The median duration of breastfeeding is 6.9 months. Since most children receive supplementation of foods and nonhuman milks very early, however, these supplements may be a major source of infant nutrition quite early. The frequency of breastfeeding in a 24-hour period can give an idea of the portion of nutrients being supplied by breastmilk. At birth, the mean frequency of breastfeeding is eight per day from which point it quickly declines. By the end of the third month, less than half of the

Table 3.2   FEEDING PATTERN BY AGE OF CHILD (PERCENT)

	Age in Months				
	0 (n=76)	1 (n=66)	3 (n=61)	6-8 (n=149)	9-11 (n=156)
Breast Only	46	14	2	2	0
Breast & Bottle	29	18	5	0	0
Bottle Only	4	6	2	0	0
Breast, Bottle, & Food	7	33	41	37	21
Breast & Food	13	14	16	12	7
Bottle milk and Food	1	15	31	46	71
Food Only	0	0	3	4	2

women are breastfeeding more than three times a day. This has implications for both infant nutrition and maternal fertility.

The data suggest some differences in feeding patterns of boy and girl infants. There is greater exclusive breastfeeding of boys (21%) than girls (6%) in the second month of life. On the other hand, although more boys are exclusively breastfed, they are also more likely to have been completely weaned (38% vs. 16%). Thus, one of the most striking gender differences is the apparent predominance of two sources of milk for girls (breast and bottle) versus only one (either breast or bottle) for boys. More mothers with sons than with daughters believe crying is an indication of "insufficient breast-milk." This suggests a cultural as well as an individual response: emphasis on the survival of males may result in earlier supplementation if boy infants appear to be unsatisfied with mothers' milk alone. Food supplementation also shows a different pattern among girls and boys. By the second month of life, 18 percent more girls receive

Figure 3.1   BREASTFEEDING PATTERNS IN BOGOTÁ

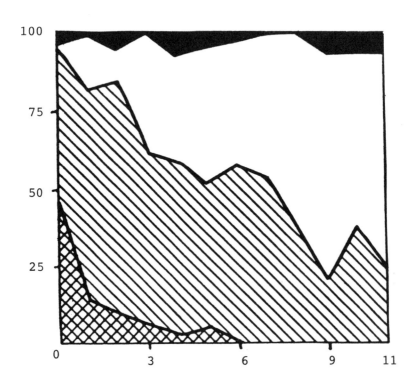

 Never breastfed (n = 23, 3%)

Ever breastfed but stopped (n = 273, 62%)

Currently breastfeeding (n = 411, 58%)

Exclusively breastfed (n = 58, 8.4%)

foods than do boys. The reasons for these differences in feeding behavior need further investigation.

Insufficient Milk and Weaning

Almost 60 percent of the women who stopped breast-feeding did so because of "insufficient milk." Fifty-three percent of these said their milk "failed to come"; 28 percent believed their child's crying indicated insufficient milk, 11 percent reported the child did not suckle, and 9 percent blamed their own malnutrition. When mothers were asked what a woman can do in order to produce more breastmilk, 53 percent indicated that they should drink more liquids (including soup); 16 percent suggested eating more; and 27 percent said they could eat brown sugar water, alone or with other liquids, herbs, or foods. Only 4 percent suggested breastfeeding more often.

Ethnographic data indicate that the hot and cold (humoral) theory of disease is widespread among the Bogotá women and is reflected in mothers' interpretations of illness and health, including breastfeeding problems such as insufficient milk. In general, the theory rests on the assumption that a healthy body is somewhat "wet" and "warm" and that disease is a deviation from this state either toward "cold" or "hot" conditions. Unfavorable states may be produced by a change in body temperature, by eating too much food, or by particular substances which are also classified as "hot" and "cold." Usually therapies consist of treating "cold" classified states with "hot" foods and medications and "hot" states with "cool" substances.

Lactating mothers are considered to be in a vulnerable state, potentially dangerous to both mother and child. This belief can cause a woman to stop breastfeeding when an illness or some other factor "thins" her milk. If a mother catches cold, she may stop breastfeeding because it makes the child "feel uncomfortable and cry during the night." Worry, anxiety, tiredness, and fright all affect consistency and quantity of breastmilk, resulting in diarrhea in babies. This can be avoided only by cessation of breastfeeding. Sixteen percent of the sample attributed the "drying off" of their milk to changes in temperature, for example the result of exposure to cold when doing laundry or to kitchen heat.

One can prevent decreased milk supply by adhering to pre- and postnatal diets (including use of herbs and herbal baths) and especially to the traditional 40-day postpartum rest period. Many women are aware of traditional diet prescriptions and believe in their importance.

Few appear able to follow the specifications, however. Recaida, with symptoms of chills, fever, tiredness, and depression, is believed to develop if dietary prescriptions are not followed. Women believe that suspension of breastfeeding is necessary to prevent this illness from being passed on to the infant.

Poor women state that they are living and working under increasingly difficult conditions. The inability to feed their families well is a serious source of anxiety to these women whose resources cannot assure a ready supply of all types of food. They claim that their children born in Bogotá weighed less than those born elsewhere. Grandmothers corroborate this, saying that their own children ate a better and wider variety of foods, were breastfed for longer durations, and appeared healthier than their Bogotá-born and -raised grandchildren. Many of the mothers are unable to avoid work or strenuous exertion after delivery and cannot follow postpartum diets, resulting, it is felt, in poor quality and inadequate breastmilk. Moreover, belief in the hot and cold theory may predispose women to expect drastic changes in milk supply with changes in lifestyles.

While mothers have limited control over the quality of their own milk supply, they may feel more in control of their child's nutrition when using bottle milks. In addition, social pressure for women to stop breastfeeding, as well as the availability of milks at some health clinics and hospitals and at drug stores that extend credit, contributes to the introduction of bottle formulas and early cessation of breastfeeding. Ethnographic material describes husbands who bring home formula for their wives to use. Some health professionals in Bogotá also recommend to mothers the use of bottle formula as a superior food. Moreover, there is a widespread belief, reinforced by doctors and pharmacists, that if the mother is ill or experiences "insufficient milk," then she should suspend breastfeeding to avoid communicating illness to the baby. In this study, the male doctors appear to create a sense of personal failure in the women and undermine their ability and will to breastfeed for longer durations. Thus, the "insufficient milk" syndrome may be a manifestation of a deteriorating position of women in Bogotá, with lowering of their status as mothers along with perceived worsening of living conditions.

Details of Supplementation

Initiation of breastmilk substitutes and foods occurs very early, with over 60 percent of the infants receiving both before the end of the second month of life. Forty percent of 0-1-month-old breastfeeding infants receive a bottle as do 65 percent of 1-2 month olds. Thirty percent of the women who breastfeed and provide milk supplements feed them to their infants immediately before or after breastfeeding. Total wean-ing, on the average, takes place less than two months after the introduction of the bottle. Use of supplementary foods is more common at all ages than the bottle, except in the first and second months. By the third month, 50 percent or more of children eat juice, fruits, vegetables, grain, sugar, and meats, fish, or eggs. At seven months, children are expected to eat "anything." Forty-six percent of those in charge of feeding the children over-dilute the milk preparations. These additions are either extra liquids (sugar water, herb water, or vegetable water); more water than producers indicate for infant formulas; or replace-ment of part of powdered milk with flours (plantain, corn, etc.) and sugars. In all socioeconomic groups, women use bottles for liquified foods and add foods to formulas in varying degrees. The use of starches, flours, and sugars is much higher among the poor. According to pharmacists interviewed, dilution with brown sugar water and cornstarch is a widespread cause of malnutrition. Closely associated with dilution of milks is the reported lack of cleanliness of bottles. A quarter of the sample indicated they wash out their baby's bottle only once or twice a day. Methods vary from boiled water and no soap to rinsing in any available water.

Overall, it is the middle- and lower-middle-class women who spend a greater proportion of their income on infant formulas and processed foods, however. Among these women, bottles are boiled, and a major problem of dilution with water is not observed. Here, the addi-tion of brown sugar or apple or vegetable (spinach and carrot) water is for taste, nutrition, and aesthetics rather than as a way to conserve the milk product.

Sugar appears to be a major food source for both adults and children. In some sectors, its use is so extensive that panela (brown sugar loaf), a product produced with no health quality control, is purchased wholesale.1 In the seventeenth century large-scale production of sugar began for both export and self-consumption throughout South America. Colombia is the world's third largest panela-producing country. Given its history, it is not surprising that Colombians view panela as an item of direct consumption as well as hav-ing medicinal properties. Sugar was used as a medicine in ancient Arab pharmacology. It entered Europe as both a spice and a medicine where it was commonly prescribed with combinations of foods. The ease with which sugar can be combined with other foods, especially in liquid form, is well appreciated by the Bogotá mothers. Although panela is a favored food, the ethnography indicates widespread knowledge of a whole range of infant foods and awareness of their nutritional qualities. Since the extensive use of panela appears closely linked to cost and availability, enabling women to increase the purchase of more nutritious food might decrease the use of panela.

Clearly many mothers are aware of aspects of appropriate nutrition and food supplementation. The only women who appear not to have this knowledge are very young women who live more isolated lives far from their own mothers. These younger women most often use bottle milks to wean. This is a group that may be in need of special help, education, and intervention. In all sectors, women used bottles for liquified foods and added foods to formulas in varying degrees. Naturally, the use of starches, flours, and sugars was much higher among the poorer classes. The use of baby bottles presents a serious public health problem, not only in terms of microbial contamination, but in the potential for destruction of children's teeth through the "nursing bottle syndrome." It is the major cause of caries and premature loss of deciduous teeth. Milk or formula can produce this picture because of the lactose present. Milk with panela and cornstarch or juice may produce an even more marked picture.

DETERMINANTS OF INFANT FEEDING PRACTICES
Influence of Background Factors

Since infant feeding research generally shows an association between socioeconomic characteristics and infant feeding behavior, background variables were examined for their relation to infant feeding choices. As expected, since breastfeeding initiation is high, none of the socioeconomic factors appear associated with initiation of breastfeeding. Increasing family income, in general, is associated with shorter breastfeeding duration. Education is not related in a straightforward way, but women at both the lowest and highest ends of the educational spectrum appear to breastfeed longer than women with a modest amount of schooling. Women of the highest parity and age breastfeed longer than other women. Mother's place of origin appears unrelated to breastfeeding duration (Table 3.3).

Older women, parity-one women, and women born in Bogotá are at greater risk of introducing an early bottle. Income level appears unrelated to the propensity

to use early bottles. Mothers with more years of education and higher parity are less likely to do so. The
negative relationship between education and introduction
of a bottle is interesting and in contrast to findings
in other developing countries. It may reflect a high
level of public information about nutrition in Colombia
in recent years or the extent to which educated women
in Colombia are influenced by trends in Western Europe
and North America.

Logistic regression analysis was used to evaluate
the individual effect of these background variables on
specific infant feeding outcomes while controlling for
the other predictors (statistics not given). None of
the variables used (including mother's education, age,
family income, mother's birthplace or parity) had any
significant association with duration of breastfeeding
to three or six months. Breastfeeding for much longer
than the norm in Bogotá (nine months or more) was highly
significantly associated with lower family income. The
ethnography indicates that the poorest women may have
minimal postpartum contact with the formal health sector
and, therefore, may be less exposed to external influences promoting early cessation of breastfeeding. Also,
poor women have little, if any, disposable cash and may
not be able to rely on purchased milks as the sole
source of infant nutrition.

Background predictors are more highly associated
with early bottle feeding than with breastfeeding durations. Mothers with more years of schooling are less
likely to bottlefeed early. Lower parity and higher
maternal age both increase the likelihood of introducing an early bottle. In the group of women over 35 with
one child, 81 percent introduced a bottle by two months
as compared with 47 percent of all women. Although the
combination of low parity and older age may be associated with higher economic status, income, by itself,
has no significant relationship to early bottle use.
Early bottle feeding itself is strongly associated with
the probability of early discontinuation of breastfeeding. Introduction of a bottle by one month is a powerful
predictor of the chances of not breastfeeding to three
months or six months. There is no way to separate those
mothers for whom use of the bottle represents an intent
to wean from those for whom it is associated with unintended termination of breastfeeding.

Table 3.3   BREASTFEEDING AND BOTTLE FEEDING PRACTICES BY
             SELECTED VARIABLES

	Breastfed 3 months		Breastfed 6 months		Bottle by 2 months	
	n	%	n	%	n	%
Mother's Age						
12-17 years	10	62.5	57	1.4	12	52.2
18-19	30	71.4	17	58.6	32	53.3
20-24	119	77.3	54	56.8	87	43.7
25-29	69	72.6	30	46.9	58	43.6
30-34	47	71.1	22	52.4	47	54.7
35-39	18	81.8	7	70.0	20	62.5
40+	10	90.9	8	88.9	9	60.0
Education						
None	9	90.2	6	100.0	6	46.2
1-4 years	60	71.4	31	59.6	58	50.9
5-7	116	75.8	53	54.1	104	50.5
8-10	66	68.7	27	50.9	66	50.4
11-12	41	82.0	18	50.0	27	39.7
13+	10	83.3	7	70.0	4	25.0
Parity						
1	103	74.6	43	53.8	111	55.0
2-3	144	73.8	72	56.7	113	44.5
4-5	42	75.0	20	56.6	31	44.9
6-12+	11	91.6	5	62.5	7	41.2
Mother's Origin						
Elsewhere	189	75.3	91	55.5	176	51.5
Bogotá	107	72.8	46	54.1	84	42.9
Family Income*						
Low-6,000	57	79.2	30	71.4	48	48.0
6,001-9,800	58	77.3	30	60.0	45	44.6
9,801 14,900	65	69.9	29	48.3	75	55.6
14,901-29,000	72	80.0	29	52.7	50	44.2
29,001 Hi	27	65.9	14	48.3	31	52.5

*Pesos

Table 3.3 BREASTFEEDING AND BOTTLE FEEDING PRACTICES BY
(Cont'd)   SELECTED VARIABLES

	Breastfed 3 months		Breastfed 6 months		Bottle by 2 months	
	n	%	n	%	n	%
Maternal Employment						
Yes	84	65.1	45	47.9	58	51.6
No	241	80.6	113	63.8	146	47.2
Place of Infant Birth						
Public hospital	140	73.3	74	59.7	119	45.4
Private hospital	59	76.6	27	58.7	48	47.1
Social Security hospital	64	71.1	23	43.4	67	54.5
Home	38	80.9	18	56.2	29	48.3
Rooming-In						
Yes	259	75.3	127	41.2	220	47.1
No	40	71.4	14	58.3	43	56.6

Influence of Infant Foods Marketing

Commercial infant foods are widely available in Bogotá. These include infant formulas produced by multi-national companies and infant foods produced locally. Some locally produced products appeared to be of low quality, some showed evidence of mislabeling and mis-statements of nutritional value or misrepresentation of their suitability for infants. Mass market advertising was not observed, although approximately one-half of the sample recall prior advertising of infant formulas. Evidence indicates that promotional activities of multinational producers are now focused on hospitals and health professionals (Chapter 7). Hospital personnel are regularly visited by company representatives. Nestlé, Wyeth, and Abbott provided educational materials, posters, product samples, free supplies, and sometimes pediatric equipment to health facilities. The distribution of free samples of infant formula to mothers was not widespread (6.2%). Health care workers interviewed by the ethnographers mentioned that brand endorsement was routine and had a high probability of establishing brand loyalty. Approximately 25 percent of the mothers who were bottle feeding indicated that they were using a brand recommended by their physician. In a climate where price competition exacerbates problems of quality and mislabeling, and where economic conditions can lead consumers to shift from higher-priced humanized formulas to lower-priced milk products (powdered milks, cereals, flours, etc.), it is especially important for health professionals to concentrate their recommendations on breastfeeding.

Influence of Maternal Employment

At the time of the survey, 25 percent of the women were engaged in some form of income-generating activity away from home. Because of the particular questionnaire used in Bogotá, there is no way to identify the women who earn money at home. In general, mothers in the labor force are of lower parity. Almost 50 percent of the employed women had only one child. Women with more than thirteen years of education were employed relatively much more frequently than other women, but they constitute only 7.4 percent of all income earners because they are such a small fraction of the entire study sample. Women from the two highest income categories are also more likely than average to be employed.

As expected, very few mothers return to their jobs immediately after the birth of the child. The usual period allowed for maternity leave is about two months. In fact, mothers of two month olds report employment at a higher rate: 23 percent. The prevalence of employment remains steady to about age six months and rises to over 30 percent from then on. Three-quarters of the employed women reported how many hours they spent out of the house. Of these, over 80 percent spent eight or more hours away. Over 85 percent of all employed mothers reported being separated from their infants during work.

Women employed away from home have a greater tendency to wean their children early. Eighty-two percent of such women with children over seven months had weaned compared with 66 percent of the other mothers. Many more mothers who work away from home use bottles early: 82 percent of employed women with babies 0-2 months reported use of the bottle as compared to 55 percent of mothers of 0-2-month-old babies who did not report outside employment.

In a regression model, breastfeeding to three, six, or nine months is strongly and consistently negatively associated with working outside the home (statistics not shown). Women employed away from home are only about one-half as likely to breastfeed for three, six, or nine

months as those who are not. This is also evident in
life table analysis where the median duration of breastfeeding is much longer for women who are at home (8.5
months) than for those who also hold jobs away from home
(4.5 months). Bottle feeding behavior, on the other
hand, does not appear to be strongly influenced by paid
employment status per se. Women working outside the home
are only slightly more likely to bottlefeed their children at an early age.

Separate analyses (not shown) of women working
outside their homes and other mothers show that for
women who are not so employed, family income has a
highly significantly negative association with breastfeeding to six and nine months. This association does
not hold for the employed women, however. For these
women, the only significant predictor of breastfeeding
is higher educational status, associated with shorter
breastfeeding duration (p <.01) for six months only
(and not for three or nine months). The introduction
of a bottle by one month is more strongly and consistently negatively associated with breastfeeding duration for women not working away from home than for
employed mothers. It is possible that introduction of
early bottles may signal the intention to wean for women
who are not employed away from home, whereas bottle use
is more a matter of necessity, unrelated to the desire
to continue breastfeeding, for employed women.

Ethnographic descriptions vividly illustrate the
relationship between maternal employment and infant
feeding behavior. Some mothers who are employed outside of the home replace daytime breastfeeding with bottles of artificial or canned milk with starch. Usually
these prepared bottles are made at a single time for
an entire day's use. One pharmacist said he knew of
cases where poor women express breastmilk to be fed by
an older child of six or seven years, and the hungry
older child drinks the milk, leaving the infant without
food. This pharmacist advises women to use complete formula milk and to leave it for both the infant and older
children.

Interestingly, the case studies also strongly
suggest that poor women who can earn some money have
an advantage over those who depend solely on their
husbands' incomes. Independent income can result in
supplementation of all children's nutrition with more
and higher quality foods. This alone must be a great
incentive for women to return to paid work. As one
mother poignantly stated:

One day that I do not work is a day that I

do not give soup to the children. When I have money I make them soup with a lot of bones, and always I try to give them vegetables, lentils and beans, but one week that the children do not eat well is sufficient time for them to become malnourished...... sometimes on weekends I make them chicken soup, but that is the same as having chicks and giving them corn only once a week; it is not the same as giving it to them every day...... also, if I have to work away from home, it is my fourteen-year-old son who makes the soup any which way he can.

Influence of Health Services

Although most women (88%) received some form of prenatal care, many were not seen by a health worker until after the sixth month of pregnancy. Ninety percent of the births were in hospitals (Table 3.1). Approximately 30 percent of the sample received advice on feeding prior to delivery, and 30 percent received advice in the course of neonatal care. Professional medical personnel appear to be the primary source of information and advice to women regarding supplementation.

The survey data show that public health sector professionals are more likely to recommend the use of bottle milks (59%) during a prenatal visit than workers in other health facilities (6%). Families of employees covered by the Social Security Institute's benefits were eligible to receive canned milk up until six months of life for "needy infants." This policy may predispose some workers to value these products as nutritional supplements. Postnatally, private physicians appeared to recommend the use of artificial milks to a much greater extent than they did during prenatal visits (i.e., 3 percent prenatally, 20 percent postpartum). Mothers reported that approximately one-quarter of the advice in the first few days after birth was to bottlefeed infants.

Bivariate analyses of the type of advice reported and feeding outcomes show a relationship between reported recommendations by health workers to use formulas and shorter breastfeeding duration. Weaning appears to be related to both prenatal and postpartum advice. For example, 83 percent of the women who remembered being told about breastfeeding during a prenatal visit were still breastfeeding at three months compared with 67 percent of those who remembered receiving bottle feeding recommendations. Conversely, by two months, 67 percent of the mothers who recalled advice on formula feeding had introduced a bottle to their infants compared with 40 percent of those who recalled breastfeeding advice. Thus, women seem to act according to the professional advice they remember.

Additional supporting evidence is provided by qualitative data. Both women who use health centers and those who use private pediatricians appear to be at high risk of introducing bottle milks too early. The ethnography notes private physicians who recommend S-26 to be given immediately after birth and also advise commercial tonics to enhance the newborn's appetite. Physicians were reported to have given advice against night feeding because it caused "indigestion" and also recommended weaning with formula. The ethnography relates that some mothers do not breastfeed because they do not trust the quality of their milk, a perception reinforced by health professionals who suggest, for example, that clear milk indicates poor quality.

The in-depth interviews are replete with examples that highlight the extent of misinformation and poor advice given by physicians. Doctors suggested that women cease breastfeeding when their children have diarrhea or when the mother has a cold or other illness. In an interesting incident, a physician recommended weaning a child who was over twelve months of age because "he [the physician] said it would finish me off." In another instance, a two-month-old infant had amoebic dysentery, and the doctor recommended that the mother cease breastfeeding. He then suggested different milks, "first, AL 110; then Isomil because the baby wouldn't assimilate sugars or fats well. But after the fourth month the baby refused this milk, so the doctor recommended S-26."

Although these examples do not demonstrate causality between advice from medical personnel and diminished duration of breastfeeding, the data capture the predilection of these professionals to recommend artificial milks too early in infants' lives.

Many factors are responsible for physicians giving inappropriate advice to mothers of young children, and, clearly, inadequate education is involved. Whatever the reason for the poor advice, the damage done can be far reaching. Recommendations to cease breastfeeding convey the idea that breastfeeding can harm children. In effect, the advice given to these breastfeeding mothers suggests that they are incompetent and in need of guidance by health professionals in their reproductive and caretaking roles. In this sense, traditional female control over children's health becomes appropriated by the male professional, thus perpetuating and intensifying sexual inequalities. Chapter 7 explores this issue in more general terms as part of the process of incorporating women's reproductive roles into the curative model of obstetrics.

Factors other than advice of physicians or pharmacists also appear to influence feeding decisions of mothers in Bogotá. For example, the cross-sectional data demonstrate a trend in infant feeding choices by place of child's birth (Table 3.2). Social Security hospitals have the lowest rates of initiation, the lowest proportions of breastfeeders at all durations, and the highest percentage introducing early bottles. Life table analysis clearly shows that women who deliver in hospitals where rooming-in is practiced have a higher proportion of breastfeeders at each age interval, with greater differences after four months of age.

Several of these issues were explored in a logistic regression model (which expanded the original model of background variables) in order to locate a predictive health service variable (statistics not shown). Pre- and postnatal advice, location of birth, receipt of a free formula sample, and birth by Cesarean section are either too rare or not defined clearly enough to serve in the model. Rooming-in does not have a statistically significant relationship to any of the dependent variables in a model including all mothers. In a separate analysis (not shown) of the women who do not work away from home (i.e., the majority of the sample), however, rooming-in is highly significantly associated with breastfeeding for at least six months and for both three and six months when early use of bottles is controlled. A woman not working away from home who has roomed-in with her infant in the hospital is six times as likely to breastfeed at six months as one who was separated at birth from her child.

The interaction between aspects of health services, background parameters, and infant feeding behavior may be much more complex than regression techniques alone can assess. This is seen in part by the statistically significant outcome for the rooming-in variable only when two groups of mothers are examined separately. The ethnographers, after extensive interviewing, attribute early introduction of milk bottles largely to the influence of the professional health sector. In one area of the city, all women interviewed in-depth related a period of separation from their infants at birth in the hospital. Their children were given either dextrose or artificial milks. Doctors affiliated with the health

care facilities recommended specific milk brands to
their clients. Thus, the idea that breastmilk is not
the most nutritious or complete food is established at
birth or shortly thereafter for many of these women.

On the other hand, poorer women utilize druggists,
non-licensed pharmacists, and herbalists as well as the
formal health care system. Many of the informal health
care workers are more aware of the life circumstances
of the women and the potential for dilution of formulas.
The reliance on informal sources of health care is an
important cultural preference that can be utilized in
health policies or educational campaigns.

The Overall Model

In an effort to create an overall model of the
determinants of infant feeding in Bogotá, the entire
set of predictor variables was fit in a logistic
regression model. Very few of the variables have
significant associations with breastfeeding duration
and none is significantly related to all durations
examined. Employment away from home is significantly
negatively correlated for three and nine months duration
and higher income is significantly negatively associated
with breastfeeding nine months or more. (Tables 3.4,
3.5). Many more variables are significantly correlated
with propensity to use early bottles. More maternal
education significantly <u>decreases</u> the probability of
introducing an early bottle as does higher parity. Older
age increases the chances of early bottle use.

In an analysis of the determinants of breastfeeding
duration which controls for early bottle use (statistics
not shown), paid employment outside the home is
correlated at an even higher level of significance with
not breastfeeding for three months but loses its
association with breastfeeding to nine months. Higher
family income retains a significant association with
weaning by nine months. Early introduction of bottles
is itself highly significantly associated with not
breastfeeding to three or six months. A woman who
introduces a bottle by one month is four times less
likely to be breastfeeding at three months than a mother
who did not use a bottle by one month. No relationship
is seen, however, between introducing a bottle early
and breastfeeding to nine months.

Similar separate analyses were done for women employed outside the home and women without such jobs
(statistics not shown). A woman who experiences hospital
rooming-in and who does <u>not</u> work away from home is

Table 3.4   OVERALL LOGISTIC REGRESSION MODEL (BETA STATISTICS)

	Breastfed 3 Months	Breastfed 6 Months	Breastfed 9 Months	Bottle by 2 Months
Education	0.1641	-0.0098	0.2894	-0.2946**
Mother's Age	0.0041	0.0086	0.0407	0.0470**
Family Income	-0.0935	-0.1444	-0.5429**	0.0541
Mother's Origin	-0.1865	0.0300	-0.470	-0.2468
Parity	0.0855	-0.0822	0.0749	-0.4975**
Maternal Employment	-0.7975**	-0.5135	-0.9757*	0.1372
Rooming-In	0.2700	0.5792	0.1526	-0.3575
Model Chi^2	13.27	10.62	13.22	24.100**

Statistical significance: p *$\leq$.05 level; ** $\leq$.01

62

Table 3.5   ADJUSTED RISK ODDS RATIOS AND 95% CONFIDENCE INTERVALS FOR
PREDICTOR VARIABLES WITH SIGNIFICANT P VALUES

	Breastfed 3 Months	Breastfed 9 Months	Bottle by 2 Months
Education (Years) 5-7 vs. 1-4	NS	NS	(0.61, 0.9) 0.745
Mother's Age 40+ vs. 20-24	NS	NS	(1.6, 1.25) 1.207
Family Income* 9,801-14,700 vs. Low-6,000	NS	(0.22, 0.51) 0.338	NS
Parity 2-3 vs 1	NS	NS	(0.45, 0.81) 0.608
Maternal Employment	(0.27, 0.80) 0.450	(0.14, 0.99) 0.377	NS

*Pesos

almost three times as likely to breastfeed for three months and five times as likely to breastfeed for six months as a woman separated from her child at birth. Rooming-in does not affect the odds of breastfeeding to any duration for those women who work away from home, but higher education is a negative influence on the chances of breastfeeding to six months and beyond. For mothers at home, on the other hand, education is <u>positively</u> correlated with breastfeeding duration but not significantly so. Older women and women with higher family incomes <u>if</u> <u>they</u> <u>do</u> <u>not</u> <u>work</u> <u>outside</u> <u>the</u> <u>home</u> are significantly less likely to breastfeed for longer durations. These relationships are not present among the women who hold jobs outside the home. In almost all cases, the use of bottles is itself highly predictive of early weaning. A paradoxical exception is that, for mothers working away from home, early bottle feeding is <u>positively</u> associated with breastfeeding for nine months or more (p<.01).

CONCLUSION

This examination of everyday life of low-income mothers in Bogotá, Colombia, demonstrates that in many ways, the difficulties of feeding infants are an integral part of life in poverty. Unemployment and underemployment, substandard housing, and poor sanitary facilities compound the problems of child care. Infants are often given early supplementation with insufficient quantities of bottle milks strongly diluted with <u>panela</u> water and starch. Few infants receive their mother's milk exclusively for the recommended duration. Very early supplementation is correlated with both older-age and lower-parity mothers, neither of which are characteristics that can be modified by intervention programs. On the other hand, more education is independently associated with less early supplementation, suggesting that improving education may also help improve infant feeding practices in Bogotá.

Although almost all mothers in Bogotá use bottle supplements early, employed women are at greater risk for early cessation of breastfeeding. In fact, virtually no predictors of breastfeeding duration are strongly and consistently associated with time of weaning in the group of employed mothers. Employment outside the home itself seems to have the predominant effect. In order for poor women, their infants, families, and society to benefit from paid female employment, it is necessary to ensure that a proper support system is available. This includes, but is not restricted to, adequate minimum wages, job training, quality child care alternatives, maternity leaves, breastfeeding breaks, and other social security measures, such as supplemental income to poor women in order that they have the option not to enter the labor force. If these policies were implemented, women would find it easier to continue breastfeeding for longer periods and redirect money now spent on formula to buying better food for the entire household.

Women who do not hold outside jobs are more open to the influences of other factors in their feeding practices. Family income, of no significant relationship to breastfeeding duration for employed women, shows the expected strong negative relationship among women who do not work for pay outside the home. In addition, for this majority of women, the experience of rooming-in is strongly correlated with longer breastfeeding. This is, of course, an area in which health policies can be modified to increase the probability of improved infant feeding practices.

Although the belief that bottle milks are nutritionally superior has clearly penetrated Bogotá households, the common mixed feeding regimes can be explained only partially by this notion. The study identified many women with knowledge of appropriate infant weaning foods who, although they believed breastfeeding was superior nutritionally, nonetheless faced structural and ideological barriers to implementing their preferences in their own families. The common practice of weaning onto bottle formulas can often be traced to the appropriation of infant feeding decisions by others, that is, dominating family members and medical institutions.

The "insufficient milk syndrome" is part of a complex change in women's status. The syndrome is related to utilization of hot and cold classifications of behavior and foods as well. The consequence can be lactation failure or unnecessary supplementation. Although similar perceptions of insufficient milk exist among mothers worldwide, it is necessary to understand its cultural context in order to formulate approaches to the problem in particular nations.

The intersection of Western medicine and commercial marketing has begun to transform Bogotá women into consumers instead of producers of milk. This study has specifically identified advice and practices of physicians and health professionals at public facilities as effectively discouraging good infant feeding practices. A very directed educational program for physicians and other health professionals is needed in order to reverse misconceptions. Fathers should be included in health

education campaigns as well, so that attitudes and behaviors suggested by health workers will not meet
with opposition in the home.   Rooming-in practices
should be established in all hospitals and prelacteal
feeds of formula and dextrose discouraged. Marketing
of commercial infant feeding products (whether of local
or transnational origin) through health delivery institutions and personnel should be limited. These recommendations can help reverse the institutional tendency
to introduce bottle formulas at the expense of breastfeeding.

There is an internal consistency in the data which
suggests an integrated approach to the problems of infant feeding found in Bogotá;

- o   if women can be less constrained by meager in-
       comes, through income supplementation, higher
       minimum wages, and paid job training programs;

- o   if they have an influential position regard-
       ing the distribution of household resources;

- o   if they can secure quality childcare, and get
       adequate rest and nutrition as suggested by
       tradition;

- o   if they can be properly supported when they
       experience breastfeeding problems and receive
       professional approval of breastfeeding and
       child care decisions;

then, perhaps, some of the negative attitudes associated
with women's social and reproductive roles will begin
to change. Childbirth and raising children may, then,
be a source of pleasure and happiness rather than merely
an addition to life's burdens for these women.

NOTE

1.   Morales de Look et al., "The Food Industry in
     Bogotá," Report to the Population Council
     (Javeriana University, 1982), p. 8.

4 Infant Feeding in Nairobi, Kenya

Michael C. Latham, K. Okoth Agunda, and
Terry Elliot

> When the baby cries
> Let him suck
> From the breast.
> There is no fixed time
> For breastfeeding.
> When the baby cries
> It may be he is ill;
> The first medicine for a child
> Is the breast.
> Give him milk
> And he will stop crying.

This excerpt from the lyric poem Song of Lawino by the East African poet Okot p'Bitek illustrates traditional views on breastfeeding.1 It suggests breastfeeding on demand, during sickness and in health. This is a pattern that appears to be changing in urban Kenya today, to the detriment of children and their families.

Kenya has a population of about 20 million people, a reported infant mortality rate of approximately 80 per 1,000 live births, a GNP of some $340 in 1983, and life expectancy at birth of around 53 years. Judged from these indicators Kenya would be in the top one-third of sub-Saharan African countries in terms of development. The annual rate of population increase is now said to be 3.9 percent which is higher than that of any other country in the world.

Kenya straddles the equator but has major differences in altitude, rainfall, and ecology between one area and another. These differences, together with great cultural diversity, result in major variations in population density, in foods grown and consumed, and in ways of life.

The vast majority of the population still resides in the rural areas, where agriculture, including livestock management, is the main occupation. Nairobi, the capital city, now has a population of over one million people and it, together with another dozen towns, are increasing in population at a rapid pace.

Although by far the greater numbers of people still reside in rural areas, it is likely that changes in infant feeding practices influenced by modernization will begin in the cities and only later spread to communities in the countryside. This has been the rule in most other countries. In rural Kenya, even very recently, W. M. Van Steinbergen and others have noted a high prevalence and long duration of breastfeeding.2

The Nairobi Infant Feeding Study included a large cross-sectional survey of a weighted sample of 980 low- and middle-income Nairobi mothers who had given birth in the previous eighteen months. The mothers were interviewed in their homes between March and June 1982. They were selected using the Kenya Central Bureau of Statistics urban sampling frame based on the 1979 national census. Twelve upper-income clusters were eliminated from consideration, and the remaining 43 clusters were covered by the survey. A description of the sampling, the survey methodology, and the instrument development can be found in Chapter 1. Both the weighted sampling and the exclusion of upper-income strata were somewhat different from the study design used in the other three sites. Since case weights were assigned to each individual and tabulations are always reported as rounded to the nearest whole number of "respondents," some totals appear to be based on numbers larger than the entire number of women interviewed (e.g., 982 or 983 instead of 980, Table 4.1). Because of the sample selection, it should be recognized that these data, and statements based on them, apply only to low- and middle-income families in Nairobi.

HOUSEHOLD AND DEMOGRAPHIC CHARACTERISTICS

Characteristics of the households varied considerably. Some families lived in apartment buildings and others in separate houses, many of which were small and overcrowded. The mean household size was 5.5 persons (range 2-13). Only 30 percent had piped water in the house; 40 percent of families had access to a flush toilet (often outside the house); 29 percent had electricity; and 7 percent had a refrigerator. Over half the mothers cooked using wood or charcoal and another one-third using kerosene. Only 12% cooked with gas or electricity.

Table 4.1 provides information from the mothers
on age, tribal origin, education, parity, length of residence in Nairobi and location of birth of the index child,
socioeconomic status, and maternal employment. Ninety-
seven percent of the infants had at some time been breastfed, and 77 percent were still being breastfed at the
time of the interview. One hundred and sixty-two (17%)
of the children were reported to have been hospitalized
as in-patients since birth. The most common causes of
admission were gastro-intestinal problems, respiratory
infections, and measles. Forty-four percent of the mothers
reported that the index child had been ill in the last
two weeks.

Table 4.1   SAMPLE CHARACTERISTICS*

Mother's Age	n	%	Education	n	%
19 & under	164	16.7	None	175	17.8
20-24	422	43.0	Standard 1-7	485	49.4
25-29	262	26.7	Form 1 & above	321	32.7
30-35	84	8.6			
35 & over	49	5.0	Total	981	99.9
Total	981	100.0			

Mother's Tribal Origin	n	%	Parity	n	%
Luo	300	30.6	1	255	26.0
Kikuyu	269	27.4	2	254	25.9
Luhya	217	22.2	3-4	278	28.3
Other	195	19.8	5+	196	20.0
Total	981	100.0	Total	983	100.2

Table 4.1   SAMPLE CHARACTERISTICS*
(Cont'd)

Residence in Nairobi			Socioeconomic Status		
	n	%		n	%
<1 year	150	15.3	No electricity	634	65.0
2-5 years	489	49.8	or inside		
>5 years	342	34.9	water		
			Electricity	119	12.0
Total	981	100.0	or inside water		
			Electricity	229	23.0
			and inside		
			water		
			Total	982	100.0

Place of Infant Birth			Work Out		
	n	%		n	%
			No	846	89.0
At home	232	23.7	Yes	103	11.0
Gov't.					
facility	645	66.1	Total	949	100.0
Other	99	10.1			
Total	976	99.9			

---

* Total "n" for each category varies because a different
case-weight was assigned to each respondent. Subtotal
are rounded to nearest whole number, resulting in occa
sional category totals larger than numbers interviewed

INFANT FEEDING PRACTICES
Overall Patterns

     Almost all of the women interviewed started breast-
feeding, and 85 and 50 percent were still breastfeeding
at six and fifteen months respectively (Figure 4.1).
Data in Table 4.2 refer to feeding patterns by age of
the child at the time of the interview and do not include
retrospective information. Six feeding patterns are shown,
including combinations of breastmilk, breastmilk substitutes, and food supplements. While almost all infants

are initially breastfed, rather few are exclusively breastfed for very long. At less than one month of age, 70 percent receive only breastmilk, but between three and four months of age this percentage drops to 11 percent. Only eleven infants were said to be exclusively breastfed beyond six months of age.

Use of breastmilk substitutes was around 25 percent at one month, rising to over 60 percent at two months, and 85 percent at three months. During the early months, more of the breastmilk substitutes consist of infant formula. As the infant gets older this is replaced by cows' milk (Table 4.3). Ninety-two percent of mothers feeding formula and 74 percent of mothers feeding cows' milk use a bottle and teat. At younger ages, most of the formula and a good deal of the cows milk is fed using a baby bottle. The use of food supplements rises sharply from less than 20 percent at one month of age, to 60 percent at three months, and over 90 percent after six months.

The items consumed by the study children in the previous 24-hour period, as recalled by the mother or guardian at the time of the interview, are presented in Table 4.3, illustrating the early age at which foods other than breastmilk are introduced into the diet of the infant. In the first four months, this is mainly formula or cows milk, or glucose drink. Since medical research shows exclusive breastfeeding to be optimal for most infants for the first four months to six months of life, this extremely early unnecessary addition of breastmilk substitutes and glucose is economically wasteful and biologically dangerous. At older ages, the study infants are usually receiving both traditional gruels (locally termed uji) or packaged cereals which, though sometimes convenient, are very expensive. Fruits (other than bananas) and vegetables (other than potatoes) are not widely consumed.

Breastfeeding

The data presented show that most of these Nairobi women breastfeed their babies, with 97 percent initiating and the majority continuing to breastfeed for over twelve months. The median duration of breastfeeding was calculated, using life table analysis procedures, at 16.2 months. About three-quarters of mothers stated that they initiated breastfeeding within 24 hours of the babies' birth. Only a small minority of mothers stated that they had been given advice on breastfeeding, and over 95 per-

Figure 4.1   BREASTFEEDING PATTERNS IN NAIROBI

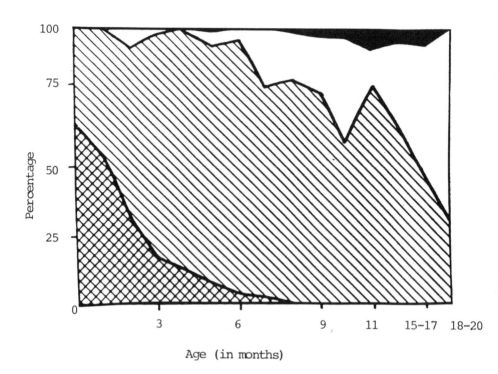

Age (in months)

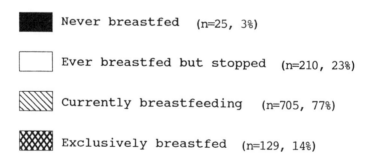

Never breastfed (n=25, 3%)

Ever breastfed but stopped (n=210, 23%)

Currently breastfeeding (n=705, 77%)

Exclusively breastfed (n=129, 14%)

Table 4.2   FEEDING PATTERN BY AGE OF CHILD (PERCENT)

	<1 (n=75)	1-2 (n=69)	3-4 (n=39)	5-6 (n=60)	9-10 (n=62)	12-13 (n=54)	15-16 (n=44)
Breast Only	70	53	11	6	3	5	0
Breast & Bottle	16	32	27	17	4	0	0
Breast, Bottle & Food	8	6	35	55	38	39	27
Breast & Food	6	10	23	12	17	25	22
Bottle & Food	0	0	3	10	27	28	46
Food Only	0	0	0	0	10	4	4

Table 4.3   PERCENTAGE OF CHILDREN CONSUMING
                   SELECTED FOODS

Foods			Child's Age in Months				
	≤2	2-4	4-6	6-8	8-10	12-14	16-18
Breastmilk	96	95	92	80	66	59	40
Cow's Milk	9	14	23	31	37	37	50
Infant Formula	25	44	38	28	21	10	3
Glucose Drink	21	19	12	15	9	3	0
Tea With Milk	0	0	4	3	8	9	23
Uji With Milk	2	9	30	43	54	54	40
Uji Without Milk	2	7	16	20	17	16	24
Packaged Cereal	9	18	21	12	9	3	2
Ugali	2	2	10	20	29	44	60
Potatoes	1	5	13	29	32	27	36
Bananas	3	8	18	34	41	37	36
Eggs	0	3	3	11	9	14	16

cent reported breastfeeding as being pleasant rather than unpleasant. Eighty-five percent of mothers said that they had no problems with breastfeeding. The most prevalent problems that were reported were: engorged breast (6%), sore nipples (3%), and breast infections (2%). Less than 4 percent of women reported that they had insufficient milk.

In rural Kenya and in many traditional societies, breastfeeding is often practiced on demand. Many mothers breastfeed their infants very frequently during the day, and they often sleep with their infants at night, allowing the infant to suck at the breast whenever hungry. Under these circumstances, it might be difficult to obtain

accurate answers to the question "How often do you breastfeed your baby each day?" Most of the Nairobi women were
able to answer this question, however. The mean frequency
of breastfeeding per 24 hours was about 9.5 at ages 0-
4 months, 8 at 4-8 months, around 6 from 8-16 months,
and about 5 in the 16-18 month age range. This reported
decline in the frequency of breastfeeding, associated
with the very early introduction of breastmilk substitutes, almost certainly contributed in these Nairobi
mothers to a shorter than expected mean length of postpartum amenorrhea (6.9 months). The relationship of infant
feeding to fertility is discussed further in Chapter
10. Of concern is that changing infant feeding patterns
are contributing to narrower spacing between births.

In this regard, it was interesting that most mothers
were aware of the effect of breastfeeding on delaying
postpartum ovulation, menstruation, and pregnancy. Some
75 percent of women believed that, at six months postpartum, a woman who is still breastfeeding is less likely
to get pregnant than one who has ceased breastfeeding
at three months. The ethnography also documented this
knowledge. Only 18 percent of the women interviewed had
used any contraceptive method since the birth of the
last infant.

MOTHERS' ATTITUDES AND KNOWLEDGE

Mothers' knowledge and attitudes concerning infant
feeding were assessed by obtaining responses to a series
of statements. An important finding is that the vast
majority of mothers (85%) wrongly believe that an infant
will be healthier if it receives infant formula in addition to breastmilk in the first three months of life.
It was also surprising that more than 75 percent of
mothers feel that "it is better to bottlefeed a baby
if you are out in a public place."

Most mothers believe that babies should be breastfed
whenever they are hungry. On the other hand, one half
of the women think that they should not breastfeed when
they have a fever. It was also clear from the questions
that mothers believe that bottle feeding encourages
fathers to take an interest in a new baby and that they
believe that wealthy women in Kenya bottlefeed their
babies.

Other questions, and the ethnography, revealed that
most mothers feel that breastfeeding takes more of a
mothers' time than does bottle feeding. The belief that
the bottlefed baby "feeds itself" is supported by one

woman's statement that "it is very easy to feed a baby with a bottle. You can just prop the bottle with a pillow and the baby will feed itself." Very few women use the cup and spoon method of feeding breastmilk substitutes even though this is the method advised by health experts.

When asked how long mothers' breastmilk, without other foods, is enough for a baby, 22 percent said two months or less and 53 percent said three months or less. The mean age recommended for how long babies should be breastfed was 17.5 months, which is rather close to the actual median duration of breastfeeding calculated from the sample (16.2 months). Sexual abstinence after childbirth was recommended for from one week to two years, with three months the most frequent response.

DETERMINANTS OF INFANT FEEDING PRACTICES
Influence of Background Factors

The relationship between selected background characteristics of particular interest (i.e., maternal age, maternal education, parity, urban orientation of the mother, and family economic status) and feeding patterns was examined. Family economic status was represented by a variable based on household possession of piped water and/or electricity. A mother was considered "urban" if she had lived in a city for most of her life. Table 4.4 presents the results of these bivariate analyses.

Both the oldest and most highly parous mothers are most likely to breastfeed and tend to breastfeed for longer durations. Durations are lower for the most highly educated group. The highly educated group has a substantially lower likelihood of breastfeeding for six months and also for nine and twelve months. Interestingly, the group of women with no education is also less likely to breastfeed for nine or twelve months than women with one to seven years of education. While the probability of longer breastfeeding is substantially lower among women with no education, it is not quite as low as among those with more than eight years of schooling.

The associations of both economic status and urban residence with infant feeding outcomes are quite consistent. Generally, there is a decline in the duration of breastfeeding as household economic status rises. Higher family economic status is associated with more early bottle feeding. Consistently fewer urban mothers breastfeed for the different durations under consideration, and they also have a greater propensity to introduce early bottle feeding.

Thus, for the infant feeding outcomes of interest, this study has documented important differences in various segments of the Nairobi population. These apparent associations were examined in more detail through the use of multivariate analysis (Chapter 1). Such analysis provided an opportunity to evaluate the strength of association between particular variables while simultaneously controlling for the confounding effects of the others.

The results of the logistic regression analyses using background variables only (statistics not shown) did indicate that the single most powerful independent predictor of breastfeeding duration is urban orientation of the mother. Maternal education is independently, significantly negatively correlated with breastfeeding only to six months but not to nine or twelve months duration. The economic status of the households is not significantly related to breastfeeding for six months but is for nine and twelve months. On the other hand, urban orientation of mother is highly significantly related to all three durations. The adjusted risk odds ratios for these models suggest that urban mothers have <u>one-third</u> of the probability of non-urban mothers of breastfeeding to longer durations. When controls are applied for urban orientation (more likely in educated, higher status households) the significance of the association between education and shorter breastfeeding almost disappears. On the other hand, both higher household economic status and urban orientation of the mother are independent predictors of early bottle feeding. In particular, high economic status is strongly associated with use of a bottle by two months of age.

A model which considers early bottle feeding as merely a feeding outcome does not account for the fact that this behavior may, in itself, exert an independent influence on breastfeeding duration. Bottle feeding has been thought to disrupt the biological process of lactation and hasten the cessation of breastfeeding. Since, in this sample, the introduction of bottle feeding occurs rather early and the median duration of breastfeeding is over sixteen months, it is likely that the two events are not consciously linked by mothers. The effect of introduction of bottle feeding on the probability of breastfeeding several months later was, therefore, examined (statistics not shown). Any effect of bottle feeding at two months on weaning by three months might be heavily influenced by mothers who intentionally substituted bottle for breast within the first three months. Longer durations

Table 4.4   BREASTFEEDING AND BOTTLE FEEDING PRACTICES BY SELECTED VARIABLES

	Breastfed 3 Months		Breastfed 6 Months		Breastfed 9 Months		Breastfed 12 Months		Bottle By 2 Months	
	n	%	n	%	n	%	n	%	n	%
Mother's Age										
< 20	128	99.2	99	85.1	71	85.9	49	75.5	137	31.4
20-29	503	94.6	411	83.9	296	73.3	202	69.3	583	30.0
30-39	96	95.8	80	87.5	55	80.0	32	81.3	104	32.7
> 40	9	100.0	5	100.0	5	100.0	5	100.0	11	38.8
Education										
None	130	96.0	104	91.8	79	75.9	46	65.3	147	25.2
1-4 years	63	96.2	52	91.3	36	92.6	22	93.5	71	30.4
5-7 years	301	96.0	244	87.9	171	78.9	117	80.6	342	26.9
≥ 8 years	242	94.2	192	79.2	145	71.0	102	59.8	276	38.0
Parity										
1	197	96.4	163	88.4	113	76.2	80	68.8	221	35.3
2-3	302	94.9	248	84.7	174	74.7	118	68.3	342	26.1
4-5	156	94.2	129	84.4	99	74.8	64	79.9	183	29.8
6-12	81	98.8	54	90.1	40	90.0	25	76.0	91	38.5

Table 4.4   BREASTFEEDING AND BOTTLE FEEDING PRACTICES BY SELECTED VARIABLES
(Cont'd)

	Breastfed 3 Months		Breastfed 6 Months		Breastfed 9 Months		Breastfed 12 Months		Bottle By 2 Months	
	n	%	n	%	n	%	n	%	n	%
Urban Mother										
No	575	95.7	463	88.9	331	81.4	221	78.2	645	28.5
Yes	161	94.9	132	76.5	95	59.8	66	50.7	190	37.8
Economic Status*										
1	483	95.5	390	88.6	274	81.3	180	77.1	544	25.3
2	91	100.0	77	94.6	52	79.0	32	75.8	101	30.9
3	162	93.0	128	73.6	100	62.4	75	57.4	190	45.7
Work Out										
No	639	96.1	529	88.6	362	79.4	234	76.7	723	29.0
Yes	86	92.1	65	66.9	58	61.3	48	51.1	94	37.1
Hospital Birth										
No	165	98.6	134	94.5	95	91.9	65	88.2	181	22.6
Yes	565	94.8	457	83.9	328	72.3	221	67.0	646	32.5

*Economic Status: 1. No electricity or inside water;
                   2. Electricity or inside water;
                   3. Electricity and inside water

79

of breastfeeding (four to seven months after the introduction of bottles) would be less likely to be weighted
by such cases. Since most babies who did not breastfeed
six months and nine months did breastfeed for at least
three months (64% and 77% respectively), the introduction of the bottle by two months was probably not, in
their cases, an indication of mother's intention to
cease breastfeeding.

Thus, a logistic model (not shown) was fitted for
six and nine months of breastfeeding using bottle feeding by two months as a predictor variable. A strong,
negative independent correlation of this variable with
both durations is apparent. This suggests that even when
controlling for the effects of other background variables, the introduction of early bottle feeding reduces
the likelihood that a child will breastfeed for as long
as six months or nine months. For twelve months duration, early bottle feeding no longer exerts any significant impact. To be sure that these results do not
reflect introduction of the bottle for the purpose of
weaning immediately, the six and nine month models were
fitted again, deleting mothers who did not breastfeed
for three months. The effect of early bottle feeding
remains significant in both models (p<.01 for six months
and p<.05 for nine months). Adjusted risk odds ratios
suggest that if bottle feeding is begun by two months,
the odds that the child will breastfeed for six or nine
months are less than half what they would have been had
bottles not been introduced so early. The possibility
of decreasing early bottle feeding may have considerable
policy relevance because it is amenable to change, unlike parity or age or urban residency and is not in
conflict with other humanitarian or development goals,
such as raising educational levels or socioeconomic
status.

Influence of Infant Foods Marketing

Investigation of the marketing and promotion of
breastmilk substitutes showed that infant formula was
very widely available in Nairobi in large shops and
small kiosks, both in more affluent and in the poorest
neighborhoods. A Nestlé subsidiary, Food Specialties
(Kenya) Ltd., dominates the market with its two products,
Lactogen and Nan. The same company has the highest sales
of manufactured weaning foods, its product Cerelac being
the most widely sold. Of the 107 retail outlets that
were audited, over 90 percent stocked infant formula,
and Nestlé had by far the highest market penetration.
Mass media advertising of infant formula seems to have

been discontinued several years before the study, but evidence was found from mothers that advertisements are still remembered.

It was clear that much promotion now is directed at health care workers. Free supplies of formula are still provided by the manufacturers to several hospitals, free samples are still being issued to mothers following delivery, and a good deal of promotional literature is still being distributed. Some 59 percent of the mothers who delivered in a private hospital, compared with only 5 percent of those delivering in a government facility, report receiving company literature on formula feeding. It seems that government hospitals are complying more closely with the World Health Organization Code's provisions than private hospitals which are often flouting them.

The high cost of feeding infant formula is evident from a comparison of the costs of infant formula with minimum wages in Kenya at the time of the study. A wage earner at the minimum wage would need to spend between 32 percent and 67 percent of total income to formula feed one infant adequately for the first six months of life, depending on the brand of infant formula chosen.

Influence of Maternal Employment

At the time of the interview, only 11 percent of the women had jobs outside their homes, and only about 5 percent of the entire sample were not able to see the child during the working day. This suggests that paid employment away from home does not account for very much of the use of breastmilk substitutes by infants under six months of age.

Results of bivariate analysis of feeding outcomes and employment away from home are presented in Table 4.4. There is slightly less breastfeeding to three months of age among mothers who are employed away from home but a substantially lower likelihood of breastfeeding to six, nine, or twelve months. This is corroborated by life table analysis which indicates a significant difference (at the .01 level) in median duration of breastfeeding for women who are employed outside the home (12 months) and for those who remain at home (16.2 months). Even here, however, it should be noted that over half of all women who are employed away from home are still breastfeeding at the first birthday. Early bottle feeding is somewhat more common among the women working outside their homes for pay. The mean weaning interval (defined as the time between the introduction of the first supplement and weaning of the infant from the breast) is also significantly different for mothers employed away from home (4.8 months) as compared to mothers working for pay at home or not employed (5.8 months).

When a variable representing work for pay outside the home was added to the set of background variables in logistic analysis, no significant independent effect is seen on the probability of outcome for the breast-feeding duration variables or for introduction of early bottles (statistics not shown). This is discussed in Chapter 6. In this Nairobi population, employment out-side the home is closely associated with higher socioecon-omic status and being an "urban" mother, both of which exert significant independent effects in the above models. Thus, while working outside the home appears to be associ-ated with several of the infant feeding outcome variables, once other background factors are controlled, the apparent association is no longer evident.

Influence of Health Services

Information obtained from ethnographic observations, from the cross-sectional survey, and from questionnaires administered to health workers provides a picture of a health care system which is unsupportive of breast-feeding. The survey revealed that while 85 percent of the mothers receive some sort of prenatal care, less than half of these women recall being told anything about infant feeding. Of those given information, 25 percent recall being misinformed that either exclusive bottle feeding or mixed bottle and breastfeeding was best for their baby. While 77 percent of the mothers gave birth in a health care facility, only 14 percent of this group recall being told anything about infant feeding at that time. Fully 80 percent of the children born in hospital roomed-in with their mothers, and 75 percent of the mothers reported breastfeeding in the health facility. Yet, 58 percent of study children born in hospitals, compared with 37 percent of those born at home, were being fed infant formula at the time of the survey. At twelve to eighteen months of age, 84 per-cent were still being breastfed if the delivery was conducted by a traditional birth attendant compared with 52 percent if delivered by a modern health worker. Of course, the type of delivery is influenced by mothers' level of education and income and so are feeding prac-tices.

A questionnaire administered to 271 health workers (mainly registered nurses, nurse-midwives, clinical officers, and upgraded traditional birth attendants) revealed that they were not very well informed about breastfeeding and had views different from stated government policy concerning promotion of breastmilk substitutes. Only 36 percent believed that the government should legislate against formula promotion, and yet the Kenya government had voted in favor of the 1981 WHO Code of Marketing of Breastmilk Substitutes and was in the process of introducing a Kenyan Code. Some 39 percent of the health workers said that they encouraged mothers to use infant formula, and 22 percent stated that formula company representatives regularly visit their health units.

As part of the research, visits were made to a number of government and private hospitals in Nairobi. These revealed several health care facility practices that are not supportive of breastfeeding including: the provision of free infant formula samples and literature to mothers in private hospitals; the separation of mothers from their newborn infants in many maternity facilities; the routine feeding of breastmilk substitutes; and the scheduling of breastfeeding in some institutions.

Given the practices described in Nairobi hospitals, there is a possibility that the location of a birth may influence future infant feeding decisions among mothers. In fact, as Table 4.5 shows, it appears that giving birth in a hospital is associated with lower percentages of women breastfeeding to durations of three, six, nine, and twelve months.

A consistent association is also seen between hospital births and early bottle feeding. Thirty-three percent of hospital-born children were introduced to a bottle by two months compared to 23 percent of those born elsewhere. Exclusive breastfeeding is clearly more persistent in the group of women experiencing "traditional" delivery (traditional birth attendant, family, friends, or unattended) than among those who delivered in hospitals. For children two and three months old, 40 percent of the "traditional" delivery group are exclusively breastfed while only 18 percent of the modern delivery group are fed in this manner. Mothers who deliver in a traditional manner are more likely to favor a diet of breastmilk and food, and mothers who experience modern deliveries choose diets composed of breastmilk substitutes and food more often. More children delivered in hospitals were fed formula than those delivered at home. Babies delivered by health workers were more often fed infant formula than those delivered

Table 4.5   OVERALL LOGISTIC REGRESSION MODELS
                          (BETA STATISTICS)

	Breastfed 6 months	Breastfed 9 Months	Breastfed 12 Months	Bottle By 2 Months
Education	-0.238*	-0.028	-0.013	-0.010
Socioeconomic Status	-0.154	-0.316	-0.255	0.395***
Parity	0.049	0.239	0.319	0.051
Mother's Age	-0.191	-0.085	-0.079	-0.074
Hospital Birth	-0.816*	-0.889*	-0.605	0.326
Work Out	-0.120	-0.300	-0.759	0.038
Urban Mother	-0.639*	-1.016***	-1.050**	0.351
Model Chi^2	31.28***	37.23***	31.16***	26.50***

Statistical significance: * p ≤ .05, ** p ≤ .01,
                             *** p ≤ .001

by traditional midwives or family, friends, or unattended (P<.001). These differences may be caused partially by income variations. The poorest women in the sample may be unable to afford either a hospital delivery or infant formula.

Paradoxically, those mothers reporting having heard from a health worker that it is good to breastfeed are significantly more likely (p = .02) to report the use of infant formula. This surprising result may be due to the fact that upper-income mothers are more likely to receive all kinds of information than poorer mothers, but also more likely to bottlefeed. It may be due also to the mixed signals that mothers receive in health care facilities. The institutional profiles from the medical infrastructure study are full of examples of mothers being told to breastfeed but being taught formula feeding by posters or example. In such situations, any contact with modern medical facilities, even where breastfeeding information is dispensed, may encourage bottle feeding.

On the other hand, no relationship was found between rooming-in practices or what the baby was fed in the hospital and the introduction of breastmilk substitutes. Too few mothers in the sample received feeding bottles or booklets on discharge or purchased formula from the hospital at a reduced price to analyze the effects of these practices. Clearly, however, more needs to be done by health care facilities to educate mothers effectively about infant feeding.

When the influence of place of birth of the index child is examined by multivariate analysis, evidence is seen for an independent effect of hospital births on breastfeeding duration, even after controlling for other background factors (statistics not shown). Being born in a hospital independently reduces the likelihood of being breastfed for six months or nine months but is not significantly associated with twelve months of breastfeeding or more. This appears logical, since influences from the experience surrounding the baby's birth might be strongest in the earliest months of life. The effect is, in fact, substantial: a child born in a hospital is only about 40 percent as likely to be breastfed for as long as six or nine months as a child not born there. It is not possible to specify exactly what it is about being born in a hospital that influences feeding patterns. There is, nonetheless, compelling evidence that there is an independent influence on duration of breastfeeding of the environment and practices surrounding institutional births among Nairobi mothers.

The Overall Model

Logistic regression was used to examine how combinations of variables relating to maternal employment, health services, and background factors are related to different infant feeding outcomes. In this overall model, the principal determinants of breastfeeding continue to be urban orientation of the mother (for all durations), hospital birth (for six and nine months duration), and mother's education (for six months duration only). Higher socioeconomic status is the only variable significantly associated with likelihood of early bottle feeding (Table 4.6), although socioeconomic status has no significant relationship to duration of breastfeeding.

The risk ratios for the significant variables give an indication of the magnitude of the individual effects (Table 4.6). Urban orientation of the mother remains the single most powerful factor that reduces the likelihood that a Nairobi child will be breastfed for any

Table 4.6   ADJUSTED RISK ODDS RATIOS AND 95% CONFIDENCE INTERVALS FOR
            PREDICTOR VARIABLES WITH SIGNIFICANT P VALUES

	Breastfed 6 Months	Breastfed 9 Months	Breastfed 12 Months	Bottle by 2 Months
Education 5-7 vs. 0	0.62 (0.49, 0.79)	NS	NS	NS
Socioeconomic Status High vs. Low	NS	NS	NS	2.20 (1.75, 2.77)
Hospital Birth	0.44 (0.20, 0.98)	0.41 (0.20, 0.86)	NS	NS
Urban Mother	0.53 (0.30, 0.92)	0.36 (0.21, 0.63)	0.35 (0.18, 0.66)	NS

length of time. Children of "urban" mothers are only
about one-third as likely to breastfeed for nine or twelve
months as children of other mothers. Being born in a
hospital reduces the odds of being breastfed six months
or nine months to less than half of those of non-hospital-
born children. Higher maternal education also reduces
the odds of breastfeeding for at least six months, but
the magnitude of the effect is not as large. In higher-
income families, a child is twice as likely to be introduced to bottle feeding by the second month of age. It
is interesting that once socioeconomic status is controlled, none of the factors associated with breastfeeding duration (urban mother, hospital birth, higher
education) are independently related to earlier use of
bottles.

When a variable representing bottle use by two months
is added to the set of predictors of breastfeeding, it
is highly significantly related to breastfeeding duration
of six and nine months (statistics not shown). At the
same time, hospital birth loses its significant association with six months duration. The relationships of
all other variables to breastfeeding duration remain
virtually unchanged.

The identification of urban orientation, higher
education, and institutional birth as factors predisposing
toward shorter breastfeeding suggests that this pattern
may become more common as trends toward urbanization
and improved access to health facilities continue. On
the other hand, it is reassuring to note that higher
family socioeconomic status does not seem independently
to predict shorter breastfeeding, and the effect of higher
educational levels is only marginal.

The importance of identifying the significance of
early bottle feeding and hospital births as determinants
of infant feeding behavior in Nairobi is that both may
be subject to modification. The preceding analyses suggest
that if practices and procedures in hospitals are modified, less ambivalent messages about breastfeeding may
be imparted and less mixed feeding early in life may
occur.

The only variable which appears related to early
bottle feeding is higher socioeconomic status. Employment
outside the home does not appear to predispose mothers
to this behavior nor does higher maternal education.
Since early bottle feeding is associated with higher
income families, who are generally accessible to educational messages via all media, attempts to change this
practice could potentially be the subject of educational

campaigns. As in the United States and Western Europe, higher income families may, in fact, be amenable to changing their infant feeding practices once the benefits of breastfeeding are made explicit and widely known.

CONCLUSION

In summaries of changing infant feeding practices, what is most discussed in the literature is the reduced prevalence and shorter duration of breastfeeding in many developing countries. It is generally believed that this new pattern occurs first in large cities, particularly in women of higher socioeconomic status, then spreads to smaller towns, and finally permeates the rural areas. A belief in this view was one of the reasons for conducting this research and for confining the studies to large cities in each of the four countries.

The above view is that promulgated by two recent WHO papers which describe a typology of three phases and eight stages of breastfeeding situations found in countries around the world.3 These range from a widespread, long-duration traditional breastfeeding pattern through a series of patterns of declining breastfeeding, and finally to a breastfeeding resurgence as currently evident in the Scandinavian countries. The WHO scenario suggests a progression through nine sequential stages with change occurring in each country first among urban women of high socioeconomic status and last by the rural poor.

The findings in Nairobi suggest, however, that the common pattern is less one of early total abandonment of breastfeeding and more one of early introduction of breastmilk substitutes and other foods, while breastfeeding continues. One of the problems with the WHO typology is that it analyzes only one component of the infant diet (breastmilk) and only certain aspects (prevalence and duration) of breastfeeding. The women interviewed in Nairobi would be classified, using the WHO criteria, as in Phase 1, the "traditional phase" with high prevalence and duration of breastfeeding, and in Stage 1, "all groups in the traditional phase."

The findings in Nairobi do show a high prevalence and long duration of breastfeeding, but accompanied by a pattern of very early mixed feeding. Even in the first few months of life, a high proportion of Nairobi infants are receiving breastmilk substitutes. Most commonly, this is infant formula from a baby bottle. This situa-

tion, where a very young infant is on the same day receiving both breastmilk from his mother and formula from
the nipple of a baby bottle, we have termed "triple
nipple infant feeding."4   It is the prevailing pattern
in Nairobi. The unnecessary very early supplementation
or replacement of breastmilk with breastmilk substitutes
from a bottle introduces risks and disadvantages for
the infant, the mother, and family.5 These include a
greater likelihood of infections; the possible problem
of overdilution of breastmilk substitutes; the economic
disadvantages because of the high cost of formula; and
finally the increased risk of an early pregnancy for
the mother because the period of lactational anovulation may be significantly reduced by partial breastfeeding.

    A very important result of the Nairobi study is
the clear illustration and the presentation in several
fora of this dominant pattern of early mixed feeding,
or "triple nipple infant feeding." The ethnography and
the cross-sectional survey confirm the existence of this
pattern. Some of the reasons for it were evident from
the marketing study, from the attitudes of mothers and
health personnel, and from hospital practices. Unexpec-
tedly, perhaps, there is not much evidence of reduction
in the prevalence of breastfeeding nor in its duration.
Almost all women in the study initiate breastfeeding
and the majority breastfeed for well over twelve months.
While breastfeeding is successfully initiated and goes
on for a long time; while mothers enjoy breastfeeding
and have few problems with it; nevertheless, the majority
believe there are advantages in the early introduction
of breastmilk substitutes. They act on this belief while
continuing to breastfeed the child into its second year.
While the causes and effects of exclusive breastfeeding
and exclusive formula feeding have been widely studied,
this mixed pattern of "triple nipple infant feeding"
has not been much investigated.

    Greiner suggests three categories of activities
on behalf of breastfeeding: protection of breastfeeding,
support of breastfeeding, and promotion of breastfeed-
ing.6 Protection of breastfeeding refers to policies,
programs, and activities which guard women already
breastfeeding from forces which would influence them
to do otherwise; support of breastfeeding refers to
providing assistance to women who are motivated to
breastfeed but who find themselves facing conditions
which make this difficult; and promotion of breastfeeding refers to convincing women who are not motivated
to breastfeed that they should consider doing so.

The data show the Nairobi women studied almost all successfully breastfeed their infants and are well motivated to do so. Because breastfeeding, even in the urban areas, is so prevalent and so much a normal part of infant feeding, protection of breastfeeding should receive first priority in policy related to infant feeding in Kenya. If breastfeeding is to be protected, then attention needs to be given to at least two influences which might undermine it, namely the availability and promotion of breastmilk substitutes.

The widespread availability of infant formula, even in the smallest kiosks and shops (over 80%) in the poorest neighborhoods of Nairobi, is believed to encourage its unnecessary use and, therefore, to undermine breastfeeding. The survey showed that more than 50 percent of the infants had at some time received infant formula. A National Infant Feeding Practices Workshop held at the conclusion of this study in 1983 recommended no further importation of infant formula into Kenya; that special infant formulas (for example, lactose-free formula) be available only on prescription; that certain controls and restrictions be placed on donated breastmilk substitutes; and that government pricing policies which help discourage infant formula use be continued.7

The most commonly used purveyor of breastmilk substitutes, judged from findings in the ethnography and survey, was the feeding bottle, usually a plastic bottle. Many women interviewed used a bottle because with it, they stated, a baby could "feed itself." Experts generally agree that feeding from a cup and spoon is a safer way to feed breastmilk substitutes to an infant. The workshop therefore recommended both that the importation and the local manufacture of feeding bottles be restricted.

Another important influence that might undermine breastfeeding is the promotion of breastmilk substitutes. Protection of breastfeeding needs to address this issue. Following the move away from mass-media advertising, more promotion, including advertising, is currently being directed at health workers through the health care system and medical journals and publications. To protect mothers and their infants from the promotion of breastmilk substitutes, the workshop recommended the immediate implementation of the Kenya Code for Marketing of Breastmilk Substitutes based on the 1981 WHO Code. When implemented, rules and necessary legislation would restrict some current promotional activities used by the infant formula manufacturers, including promotion to health institutions. Some months after the workshop, Kenya did adopt a code very similar to the International Code.

Support for breastfeeding is viewed as the second policy priority to improve infant feeding practices in Kenya. Breastfeeding support would provide assistance to women who are motivated to breastfeed but who face certain problems which make breastfeeding difficult, including jobs away from home, unsupportive health facility practices, and breastfeeding problems. The study suggests that paid employment resulting in separation of mother and child does not now account for the widespread formula use seen in the sample. The percentage of women affected by paid, outside employment may be higher in the upper-income groups which were not included in the survey, however, and it may increase in all groups in the future as more Kenyan women seek paid employment away from home. The workshop recommended that all employers enforce the policy to provide two months' maternity leave. Women should be allowed also to take annual leave (usually one month) in addition to maternity leave, for a total of three months away from work after delivery. Employers should also be encouraged to provide child care facilities at places of work, and women should be encouraged to breastfeed their infants at home before and after work. Job sharing and extended unpaid leave should be considered.

Ethnographic observations, questionnaires administered to health workers, and mothers' responses in the cross-sectional survey draw a picture of a health care system often totally unsupportive of breastfeeding. The practices of many health care institutions may undermine the ability of women to successfully establish breastfeeding, therefore, recommendations were made to change such practices. As a result of the workshop recommendations, the Director of Medical Services issued a directive to all government and non-government hospitals to ensure that infants are breastfed very soon after delivery, that rooming-in is practiced, that mothers are given unrestricted access to their infants, that prelacteal feeds of glucose water, infant formula, or other substances are not given in hospital, and that all commercial promotion of breastmilk substitutes through maternity units is stopped.

Maternal morbidity and breastfeeding problems appear not to be serious obstacles to breastfeeding for most of the Nairobi women in this study. Support to breastfeeding mothers should be easily available through the various health services, through women's groups such as local branches of Maendeleo ya Wanawake, and through organizations like the Breastfeeding Information Group, which currently provides counseling and sound informational material for mothers.

The widespread misconception that babies will be healthier if given formula as well as breastmilk and the fact that many women stated that they would use formula if they could afford it suggest that lack of financial resources, and not desire, has helped contain formula use to its current levels. This indicates a need to reeducate women and health workers concerning the financial, health, and other benefits of exclusive breastfeeding in the first four to six months of an infant's life.

Greiner forcefully argues that breastfeeding promotion is more difficult and resource demanding than protection and support. Promotion includes the reeducation and motivation of mothers not inclined to breastfeed so that they understand its advantages. Some promotional activities are needed for this task, and the Workshop recommended the wide use of communications to promote sound infant feeding practices in Kenya. In addition, it was recommended that a manual on breastfeeding be written and distributed to health workers to provide clear, accurate, and consistent information for their own use and in educating the public. Subsequently, UNICEF provided funds, an author was recruited, and an excellent manual has now been published and distributed.8

Recent events and actions in Kenya suggest a real commitment on the part of some government and non-government institutions (including the Division of Family Health in the Ministry of Health, Maendeleo ya Wanawake, and the Breastfeeding Information Group) to deal with breastfeeding issues. This research suggested that health workers have not played a positive role in the past, but it is hoped that, following the directives of the Director of Medical Services and with use of the manual, they will play an active part in the promotion and support of breastfeeding in the years ahead.9 At the same time, the manufacturers of infant formula and packaged weaning foods are still actively promoting their products, often flouting both the provisions and the spirit of the WHO and Kenya codes. Some manufacturers appear still to pursue profit even when it conflicts with the well-being of Kenyan infants and children.

NOTES

1.   O. p'Bitek, Song of Lawino   (London,
      Longman Green and Co., 1960), pp. 30-31.

2.   W. M. Van Steinbergen, J. A. Kusin, C. D. With,
      E. Lacko, and A. A. J. Jansen "Lactation performance
      of mothers with contrasting nutritional status in
      rural Kenya," Acta Paediatr. Scand.72 (1983, 805-
      10).

3.   World Health Organization, "The prevalence and
      duration of breast-feeding: A critical review of
      available information," WHO Statistics Quarterly
      2(1982): 92-116. WHO, "The dynamics of breast-feed-
      ing," WHO Chronicle 37, no. 1 (1983): 6-10.

4.   M. C. Latham, T. C. Elliott, B. Winikoff, J.
      Kekovole, and P. Van Esterik, "Infant feeding in
      urban Kenya: A pattern of early triple nipple
      feeding," Journal of Tropical Pediatrics 32(1986):
      276-80.

5.   M. C. Latham, "Human nutrition in tropical Africa,"
      in F.A.O. of the United Nations, (Rome, Italy:
      1979) pp. 39-47.

6.   T. Greiner, "Infant feeding policy options for
      governments," Report for Infant Feeding Consortium,
      Cornell   University   Program   on   International
      Nutrition, 1982.

7.   Recommendations of the Kenya national workshop
      on Infant Feeding Practices (Kenya: African Medical
      and Research Foundation, 1983), pp. 1-42.

8.   F. Savage King, Helping Mothers to Breast Feed
      (Kenya: African Medical and Research Foundation,
      1985), pp. 1-151.

9.   T. C. Elliott, K. O. Agunda, J. G. Kigondu, S. N.
      Kinoti, and M. C. Latham, "Breastfeeding versus
      Infant Formula: The Kenya Case," Food Policy 10
      (1985): 7-10.

5 Infant Feeding in Semarang, Indonesia

Mary Ann Castle, Beverly Winikoff,
Moeljono S. Trastotenojo, and
Fatimah Muis

Alfred Sauvy, the great French demographer, concerned himself with the human factor in economic development and asked whether "growth goes with quality or against it."1 In a sense, that is a fundamental question raised by this study of infant feeding practices in Semarang, Indonesia. The findings suggest that the people of Semarang have experienced negative effects as well as improvements in their lives as a result of increased access to Western-trained medical professionals, hospitals, modern medical technologies, and convenient, manufactured products.

Quality accompanies quantity more certainly in public health campaigns designed to reduce mortality or morbidity by vaccination, for example. The situation is not so clear in this case study of infant feeding, however, where certain Western medical attitudes and behaviors may be undermining habits which would provide more favorable nutrition for infants.

The effects of changes in infant feeding behaviors in Semarang may include the potential for increased incidence of infant and childhood morbidity, closer spacing of births, and additional economic burdens on the family because of costs of artificial feeding. The medicalization of childrearing practices encroaches on women's authority and confidence in what has traditionally been their domain of expertise as well. Such conclusions are not a cause for optimism. On the other hand, there may be ways to reverse some of the deleterious effects of economic development and social change. This chapter presents the major descriptive and analytic results of the research in Semarang. On the basis of this information, recommendations are made for public health policies which can contribute to infant and child survival by improving nutrition and health.

HOUSEHOLD AND DEMOGRAPHIC CHARACTERISTICS

The Semarang sample is comprised of 1,356 mothers of babies aged 0-24 months. For each recorded month of age, the Semarang children are, on the average, two weeks older than the samples from the other three sites because of the procedure used for recording age in Semarang (see Chapter 1). More than half of the sample mothers are in their twenties with a median age of 26. While most of the women have had two to three live births, 12 percent have between six and nine. Fifty-four percent of mothers were born in a city and 46 percent were not. The Semarang study population has little formal education. Fourteen percent have never been to school and two-thirds did not attend beyond the seventh grade (Table 5.1).

Twenty-five percent of the women report paid employment. Most likely this is an underestimate, particularly among the poorest and wealthiest classes. Since Islamic tradition places a value on the ability of the husband to support his family, some women may omit the fact that they work because it would compromise the reputations of their husbands. In addition, poor women frequently do not hold formal "jobs," but rather move fluidly from one type of informal work to another with no real "occupation." The median aggregate monthly family income is 42,000 Rupiah (the equivalent of US $67 at the time of the study), compared to a monthly minimum wage of 16,000 Rp. Eighteen percent of the households live on an income of 29,000 Rp or less, 12 percent of the families have incomes of 110,000 Rp or higher. Most husbands (90%) live in the same household as their wives.

Fifty-seven percent of the study families had electricity. Forty-four percent reported using a closed toilet and 17 percent an open toilet. Rivers, rice fields, and home-yards served as toilet facilities for almost 40 percent of the families. The availability of refrigeration and running water in the homes was very low. Six percent of families owned a refrigerator. Only 18 percent had running water. Ten percent of the families relied on a fountain or the river, whereas 27 percent had open wells, and 10 percent used pump wells. The largest proportion of families purchased their supply of water on a daily basis (35%).

Most families thus do not have a constant supply of clean water. Water bought daily from a retailer may or may not be clean, and the cleanliness of the container used to transport the water may be a real problem. Since daily rather than monthly water subscription indicates insecurity in ability to pay, inferior sources may have been used at times and not reported here. Although 82 percent of the families had kerosene stoves, 16 percent used braziers with charcoal or firewood purchased from street vendors. The low household prevalence of both refrigeration and uncontaminated water suggests less than optimal conditions for bottle feeding of infants in most families (Table 5.1).

The majority of the households are ethnic Javanese (91%). Five percent of the mothers and 6 percent of the fathers are Chinese. Eighty-eight percent of the mothers are Moslem, 10 percent are Christian and 2 percent are either Confucian or Buddhist. Javanese is the predominant language spoken at home (92%), with Indonesian (8%) as the next largest language group.

Almost two-thirds of the mothers (62%) stated they were still amenorrheic at the time of the interview. Thirty-three percent of the women were using contraceptives, and 7 percent reported that they were pregnant. Although family planning has been a governmental priority since the 1970s, recent Islamic revivalism may be producing countervailing pressures. Ethnographic data indicate that contraceptive use has been criticized in Mangkang Kulon by some religious organizations and earlier success of the family planning program there may be eroded through the revitalization movement. Thus, lactational amenorrhea remains a significant source of protection from pregnancy for many Semarang women.

Substantial morbidity among the children was reported by these mothers. More than one-half of the children (57%) had an upper respiratory tract infection in the previous four weeks and one-third (32%) were reported to have had diarrhea in the same time period. Serious health problems were less common: only 8 percent of the babies were reported to have been hospitalized after their births. About half of the babies were born in health centers or hospitals, and 5 percent of these babies were kept in the hospital after their mothers' discharge, mostly because of prematurity (38%) or low birth weight (28%).

INFANT FEEDING PRACTICES
Overall Pattern

One striking characteristic of the Semarang sample mothers is the high initiation (95%) and generally long continuation of breastfeeding (Figure 5.1). Almost 80 percent of the children are breastfed through the first eight months of life, with a median duration of twenty

months of breastfeeding. Over 40 percent of children
24 months old are still being nursed. The mean daily
frequency of breastfeeding for the whole population is
eleven feedings per day. In fact, the mean frequency

Table 5.1   SAMPLE CHARACTERISTICS

Mother's Age

	n	%
14-19	88	7
20-24	437	36
25-29	360	30
30-34	173	14
35-40+	143	13
Total	1,323	100

Parity

	n	%
1	216	16
2-3	649	49
4-5	149	11
6-13+	309	24
Total	1,201	100

Maternal Place of Origin

	n	%
Rural	605	46
Urban	720	54
Total	1,325	100

Education

	n	%
None	182	14
1-4	248	18
5-7	435	33
8-10	233	17
11-12	183	14
13+	55	4
Total	1,336	100

Maternal Employment

	n	%
Not employed	995	75
Employed outside	239	18
Employed at home	100	7
Total	1,334	100

Socioeconomic Indicators

	n	%
Electricity	750	57
Toilet	803	61
Refrigerator	84	6
Running water in home	244	18

Table 5.1   SAMPLE CHARACTERISTICS
(Cont'd)

Place of Infant Birth	n	%	Birth Attendant	n	%
Hospital, clinic, health center	603	45	Licensed midwife (bidan)	769	58
Home	600	44	Traditional birth attendant (dukun)	348	26
Midwife's home	87	7	Physician	186	14
Other	34	3	Other	22	2
Total	1,324	99	Total	1,325	100

of breastfeeding is essentially unchanged from one to twenty-three months, ranging from about nine to eleven times per day. This implies a substantial prevalence of breastfeeding on demand. Ninety-eight percent of the cohort women reported breastfeeding at night. These frequencies are high, especially considering that almost one third of the breastfed children were over a year old.

Although extended breastfeeding is a cultural value in Semarang, the feeding of colostrum to the infant is not. Seventy-two percent of the sample did not give colostrum to the index child. According to some middle-income women in the Krobokan District, watery milk (including colostrum) can be caused by the mother drinking too much water. These women believe that if the mother gives such milk to the baby, the infant will get a swollen stomach. The colostrum is, therefore, thrown away until the milk becomes thick. Failure to give colostrum may have important consequences, including greater susceptibility to infection. Use of colostrum rather than the common purges or food supplements might improve neonatal health. (Chapter 9 provides insights on the development of culturally appropriate messages which might encourage the use of colostrum.)

Breastmilk alone is the diet for 46 percent of children less than one month of age. This declines precipitously as more mothers add food supplements and/or breastmilk substitutes to the diet. By the third month, only 12.5 percent of children are exclusively breastfed,

Figure 5.1   BREASTFEEDING PATTERNS IN SEMARANG

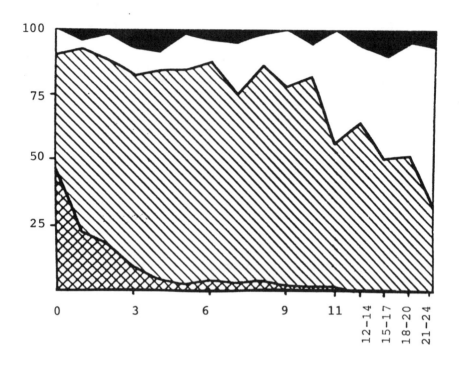

■ Never breastfed (n = 64, 4.8%)

☐ Ever breastfed but stopped (n = 355, 26%)

▨ Currently breastfeeding (n=939, 69%)

▩ Exclusively breastfed (n = 95, 7%)

yet feeding with breastmilk substitutes <u>alone</u> was rare in any age group, and no children were fed solely on food supplements until the twelfth month of life. Breastmilk remains a very common food item. Only 12 percent of the children between zero and seven months do not receive it. Although more than 25 percent of zero to two-month-old infants receive breastmilk substitutes, the number of children for whom it is the <u>only</u> source of milk is smaller: 11 percent at 0-2 months, 17 percent at six to eight months, and 36 percent at 13-18 months and does not reach 50 percent of the milk-consuming children until ages 19-24 months (Table 5.2).

An important finding is the very early introduction of <u>foods</u> along with breastfeeding. Fifty-six percent of the children zero to two months were eating various foods, rising to 86 percent of children aged three to five months. The major feeding pattern, well established by the third month of life, appears to be breastmilk supplemented with foods. Food supplementation does not appear to interfere with breastfeeding, even of long duration.

Breastfeeding Problems and Insufficient Milk

Insufficient milk was the most common breastfeeding problem cited by mothers (40%), and breast engorgement was mentioned second most frequently (19%). When women who were using bottle milks were asked why they introduced a supplement, the most common reason given was a decrease in breastmilk. Thirty-five percent of the respondents stated that they knew their breastmilk had decreased because the child was uneasy after breastfeeding. Almost 40 percent indicated that the breastmilk was either not good or was "dilute." According to the study anthropologist, this latter may be based on an inaccurate expectation as to the color and consistency of breastmilk.

Considering the high infant morbidity and mortality in Indonesia, it is not surprising that women are anxious about their ability to nourish their children. Although attempts to increase breastmilk supply were commonplace, none of the mothers knew or chose to breastfeed more frequently in order to increase milk supply. <u>Jamu</u> (medicinal herbal tonic) is a remedy commonly used (81%) by women from all socioeconomic classes who try to increase their milk production.

Most women who used <u>jamu</u> (88%) felt that their milk supply increased significantly after this treatment.

Table 5.2   FEEDING PATTERN BY AGE OF CHILD (PERCENT)

Age in Months

	0-2 (n=136)	3-5 (n=165)	6-8 (n=188)	9-12 (n=265)	13-18 (n=304)	19-24 (n=246)
Breast Only	32	12	8	4	2	0
Breast & Bottle	10	0	1	0	1	0
Breast, Bottle, & Food	11	21	14	14	13	11
Breast & Food	37	52	60	54	45	30
Bottle & Food	8	13	17	25	32	41
Food Only	0	0	0	2	7	17

Fifteen percent tried to increase milk supply by increasing the amount of fruits and vegetables they ate. On the other hand, some women curtailed the use of jamu and other liquids because they feared dilution of their milk, which would affect its quality. The potential uses of jamu in preventive health care have been discussed elsewhere, but fuller analyses of the pharmacological agents in various jamu and an assessment of their relative effectiveness would be helpful.2

Drinking jamu and eating more fruits and vegetables are both consistent with the Javanese humoral theory of illness and health: the mother is considered to be experiencing an imbalance in body elements, and health can be restored by increasing specific nutrients. This is quite different from the possible response of providing additional milk and food supplements to the baby. An alternate interpretation is that jamu is a psychological support which provides an objective, positive way to respond to fluctuations in milk supply. More than 80 percent of the entire sample agreed that they should not take drugs while breastfeeding. Women using oral contraceptives expressed similar attitudes. There was, in fact, no evidence for an association between contraceptives in general (or any particular contraceptive) and the perception of insufficient milk.

Weaning

The ethnographic data indicate that rural-born and middle-class women prefer weaning in the second or third year. Women of all classes in the urban district mentioned that exclusive breastfeeding up to three to four months with supplementation thereafter was the ideal feeding pattern. The cross-sectional data show that the three most frequently stated reasons for weaning were the baby's refusal of breastmilk (23%), the age of the child (23%) and insufficient milk (19%). Eighty percent of the mothers who weaned their children because of insufficient milk and 55 percent who weaned because "baby refused breast" did so by six months of life, whereas, in the sample as a whole, only 8 percent had been weaned by six months.

In response to direct inquiry about the techniques of weaning, only 5 percent of the sample indicated that they had a deliberate method. Of these, 42 percent each either put something bitter on the nipple (e.g., turmeric, jamu pahit, kunyit brotowali, or a crushed quinine pill) or took the baby to a traditional healer for a therapeutic technique. The ethnographer indicates that asking a traditional midwife to pray for the baby to make it separate from its mother's breast was a method used in Mangkang Kulon and Kranggan districts. Only 16 percent of the mothers reported physical separation as the weaning method of choice. Middle-class mothers in Kranggan introduced artificial formulas slowly as a weaning method. Poor mothers gradually replaced breastmilk with tea or water in a cup. Many, if not most, women appeared to add supplements of foods and artificial milk according to a developmental schedule. Weaning from the breast was gradual and related to the quantity and scope of supplementation. The ethnographer has implied that ritual methods are resorted to only if a child does not eat or, among rural mothers, if it is believed that the child is sickly.

One-third of children who first received a bottle before six weeks of age were weaned within two months. In comparison, 94 percent of children who first received a bottle later than four months of age took more than six additional months to wean. Although bottle feeding is predominantly used as a supplement and not a milk substitute for most children, when the bottle is introduced early, the child is weaned quickly from the breast. Some of the mothers may be introducing bottles with the conscious intention of weaning, but for others early weaning may be inadvertent: a woman who introduces milk supplements early may find her breastmilk decreasing, causing her to increase artificial milk feeds and hasten the end of breastfeeding.

Details of Supplementation

Early supplementation is one of the most salient aspects of infant feeding practices in Semarang. Sixty-one percent of <u>all</u> children in Semarang were given "prelacteal feeds" prior to initiation of breastfeeding. Twenty-nine percent of these feeds were either honey or sugar water, and 70 percent were milk. Honey was often used by poor women and sugar water by wealthier ones. Seventy-nine percent of all children born in hospitals were given supplemental milk while still in the hospital. The use of bottle milk as the first food in the hospital may reinforce an already established belief that colostrum is not good for infants.

The primary foods introduced at zero to two months and increasing throughout infancy are grains, fruit, and sugars. Rice, the major staple in Indonesia for generations, is introduced early: it is fed to 20 percent of the children at zero to two months and 54 percent at three to five months. Rice represents both a nutritional and ritual sign, and rice porridge is an important preferred dish mixed with vegetables and other foods for all children. Fruits are the second most important food item in the Semarang children's diet, fed to about one-quarter in the first few months of life and increasing steadily (although more slowly than grains) throughout the first twelve months.

Finally, sugar is an interesting sumptuary item of some significance. There is a long history of sugarcane production in Indonesia, so it is not surprising that sugar is included as part of the basic diet for infants. It is also, of course, a cheap source of calories. Sugar is fed to 4 percent of the babies at zero to two months, rising slowly to 25 percent by age six to eight months and to almost 60 percent of all children over the age of one year. Sugar is also included in traditional ritual. A wealthy Javanese woman described the touching earth ceremony (the tedak siti ceremony) where the child is brought into contact with the earth for the first time: part of the ceremony requires an artificial ladder of sugarcane which is constructed by the child's grandmother. The traditional midwife helps the baby step up and down the sugarcane ladder and, finally, places his/her foot on a plate of red rice porridge. Here, both rice and sugarcane appear in an important ceremonial context for infants and their families.

The ethnographic data suggest that women consider different diets appropriate for different stages of infant development. All women interviewed in the three districts appear to introduce various solid foods in accordance with the baby's age and growth. Variations in types of food used appear to reflect social, cultural, and economic differences among women. For example, middle- and upper-class women from Krobokan stated that "traditional" foods of mashed rice and bananas are less clean, not nutritious, and inconvenient, and that the custom of prechewing food contributes to "disease" in the infant. Inaccurate or incomplete information appears to influence some mothers' decisions to modify or abandon traditional feeding patterns. Mothers who avoid the traditional foods and habits replace them with "modern" canned foods such as Cerelac and Nestum. Some of the upper-class mothers also believe that "canned milk" makes babies healthier than breastmilk and "adds immunity" after weaning. The fact that higher-income women give bottles more often may be a result of the relative cost of food versus bottle feeding. Whether lower-income women would have used formula feeding had cash been available to pay for it is, unfortunately, not verifiable. The emergence of bottle feeding, however, may be an imitation of Western behavior or the expression of a subtle encouragement to be modern or efficient.

MOTHERS' KNOWLEDGE AND ATTITUDES

Virtually all women (93%) are positively oriented toward breastfeeding. Most consider it to be nutritious and believe that it confers immunity to disease. On the other hand, about 60 percent of the mothers believed that if they were ill or their child had diarrhea, they should cease breastfeeding. Ninety-nine percent of respondents agreed that breastfeeding was a Moslem woman's destiny and three-quarters agreed that Islam prescribes that breastfeeding be continued until two years of age. One-third thought breastfeeding always makes it difficult to conceive and about one-fourth thought it never did. Women who did not breastfeed were more likely to have negative attitudes about the effects of breastfeeding on breast size and shape. A large majority (84%) thought that the father knew what food was best for the child, suggesting that the inclusion of fathers in infant nutrition campaigns may be useful.

Class, religious, and geographic factors influence attitudes about breastfeeding. For example, among upper- and middle-class women in suburban Krobokan, it was suggested that it was shameful for women to breastfeed in public. Although some referred to the kodrait or innate responsibility of a mother to breastfeed, the view of bottle feeding as having some advantages appears to have diffused to these wealthier, although still traditionalist, Islamic women. While bottle feeding may not agree with fundamental Islamic tenets, it provides an acceptable solution to covert norms against breastfeeding in public. Fifty percent of the women who felt they should not breastfeed in a public place weaned their child by the sixth month compared with 39 percent of the women who indicated there were no situational restrictions. The poorer women in all districts believed mother's milk or cow's milk to be better than artificial formulas. Some of these women complained that working interfered with ideal breastfeeding, but noted that they could nurse when they returned home.

DETERMINANTS OF INFANT FEEDING BEHAVIOR
Influence of Background Variables

Since most women initiate breastfeeding in Semarang, little variation according to social and economic factors was anticipated or found. In bivariate analysis, mother's age, education, place of origin, and family income appear related to duration of breastfeeding and introduction of bottle feeding to varying degrees. A slightly lower likelihood of ever breastfeeding exists for women over 35 years, with no strong trends in breastfeeding duration or bottle use. Higher-parity women appear more likely to breastfeed for long durations and less likely to introduce early bottles. There is a sharp decline in breastfeeding duration with higher education. Seventy-five percent of women with no schooling are breastfeeding at eighteen months compared with 61 percent of those with between one to ten years of school and 43 percent of those with eleven or more years of education. Initiation of bottle feeding is clearly, consistently, and positively correlated with years of education and there is a distinctly higher probability of initiating early bottle feeding as well as less prolonged breastfeeding among city-born women.

Income also appears to be negatively related to breastfeeding duration and positively correlated with introduction of bottles: the lower the income, the greater the chance of breastfeeding for a longer time and the less the chance of early bottle use. In fact, as with education, income appears to affect the <u>bottle feeding</u> variables even more strongly and consistently than the <u>breastfeeding</u> variables. There is a stepwise increase in bottle feeding in each higher income group. Only 7.5 percent of women in the lowest income group bottlefeed by two months of age as compared with 45.4 percent of those in the highest income category. Overall, 25 percent of lower-income women use bottles versus 81 percent of higher-income women. Breastfeeding prevalence also differs in the two groups but not quite as sharply: 81 percent of lower-income women vs. 46 percent of the higher income group are currently breastfeeding. Two-thirds of the lowest income women offer their infants a diet of breastmilk and food supplements--a combination used by only 16 percent of upper income women. Thus, although the data reveal a marked homogeneity in the belief that infants should receive foods other than breastmilk early in life, type of supplementation differs considerably according to income and class.

Logistic regression analysis, using income, mothers' education, age, parity, and rural/urban origin variables (results not shown), reveals a single significant association with all durations of breastfeeding: family income. A similar model (not shown) for the determinants of bottle feeding by four months shows that lower parity, older age, higher education of mother, and higher family income are significantly positively associated with earlier bottle feeding after controlling for the other factors. The odds that women from the highest-income families will introduce a bottle by four months are almost four times as great as for women from the lowest income class, and breastfeeding to the measured durations is only 20 percent to 30 percent as likely.

The logistic data (not shown) support the contention that early introduction of bottle feeding is related to shorter duration of breastfeeding. Women who do not introduce bottles by four months are 30 times as likely to breastfeed for nine months and more than twenty times as likely to breastfeed for twelve months as those who do use early bottles. The introduction of early bottle feeding as a variable in the model dramatically reduces the independent relationship of family income to breastfeeding duration. For breastfeeding six months, the relationship is no longer significant, although income remains significant for all intervals beyond six months.

The question remains, however, whether early introduction of the bottle represents a deliberate intention to wean on the part of the mother, in which case it would be, by definition, associated with shorter breastfeeding. Logistic regression analysis (not shown) using only those children who breastfed for at least six months (for whom use of the bottle before four months was presumably not intended as a method of weaning) demonstrated a strong independent negative correlation of early bottle use with nine, twelve, and eighteen months of breastfeeding. This suggests that the introduction of early bottle feeding is independently associated with shortened duration of breastfeeding. The results of this analysis are consistent with the hypothesis that early supplemental bottle feeding disrupts the process of lactation and hastens weaning. The possibility of decreasing incentives to early bottle feeding, therefore, may have considerable relevance in the context of efforts to promote and protect breastfeeding.

Influence of Maternal Employment

Historically, Javanese women have been economically active, particularly those from poor peasant households, but, at different times, middle- and upper-class women as well (Chapter 7). Women remain the preeminent managers of family finances in the Javanese household. Twenty-five percent (339) of this sample of mothers of very young children reported employment in income-generating activities. Most (71%) are employed outside of the home, but 29 percent work at home to earn income (Table 5.1). The occupations of women employed outside the home included: 47 percent merchants or businesswomen, 27 percent laborers or peasant workers, 14 percent office workers, and 1 percent farmers or fisherwomen. Eleven percent of these economically active mothers are living without their husbands.

Most women who hold jobs away from home work between four and nine hours per day. Forty percent of women who work at home for pay, however, work for ten or more hours a day as compared with 14 percent of women with outside employment. Three-quarters of women with employment away from home have child care arrangements that separate them from their children during the workday. Increasing number of hours worked per day is generally related to shorter breastfeeding duration. The relationship of work hours with early introduction of bottles is not as clear.

There are consistent differences between employed women and those who are exclusively housewives in regard to various breastfeeding durations. For example, 93.4 percent of mothers not employed, as compared with 86 percent of income-earning mothers, breastfeed up to three months of age (Table 5.3). Women working for pay at home and outside the home have roughly the same probability of breastfeeding for three months, but women working for income in the home are more likely to breastfeed to six, nine, and twelve months than women employed elsewhere. In fact, at longer durations (nine months and longer), women who work for pay at home appear to behave more like non-employed women than like women who are employed away from the home. In logistic regression analysis (statistics not shown), employment outside the home is statistically significantly associated with less breastfeeding to six months, after controlling for parity, age, education, family income, and rural/urban birthplace of the mother. The association of outside employment with likelihood of breastfeeding disappears for durations of nine months or longer.

Sixty-four percent of all employed women with children 0-6 months use bottle milks, compared to 22 percent of non-employed women with children of the same age. Twelve percent of non-employed, 29 percent of women earning income at home, and 41 percent of women with jobs away from home introduce a bottle by the end of two months. Thus, women employed at home are much less likely to use a bottle than those with jobs elsewhere, although all employment strongly encourages women to introduce bottle feeding early in the infant's life. In logistic regression analysis (statistics not shown), a woman employed outside the home is over ten times as likely to introduce a bottle to her child's diet by four months of age as other women, controlling for all background variables. In all, employment appears to be strongly tied to use of bottles, especially for women working for pay outside the home. Breastfeeding appears less dramatically affected by employment, and, in fact, for long durations, there is no association with employment outside the home at all.

Influence of Infant Foods Marketing

Infant formula products are widely available in Semarang. Marketing of formula and related milk products involves a strategy that includes price competition among brands; widespread product availability in retail outlets; and use by hospitals, clinics, and health care workers to create a positive, modern image of breastmilk substitutes. The major manufacturer of infant formula in Semarang is the Indonesian company Sari Husada. There are other companies operating as well, including Nestlé, Nutricia, and Morinaga. Governmental regulations prevent foreign companies from establishing direct marketing channels, assuring Sari Husada's dominant position. Sari Husada has also been working with the government to develop a greater domestic market for milk products and the expansion of the domestic dairy industry.

Infant formula is available in drug stores, large department stores and shops. Some employers make arrangements with drug stores for employees to get prescription items and infant formula at no cost. In small shops consumers usually buy one tin of formula, but in department stores customers tend to be from higher income classes and are more likely to buy five or six tins. An important practice, affecting primarily low-income groups, is "breaking bulk," where a 450-gram tin is purchased and broken into 50- or 100-gram units by the merchant. This makes product purchase accessible to lower-income families by reducing the cost of the unit of sale. It also invites abuse, however, when sellers fill packets with products of lesser quality and mislabel them.

The mothers in Semarang seem to be very sensitive to product price. Disposable income determines which product a mother will purchase at any given time. Because there seems to be a weak understanding of product distinctions within the broad "infant foods" category, income fluctuations may lead to the use of a humanized formula one week, a full cream milk the next, and a formulated milk the third.

All infant food companies attempt to reach physicians, nurses, midwives, and other professionals with product information, free samples, and gratuities. Bidans (trained midwives) in Semarang play a key role

in the transmission of infant formula education and supplies to new mothers. Chapters 7 and 8 discuss in more
detail the use of the health delivery system for product
exposure and marketing of infant formula in all four
sites.

Influence of Health Services

Almost all Semarang women (90%) received some form
of prenatal care. During this care, formula feeding was
discussed with about one-quarter of the mothers. Physicians suggested bottle feeding alone (6%) or in combination (39%) more often than midwives, who discussed
exclusive bottle use with only 2 percent of their patients and bottle supplementation with 21 percent.

Licensed midwives attended 58 percent of
deliveries. Traditional birth attendants (dukuns) were
used by 26 percent of the women, 14 percent had a doctor
in attendance, and 2 percent relied on family or
friends. Although most women of all classes used bidans,
lower-income women tended also to choose dukuns (43%)
and upper-class women to use doctors (28%). Forty-one
percent of rural-born women used dukuns compared with
15 percent of women born in urban areas. Thirty-eight
percent of the mothers who used a dukun stated they did
so because of religious belief or custom. Culturally,
the dukun's role is not comparable to that of the midwife or doctor because of the additional perinatal services and Javanese rituals she provides. The dukun visits the mother and neonate every day after birth to massage both of them. She prepares the jamu that is considered essential for good quality and large quantity
of breastmilk. The dukun also organizes rituals and cer-
emonies (slametan feasts), which provide social and psychological validation and communal recognition of the
life cycle event of childbirth. Women using a dukun have
the highest prevalence of initiation and duration of
breastfeeding and are at lowest risk of early introduction of bottles. Women relying on doctors display the
reverse trend, and those who utilize licensed midwives
(bidan) fall between the two extremes.

Forty-four percent of the children were born at
home, 45 percent were delivered at a maternity clinic,
a community health center, or a public hospital; 7 percent were born at a midwife's home and 3 percent born
elsewhere. Three-quarters of all babies born in a hospital or clinic were taken to a nursery after they were

Table 5.3   BREASTFEEDING AND BOTTLEFEEDING PRACTICES
BY SELECTED VARIABLES

	Breastfed 3 months		Breastfed 6 months		Bottle by 4 months	
	n	%	n	%	n	%
Mother's Age						
14-17	8	100.0	7	100.0	--	--
18-19	56	93.3	43	84.3	13	26.5
20-24	342	94.0	270	87.9	65	21.4
25-29	283	91.3	227	84.4	64	25.6
30-34	131	85.6	108	81.2	40	29.6
35-39	68	87.2	54	80.6	22	31.9
40+	32	88.9	26	78.8	7	28.1
Education						
0	140	95.2	115	91.3	12	9.0
1-4	197	94.7	171	91.0	24	13.3
5-7	332	91.7	268	87.3	65	21.3
8-10	187	94.9	151	88.3	34	20.9
11-12	135	84.9	98	74.8	62	48.4
13+	32	72.7	20	54.1	26	78.8
Parity						
1	253	91.0	198	86.1	57	25.8
2-3	449	93.0	353	85.3	102	25.1
4-5	193	89.8	162	84.8	41	21.6
6-7	85	91.4	72	87.8	13	15.9
8-9	34	91.9	30	90.7	6	18.7
Mother's Origin						
Urban	550	89.0	390	90.1	147	28.8
Rural	474	94.8	433	82.0	75	17.2
Family Income*						
0-29	180	97.3	144	93.5	19	11.0
30-41	287	95.0	244	92.1	31	12.1
42-60	226	92.6	189	88.3	45	21.6
61-109	204	88.7	152	79.6	67	35.3
110-High	103	78.0	73	63.5	66	56.1

*In thousand Rupiah

Table 5.3   BREASTFEEDING AND BOTTLE FEEDING PRACTICES
(Cont'd)   BY SELECTED VARIABLES

	Breastfed 3 months		Breastfed 6 months		Bottle by 4 months	
	n	%	n	%	n	%
Maternal Employment						
No	782	93.4	638	88.5	106	15.0
Yes						
Work out	240	85.1	121	74.7	98	58.3
In home	70	87.5	57	81.4	17	27.4
Place of Infant Birth						
Home	544	94.3	459	90.7	75	14.7
Maternity home	300	87.0	217	75.9	108	39.4
Hospital	163	95.3	133	89.9	34	23.6
Birth Attendant						
TBA	279	95.2	237	93.7	25	9.8
Midwife	600	92.7	484	86.7	134	24.5
Physician	124	79.0	85	64.9	60	49.6
Other	22	21.0	17	89.5	4	22.2
Rooming-In						
No	332	86.5	254	78.2	111	35.7
Yes	102	96.2	78	89.7	26	30.2
Formula Sample						
Yes	46	85.2	42	80.8	19	42.2
No	979	91.9	781	85.8	203	22.6

born; the remainder roomed-in with their mothers. Most women who gave birth in health care institutions were, therefore, separated from their infants after birth. Associated with the fact that almost all private physician-attended births were in maternity clinics, the median duration of breastfeeding was fifteen months for infants born in those clinics as compared to twenty months for those born in public hospitals and 24 months for infants born at home. Women whose infants were born at maternity clinics were much more likely to use a bottle by four months (39%) as compared with those delivering at home (15%) or in public facilities (24%) (Table 5.3).

The receipt of a free formula sample at the time of birth is associated with early regular bottle use: 42 percent of mothers received formula samples versus 23 percent of non-recipients introduced a bottle by four months. There is a negative association between prelacteal milks given in the hospital and breastfeeding through twelve months of life and a positive association of such feeding with early introduction of bottles. Babies who were given sugar water in the first three days of life had feeding patterns extremely similar to those who received milk: higher prevalence of bottle feeding and shorter breastfeeding than infants given no supplements.

Logistic regression analysis was performed expanding the original model of background variables to include an additional health services variable. The maternal employment variable was not included (statistics not shown). Birth attendant was chosen as the most useful predictor for the expanded model. A woman with a physician in attendance at the birth of her child is less than half as likely to breastfeed to six months as a woman using a dukun or bidan, even after controlling for all background socioeconomic variables. The introduction of a bottle appears to be related to having a physician-attended birth and to higher education, higher family income, and lower parity independently. In particular, a woman with a physician in attendance at the birth of her child is 1.5 times as likely to introduce a bottle by four months as a mother with another type of birth attendant.

It appears that women who use physicians as birth attendants, have hospital births, experience separation from their babies at birth, and receive and use free samples of formula are at greater risk of introducing bottle milks into their children's diet. This may be viewed as the price of medical progress or, conversely, as a social cost (i.e., loss) arising from the introduction of consumer products under competitive conditions.

If only a few upper-class women bottlefed infants under ideal environmental conditions, the practice would be of less concern. In fact, the diffusion of commercial infant feeding products combines with Western medical practices to affect at least two-thirds of the women in this sample. Although only 14 percent of women use physicians, almost 60 percent are assisted in delivery and given prenatal care by medically trained bidans.

Data from the ethnographer indicate that <u>bidans</u>, who
receive training in the biomedical model of disease
similar to physicians, are concerned about differenti-
ating themselves from the traditional <u>dukuns</u> and may
be particularly vulnerable to marketing mechanisms. Infant formula companies are highly sensitive to the key
position of <u>bidans</u> and utilize it aggressively. This
may partially explain the intensity of the <u>bidans'</u> emu-
lation of Western medical opinions regarding infant
feeding. Because of their attitudes and their vulner-
ability to marketing techniques, <u>bidans</u> may become a
major source of introduction of bottle formulas for
both weaning and as a response to problems of insufficient milk and breast morbidity.

The Overall Model

In an effort to assess the relative impact of background, maternal employment, and health service variables on infant feeding practices in Semarang, a final
logistic regression model was fit with a full set of
predictors (Tables 5.4, 5.5). The dominating variables
for all the outcomes are family income, birth attendant,

Table 5.4   OVERALL LOGISTIC REGRESSION MODEL
             (BETA STATISTICS)

	Breastfed 6 months	Breastfed 9 months	Bottle by 4 months
Parity	0.191	0.198	−0.330*
Mother's Age	−0.092	0.067	0.039
Education	0.054	−0.057	0.260**
Mother's Origin	−0.167	−0.180	0.152
Family Income	−0.415***	−0.455***	0.421***
Work Out	−0.809***	−0.532*	2.391*
Birth Attendant	−0.997***	−0.774**	0.709*
Model Chi^2	83.70***	75.88***	229.48***

Statistical significance: p value * ≤ .05 ** ≤ .01,
                           *** ≤ .001,

Table 5.5   ADJUSTED RISK ODDS RATIOS AND 95% CONFIDENCE
            INTERVALS FOR PREDICTOR VARIABLES
            WITH SIGNIFICANT P VALUES

	Breastfed 6 months	Breastfed 9 months	Bottle By 4 months
Parity			
8-9 vs. 2-3	NS	NS	0.37 (0.28,0.49)
Education			
11-12 vs. 5-7	NS	NS	1.30 (1.07,1.58)
Family Income			
30-41,000 vs. Low-29,000	0.66 (0.53,0.82)	0.63 (0.51,0.79)	1.53 (1.25,1.86)
30-41 vs. 61-109,000	0.44 (0.27,0.74)	0.40 (0.32,0.50)	2.32 (1.90,2.83)
Work Out	0.45 (0.27,0.74)	0.59 (0.36,0.97)	10.92 (6.74,17.71)
Birth Attendant Physician vs. all other	0.37 (0.22,0.62)	0.46 (0.27,0.78)	2.03 (1.20,32.47)

*Rupiah

and employment. Higher income, physician as birth attendant, and mother's employment away from home lower the
probability of longer breastfeeding and increase the
odds of early introduction of bottles independent of
all other background variables. Working for pay outside
the home appears associated with decreased probability
of breastfeeding to the shortest durations measured (six
months, nine months) but has no association with breastfeeding to twelve and eighteen months or not. As expected, there is a highly significant association between
employment outside the home and the early introduction
of a bottle.

When the model is rearranged so that introduction
of a bottle by 4 months is used as a predictor, its
association with the probability of shorter breastfeeding durations is overwhelming (Table 5.6). A woman who
introduces a bottle by four months is two times less
likely to breastfeed to six months as one who does not.
The otherwise dominating factors of family income and

Table 5.6   OVERALL LOGISTIC REGRESSION   MODELS INCLUDING
INTRODUCTION OF BOTTLE BY FOUR MONTHS AS A
PREDICTOR VARIABLE (BETA STATISTICS)

	Breastfed 6 Months	Breastfed 9 Months	Breastfed 12 Months	Breastfed 18 Months
Parity	0.245	0.207	0.038	-0.054
Mother's Age	-0.205	0.144	0.195	0.405*
Education	0.097	0.068	0.139	0.183
Birthplace	0.098	-0.304	-0.248	-0.721**
Income	-0.119	-0.484**	-0.378**	-0.355**
Employment Outside home	0.481	0.522	0.505	0.385
Birth Attendant	-1.066**	-0.637	-0.795*	-0.688
Bottle by Four months	-5.167**	-3.550***	-3.234***	-2.176***
Model Chi^2	248.06	216.77**	162.71***	70.34***

Statistical significance: p value * $\leq$ .05 ** $\leq$ .01
*** $\leq$ .001

outside employment are displaced in this model as predictors of breastfeeding. Interestingly, the association
of birth attendant with breastfeeding for six and twelve
months does not disappear. This suggests that higher
income and employment outside the home primarily shorten breastfeeding because of their association with
early introduction of the bottle, whereas contact with
Western-trained physicians operates to curtail breastfeeding in other, more direct ways as well (Table 5.6,
5.7). High income does persist as an independent predictor of breastfeeding to nine, twelve, and eighteen
months. Employment outside the home is never significant
as a predictor in this model.

In general, a Semarang woman who has more education, or is a member of a high-income family, or utilizes a physician to assist in the birth of her child
or is employed away from home will be more likely to

introduce a bottle by four months of age. These conclusions are consistent with a constellation of factors which affect infant feeding and are discussed throughout this report. They reflect variability among classes of women and also the differential impact of external forces on various groups. For example, older women of rural origin, with less education, who are not employed outside the home may, at the moment, be bastions of traditional values regarding infant care and feeding. On the other hand, if maternal employment outside the home increases, its negative effects on infant feeding could become extremely significant, mostly through its impact on early bottle feeding.

Table 5.7 ADJUSTED RISK ODDS RATIOS AND 95% CONFIDENCE INTERVALS FOR PREDICTOR VARIABLES WITH SIGNIFICANT P VALUES, OVERALL MODELS INCLUDING EARLY BOTTLES

	Breastfed 6 Months	Breastfed 9 Months	Breastfed 18 Months
Mother's Age 20-24 vs. 35-39	NS	NS	3.37 (2.28,5.00)
Family Income* 30-42 vs. 61-109	NS (0.27, 0.53)	0.38 (0.27,0.53)	0.49
Work Out	NS	NS	NS
Birth Attendant Physician vs. all others	0.344 (0.17,0.71)	NS	NS
Bottle by four months	0.01 (0.001,0.025)	0.029 (0.014,0.061)	0.11 (0.54,0.24)

*Thousands of Rupiah

CONCLUSION

It has long been noted that socioeconomic status is related to differences in infant feeding choices. This research highlights the role played by health professionals and institutions which appear to be quite influential as well. Medical professionals, representing the authority of scientific knowledge, appear to be a powerful source of social influence. The result is that women question the value of their own reproductive and child care practices in favor of sometimes incorrect instructions from doctors and other health workers.

The experiences of the upper-class women from Semarang can be seen as part of a more general process of change. Changing preferences among an elite may serve as a model for women of all classes. There is thus some urgency in the protection of breastfeeding and prevention of detrimental infant feeding choices for women who live in poor conditions that do not allow them to prepare or store infant formulas properly.

These observations, together with recent advances in knowledge about the importance of breastfeeding, lead to several recommendations. Professional health workers should be educated in the virtual impossibility of disease-free bottle feeding by poor mothers with no access to safe water supplies. Bidans and physicians should receive an upgraded education on the unintended consequences of early bottle feeding. Prelacteal feeds in hospitals should not be offered. Immediate breastfeeding after birth and the use of colostrum should be promoted for all babies. Rooming-in should be the norm in hospitals. No free formula samples should be given because of the additional financial burden which is placed on poor families if they try to continue artificial feeding.

Health professionals should provide basic information to pregnant and lactating women beginning during the prenatal period. It should be emphasized that bottlefed infants are at a health disadvantage, and women should be advised to continue breastfeeding even if they or their children are ill. All identified beneficial traditional practices, including exclusive breastfeeding on demand, and prolonged weaning periods should be promoted, along with the information that exclusive breastfeeding can provide enough nutrients for the growth of infants up to six months of age. Fathers should be incorporated into health education programs, since they appear to have considerable influence in advising their wives to use formulas and/or packaged cereals.

Educational seminars in government health centers should emphasize a "promoter" role for the bidan. Basic understanding of traditional Indonesian values and beliefs should be integrated with clinical knowledge of preventive and curative medicine. This would be a first step in upgrading the bidans' education regarding maternal-infant care and, at the same time, validating their singular importance in community health.

Women who must work for pay away from home early in their infant's life need more social support to enable them to provide optimal care. Maternity leave is rare in this sample. Longer paid maternity leave, frequent breastfeeding breaks, and quality child care arrangements would improve the welfare of all employed women and their children.

Breastfeeding support groups could, perhaps, work through local women's organizations, which would provide needed encouragement and education to women who are breastfeeding. It is possible that the dukuns could play some role here, since many women, regardless of class, appear to respect their childrearing advice. Utilization of the dukun to disseminate information about increasing milk supply by increasing the frequency of breastfeeding as well as using jamu and massages illustrates how scientific knowledge can be integrated with historically recognized Javanese practices.

Many of the factors most strongly associated with early bottle feeding and shorter breastfeeding (e.g., expanded utilization of Western medicine, increased family income, and higher education) are major priorities of developing nations. Thus, increasing numbers of women in Semarang may experience the effects of one or more of these factors in the near future as development proceeds. Because this process is often uneven, use of a doctor and employment outside the home, for example, are not necessarily accompanied by the increased incomes and improved living conditions which might render bottle feeding less dangerous. Both government and social institutions are thus faced with the tasks of integrating development goals, consumerist aspirations, and the maintenance of beneficial traditional infant feeding practices. In order to do this, policies which promote a wider market for breastmilk substitutes should be discouraged. Similarly, the services provided by health care institutions must be carefully designed so as not to present incentives to bottlefeed.

NOTES

1. A. Sauvy, Fertility and Survival, (New York: Collier Books, NY, 1963), p. 110.

2. V. Hull, "Women Doctors and Family Health Care: Some Lessons from Rural Java," Studies in Family Planning 10, 11/12, (1979): 315-25.

6 The Influence of Maternal Employment on Infant Feeding

Beverly Winikoff and Mary Ann Castle

Is there a necessary incompatibility between paid maternal labor and breastfeeding of infants? Are there specific conditions of employment which interfere with breastfeeding or encourage bottle feeding? This chapter presents empirical data on the dimensions of women's employment which may affect infant feeding decisions. In the individual site descriptions of Chapters 2 through 5, employment per se does not emerge consistently as a significant independent predictor of breastfeeding duration and use of infant formula. This is not surprising, given the different contexts of female economic activities, the variations in national development, and the diverse cultural and social norms in the four cities. Thus, the impact of maternal employment in each place must be assessed with reference to other factors that may modify its effects on infant feeding choices.

GENERAL CHARACTERISTICS OF EMPLOYMENT

Thirty-six percent of all women in the Bangkok sample reported being employed in income-generating capacity both at home and away from home, compared with 25 percent in Semarang and 11 percent in Nairobi. In Bogotá, only employment outside the home was recorded. Twenty-five percent of women were engaged in such activity, a level comparable to that in Bangkok. About two-thirds of those reporting employment in Bangkok, Nairobi, and Semarang stated that their work was away from home. Proportions of women with children under the age of twelve months who held paid jobs away from home ranged from 7 percent in Nairobi to 16 percent in Semarang and 24 to 25 percent in Bangkok and Bogotá. These percentages reflect the structure of the economy in each country, availability of urban employment, and the relative tendency of women in the informal labor sector to report pay.

In Bangkok, the women who worked outside the home report the following occupations: 41 percent wage earners, 36 percent civil servants, and 17 percent merchants. Wage labor included sewing rugs and clothing, factory work, vending, and bricklaying. Civil servants encompass government administrative and office workers, teachers, and garbage collectors. Most employed women in Bogotá were domestic workers (31 percent), factory workers (15%), secretaries or office workers (9%), and teachers (8%). In Nairobi, 62 percent of the women who reported outside employment were professionals having either administrative or clerical positions. Comparatively, in Semarang 41 percent of employed women were merchant/businesswomen, and 28 percent were laborers-peasant workers. In all sites, mother's employment is more likely with increasing age of the child. As expected, employment outside of the home is much more sensitive to the age of the child than employment at home. The number of women who are employed outside the home rises steadily with the age of the child during early infancy (Table 6.1). Work for pay at home is less common and less consistently correlated with the child's age in all four sites. The relationship of outside work with age of child is most clear for Bangkok and Bogotá.

The distinction between women who work for pay in their homes and those who were employed outside of the home was not intrinsic to the design of this study but became clearly apparent during analysis of the data. Women who earned income at home had, it was discovered, feeding patterns substantially the same as women who reported no work for pay. Thus, only employment outside the home was designated as a condition under which women might have to alter their infant feeding practices. As a result, the analyses of feeding patterns among employed women were carried out using that portion of the sample who reported work for pay away from home.

Occupational categories were not useful as a basis for comparison of feeding patterns across the four study sites. There are cultural differences regarding terminology for the various job categories and, for practical reasons, investigators in each site used different groupings in coding occupations. Moreover, the conditions of work within occupational groups vary radically in some places. For example, Bangkok civil servants include both streetsweepers and administrators.

Maternity benefits and leaves, hours of work, child care alternatives, and job security vary significantly among categories of workers in the same site as well as between similar groups of workers in different sites.

Table 6.1   TYPE OF EMPLOYMENT BY AGE OF CHILD (PERCENT)

Age (months)	Outside Employment				Work At Home for Pay			
	BANGKOK	BOGOTÁ	NAIROBI	SEMARANG	BANGKOK	BOGOTÁ*	NAIROBI	SEMARANG
0-1	6	3	3	6	1	--	3	17
1-2	16	13	11	12	10	--	4	5
2-3	20	23	9	21	10	--	7	13
3-4	25	24	5	20	12	--	5	13
4-5	30	22	14	24	7	--	5	--
5-6	28	22	13	21	8	--	--	3
6-7	31	33	4	21	9	--	7	10
7-8	33	38	10	20	10	--	11	8
8-9	25	31	8	6	10	--	11	6
9-10	28	39	10	17	10	--	11	5
12-11	29	33	7	9	13	--	--	7
11-12	26	33	6	12	6	--	6	6
12+	39	-	20	17	10	--	3	5

*No data

Occupational groups are not as comparable as socioeconomic indicators across the four cities. Hence, the latter are used to assess class status.

CHARACTERISTICS OF EMPLOYED WOMEN

The probability of employment in all four cities is clearly higher for upper-income and more highly educated women. About 40 percent of Bangkok women in the two upper income groups are employed away from home as compared with about 14 percent in the two lowest income groups. Women with the highest educational attainment are almost four times as likely to be engaged in such employment as women with no education.

For Bogotá women, educational attainment increases the probability of outside employment only after thirteen years of schooling: about one-quarter of women with less education are working for pay away from home whereas over half of women with more than thirteen years of schooling report employment outside the home. Similarly, women at the upper end of the income continuum of this sample (which does not include the very top of the income range) are more likely to be employed than women with lower family incomes.

In Nairobi, women who are relatively likely to be working for pay away from their homes during the early infancy of their children are rather atypical. They are much more likely to be urban born, more highly educated, and of higher socioeconomic status than women without paid employment and women who earn income at home. Less than 5 percent of women with less than eight years of education were employed outside the home, whereas one-third of mothers with more than ten years of education were so employed.

In Semarang, employment for pay outside of the home shows little variation in lower income and education categories. Women in the highest income and education groups, however, are much more likely to be employed outside the home. For example, 40 percent of women reporting thirteen or more years of education work for pay outside the home as compared to 20 percent of women with less than five years of schooling.

Our data show that wealthier women with young infants are employed considerably more, on average, than poorer women. The fact that more upper-income women are employed for pay reflects, in part, higher education and, hence, increased access to employment in the urban centers. This is particularly true of the Bangkok sample, which has the largest percentage of employed women. Childbirth and childrearing may be more powerful in deterring poor women from paid employment. Richer women have greater access to paid child care and maids to relieve them of household responsibilities. In addition, poorer women may be more sensitive to labor market fluctuations. They have low-status, poorly paid jobs in the informal sector with no leave time. They often quit their employment with childbirth and thus have the task of locating new employment as well as "returning" to work.

By comparing prenatal and postpartum employment, it is clear that income earning declines more often for poor women with the birth of a child. For example, 77 percent of Bangkok upper-income women who were employed before childbirth are also working for pay afterwards. This compares with current employment of only 41 percent of lower-income Bangkok women who held jobs before childbirth. A similar but less extreme pattern is evident in Bogotá (57 percent versus 45 percent). For whatever reason, not working for pay immediately after childbirth may imply a reduced standard of living for poorer women and their families.

It has been shown that increased income may make available more money for food expenditures and that this can exert a positive effect on household diet. Unless the additional income earned is enough, and is used for improved infant feeding, the result can be, instead, a negative impact on the child's nutritional status.1 Even if income is spent on adequate breastmilk substitutes, such as infant formula, these may be so expensive that the nutritional needs of other small children in the family may not be met. Finally, if work keeps the mother away from home for excessively long hours, she is not available for breastfeeding, food preparation, or child care, which she may do more competently than the available child care. In this study, 16 percent of the Bangkok, 42 percent of the Bogotá, 21 percent of the Nairobi and 14 percent of the Semarang women who worked outside the home for pay did so for ten or more hours a day. In the two Asian countries, poorer women with infants work longer in income-generating activities than other women. Thirty percent of the Bangkok women from the two lowest income groups who are employed outside the home work ten or more hours per day compared to 9 percent of the highest income group women so employed. In the case of Semarang women, 22 percent of the lowest income group women employed away from home work over ten hours per day compared with only 14 percent of all women employed outside the home.

MATERNAL EMPLOYMENT AND INFANT FEEDING PRACTICES

The effect of women's employment on breastfeeding duration and use of bottles was examined in all four sites. The propensity to use bottles among women employed outside of their homes is clearly much stronger than among those women who work for pay at home. It appears to be the separation of the mother and infant that produces a reliance on bottles and not the fact of working for pay. The data demonstrate a significant association between employment outside the home and either early bottle use or curtailment of breastfeeding (early weaning) in all sites except for Nairobi. Even in Nairobi, however, early weaning among employed women is often attributed to the need for introduction of bottles. The following section will present data supporting these findings in each of the four sites.

Bangkok and Bogotá

Compared to most developing countries, labor force participation is high for Thai women.[2] Thai peasant women generally control family finances as do many of their urban counterparts.[3] Thailand's rapid development produced high literacy rates, substantial fertility declines, lowered infant mortality, and a stated family size preference for two or three children, accompanied by a high use of contraceptives. Infrastructure is well developed, including fairly good transportation, communication, electrification, and health services distributed throughout the country. Buddhism, the predominant religion, presents no opposition to contraception or smaller family size as contrasted with certain Islamic revivalist ideologies present in Indonesia, for example.[4]

Similar to Colombia, there is a high migrancy rate in Thailand. Fifty percent of the sample born outside of Bangkok stated that they migrated there for purposes of employment, and almost 40 percent of the recent female migrants to Bangkok were working at the time of the survey. Bangkok thus presents a picture of transition which includes changes in family form and childrearing practices. As the major urban center in Thailand, it also provides an example of the most rapid sociocultural change in the country. The traditionally autonomous position of women and recent socioeconomic developments appear to be strong factors influencing Bangkok women with young infants to return to paid work. This autonomy of women may also influence their feeding choices and make more acceptable the use of bottles as well as earlier separation of the infant from the breast.

There are relatively small differences between women employed at home and women with no paid labor in terms of percentages continuing to breastfeed to three and six months or introducing a bottle by two months (Table 6.2). Differences between women working outside the home for pay and all others are considerable with respect to the proportion breastfeeding at three and six months. The same trend holds for introduction of a bottle by two months. Thirty-seven percent of Bangkok women who are employed outside of their homes breastfeed to three months compared with 76 percent of mothers not employed. Seventy-three percent of women employed away from home introduced a bottle by two months compared with 36 percent of the women not employed. This difference is more extreme than that found in the other sites.

The full impact of working outside the home for pay on infant feeding outcomes is seen in logistic regression analysis (Table 6.3). Paid employment outside the home was overwhelmingly associated with truncated breastfeeding and with early introduction of a bottle. The child of a Bangkok mother who is employed outside of the home is only one-quarter as likely to be breastfed for three and six months as a child of other mothers, independent of all other predictor variables. Similarly, Bangkok women who are employed outside of the home are almost four times as likely to be using a bottle at two months of age as other women after controlling for background and health service variables. When controls for bottle feeding are included, the relationship between early weaning and employment outside of the home per se is attenuated (statistics not shown).

When women employed outside the home are examined separately, it is clear that, for these women, the background variables which are generally associated with lower probability of continued nursing do not explain differentials in duration of breastfeeding. For a Bangkok woman employed outside of the home, separation from her infant for long periods of time quickly leads to bottle use and weaning. This central circumstance of her life is so important that virtually none of the usual influences affect her feeding decisions.

Unlike Thailand which is still over 80 percent rural, Colombia has undergone extremely rapid urbanization. Historically, Colombian women have participated in peasant agricultural production, but the extent and type of employment varied and cultural support for it fluctuated. Cultural sanctions against female wage labor existed in some regions and for some classes (e.g., rich peasants) although participation was closely linked to economic

Table 6.2   MATERNAL EMPLOYMENT AND INFANT FEEDING PRACTICES

Site	Breastfeeding at 3 months		Breastfeeding at 6 months		Bottle by 2 months*	
	n	%	n	%	n	%
Bangkok						
Work out	273	37	181	27	332	74
Work in home	90	70	61	61	111	43
No paid labor	606	76	390	65	735	36
Bogotá						
Work out	84	65	45	48	58	52
No outside employment	241	81	113	64	146	47
Nairobi						
Work out	86	92	65	67	94	37
No outside employment	639	96	529	89	723	29
Semarang						
Work out	165	85	121	75	98	58
Work in home	70	88	57	81	17	27
No paid labor	782	93	638	89	106	15

*Four months in Semarang

Table 6.3   MATERNAL EMPLOYMENT OUTSIDE THE HOME AS A PREDICTOR
             OF INFANT FEEDING PRACTICES

Site	Breastfeeding at 3 months	Breastfeeding at 6 months	Bottle by 2 months[1]
Bangkok	-1.426***[2] .24[3] (.18,.33)[4]	-1.300*** .27 (.18,.41)	1.322*** 3.75 (2.78,5.05)
Bogota	-0.828** .44 (.26,.73)	-0.545* .58 (.33,1.03)	NS
Nairobi	NS	NS	NS
Semarang	--	-0.692**[1] .50 (.31,.82)	2.385* 10.58 (6.54,17.11)

Statistical significance: *p≤.05, **p≤.01, ***p≤.001

[1]Four months in Semarang

[2]Beta statistic

[3]Adjusted risk odds ratios (RÔR)

[4]Confidence interval

necessity. Shrinking employment produced a massive migration to cities.5 In fact, Bogotá has grown from a city of 21,000 in the late nineteenth century to more than four million today. Public services have not kept pace with its migrant populace. Ethnographic data indicate that alcoholism and its attendant social and financial stresses appear to be serious problems for some of this sample. Urgent financial necessity may be the reason some Bogotá women with small children assume income-generating responsibilities, regardless of distance from jobs and inadequate child care arrangements. There is no evidence that husbands of any class have generally supportive attitudes and behavior (e.g., help with child care) toward their wives' employment. In some regions, in the past, it was considered shameful for women to perform wage labor. Husbands may resent their wives' employment as a challenge to familial authority. The conditions of employment as well as the relative control men have over women appear to exert real pressures which can influence decisions regarding infant feeding.

Of the four sites, Colombia and Thailand are most similar with respect to level of development, lower fertility, higher percentage of working mothers, higher use of contraception, and higher GNP per capita.6 In Bogotá, at three months, 65 percent of employed women versus 81 percent of homemakers still breastfeed. Fifty-two percent of employed women feed their infants a bottle by two months of age compared with 47 percent of the others (Table 6.2). Bottle feeding appears to be more of a general practice and less specifically determined by employment than in Bangkok.

A logistic regression procedure shows that paid employment away from home is overwhelmingly associated with truncated breastfeeding (Table 6.3). That is to say, such employment significantly reduces the likelihood that a child will be breastfed to three and six months of age. Employment status does not appear to be a predictor of early bottle use in Bogotá: early bottle use is quite common among all mothers there (Table 6.2, 6.3). It is clear, however, that early bottle use has an extremely strong relationship to early weaning, independent of employment.

As with the Bangkok sample, when employed and other women are analyzed separately, differences emerge (statistics not shown). For mothers not employed away from home, a Bogotá-born mother has a greater chance of not introducing a bottle by two months than a woman born elsewhere. Similarly, higher family income is associated with lower probability of breastfeeding to six and nine months duration for these women, but family income is not related to duration of breastfeeding for those employed away from home. Even when early use of bottles is controlled, income maintains its strong relationships with truncated breastfeeding for women not employed outside their homes. An interconnection of social, economic, and cultural factors appears to create a positive atmosphere for bottle feeding among Bogotá women. Mothers who are separated from their children for long hours each day appear to have difficulty maintaining breastfeeding under these conditions.

Although the cultural and historical context of women's employment and control over household income is different in Colombia and Thailand, similar economic and structural factors such as migration, urbanization, and availability of employment, affect the likelihood that mothers will work away from home. In both Bangkok and Bogotá, women working for pay outside of the home are influenced to curtail breastfeeding. In Bangkok, outside employment influences women to introduce early bottles and this, in turn, truncates breastfeeding. In Bogotá, bottle use is widespread among all women and it influences early weaning whether or not a woman is in the paid work force. Employment also independently influences feeding behavior for those who are away from home.

Nairobi and Semarang

The results of the analyses of the impact of employment on Nairobi and Semarang women present a different picture. There are many respects in which these two sites are more similar to each other than they are to Bangkok and Bogotá.

As Table 6.2 shows, 92 percent of the Nairobi and 85 percent of the Semarang sample of mothers employed outside of their homes breastfeed to three months, only slightly different from the pattern of women with no outside employment. Differences in breastfeeding patterns are more manifest at longer durations in these sites. In contrast to early breastfeeding, probability of early bottle feeding seems to be relatively sensitive to employment status. Thirty-seven percent of Nairobi and 41 percent of Semarang women who are employed away from home introduce the bottle by two months of age. This compares with 29 percent of Nairobi and 20 percent of Semarang women who are not so employed.

Historically, Kenyan women (as most African women) have participated in rural agriculture. Luo women in pre-colonial times were involved in the trade of food-

stuffs.7 Enormous socioeconomic changes, including increased taxation, fragmentation of landholdings, and
large-scale withdrawal of male labor from the farm have
intensified the role of women in agricultural work. For
example, a recent study revealed that 40 percent of Luhya
women at Kakemaga were farm managers.8 In the cities,
however, there is a scarcity of steady employment for
women, which may result in an increasing dependency of
women on men.9 Poor street vendors, for example, cannot
be assured of a steady income. Although they work for
pay, they are more vulnerable to income fluctuations
than their rural counterparts. Difficulties of child
care (e.g., dangerous areas near living quarters and
no kinswomen to help) present other problems for employed
women in Nairobi.

There appears to be an undercounting of employed
women in the informal sector in this sample. The ethnographic data indicate that much informal trading may
not have been considered as employment by the mothers
interviewed. In any case, although autonomy and economic
wage work, providing household food and necessities,
appear to have been significant aspects of the traditional
female role, life in Nairobi may erode women's ability
to maintain this independence. Only 16 percent of the
women in this study reported income-earning activities.

The tribal affiliations of the employed women are
not exactly comparable to those of the entire sample.
Kikuyu are overrepresented among income earners (27 percent of the entire sample; 47 percent of employed women).
Luhya are approximately equally represented, and Luo
appear to be underrepresented among income earners. Since
most employed women reported more years of education,
the percentages of various tribal groups in the work
force may reflect the relative prosperity of the groups
in terms of education and affluence in Nairobi.

Although employment outside the home appears, in
cross-tabulation, to be associated with shorter breastfeeding and earlier use of bottles, once other background
factors are controlled in a logistic regression procedure
no significant associations are evident. That is to say,
employment outside of the home is not a significant independent predictor of either breastfeeding duration or
bottle use in Nairobi (Table 6.3).

To understand this outcome, it is necessary to know
something about the women who are likely to be employed
away from their homes during the early infancy of their
children. In fact, they are rather atypical of the sample
universe of Nairobi mothers. These women are much more
likely to be urban born, more highly educated, and of

higher socioeconomic status than non-employed women or
those earning income at home. Over 95 percent of all
women with no education were not employed outside the
home. However, about 14 percent of the mothers with more
than ten years of education were so employed. About one-
third of those born in Nairobi work away from home whereas
only 20 percent of rural-born mothers do so. Since urban
birth and higher socioeconomic status both exert significant independent effects on shortened breastfeeding
and earlier introduction of bottles, employment itself,
in bivariate analysis, may appear to be related to these
outcomes but the association disappears when controlling
for socioeconomic status. When early use of bottles is
included as an independent variable, there is a strong
association of their use with truncated breastfeeding,
underscoring the point that for _all_ Nairobi mothers,
introduction of bottles is associated with early weaning.

The lack of significant associations between employment itself and infant feeding outcomes may also reflect
the conditions of work among the predominantly upper-
status women who hold jobs. Most government and private
employers have a long lunch break of 1 1/2 hours at noon,
and many employees return home. Almost half of the mothers
employed away from home travel twenty minutes or less
to get to work, and 80 percent travel one half hour or
less. Forty-nine percent of the women employed away from
home report that they usually see the baby during the
working day. Eleven percent of workers stated they took
their children to work with them, thus allowing contact
throughout the day.

For women, then, paid labor force participation
outside of the home does not constrain breastfeeding
at noon. The opportunity to see the baby during the day
is lower for laborers: 22 percent of that group compared
with 69 percent for sales women, 79 percent for service
employees, 39 percent for administrative/clerical workers,
and 55 percent for professional women. The greater chance
of more educated women to see their infants during the
workday may counter their natural tendency to stop breastfeeding sooner than the lower socioeconomic status women.

Interestingly, the poorer employed Nairobi women
appear to introduce an early bottle at the same rate
as upper-class employed women. That is, 38 percent of
the poor and 41 percent of upper-status women employed
away from their homes introduced a bottle by two months.
Poor women employed away from the home may not have the
opportunity to return home to breastfeed their infants
or to leave them at a convenient location to visit at
the lunch break. For whatever reason, infants of these
poor women, who are living without electricity or running

water, are at high risk for contamination of feeding bottles at an age when they are highly susceptible to diarrheal infections.

Employment for pay is more common among Semarang (25%) than Nairobi mothers (11%). The duration of breast-feeding for women who work away from home is also long, albeit shorter than for other women. The median duration of breastfeeding for women in outside employment is eighteen months compared with 21 months for women engaged in income-generating work at home. Table 6.2 gives the cross-tabulation of various feeding outcomes and work status. Women employed outside the home in Semarang appear to have somewhat shorter breastfeeding durations than women not so employed. At nine months, 69 percent of those reporting outside employment, 81 percent of those employed in their homes, and 82 percent of women not reporting paid labor are still breastfeeding. As in all other sites with the exception of Bogotá, there is a clearly increased tendency to introduce an early bottle for all employed women and particularly for those employed outside the home. Women employed outside of the home introduced an early bottle twice as often as those who worked for pay at home and four times as often as those who did not earn an income.

In logistic regression analysis, outside employment in Semarang is also statistically significantly correlated with a lower probability of breastfeeding to six months, although there is no significant relationship for longer durations. Use of the bottle is highly associated with employment outside of the home, even when background variables are controlled (Table 6.3). A Semarang mother employed away from home is more than ten times as likely to introduce an early bottle as a woman not so employed. For all women, the relationship between introduction of an early bottle and early weaning is striking. Early bottle use is an overwhelming predictor of shorter breast-feeding durations. The effect is so strong, in fact, that inclusion of early bottles in the model entirely replaces the independent influence of outside employment on duration of breastfeeding (statistics not shown). This suggests that the effects of outside employment on breastfeeding duration operate primarily by increasing the chances that mothers will use bottles early in the infant's life.

Relatively long durations of breastfeeding among Semarang working women may partially reflect traditional patterns in Javanese society, including the acceptance of female economic activity and social-cultural supports which enable the continuation of breastfeeding when women leave their homes to work for pay. Historically, Javanese women from poor peasant households have been economically active. The entire household in the peasant economy was mobilized to intensify subsistence and cash crop production. During the colonial period, labor recruitment utilized the entire family work force rather than fragmenting the household production unit.10

Among the middle and upper classes, women's employment was determined by economic conditions and social norms. For example, batik marketing in the nineteenth century was predominantly conducted by the upper-status wives of court officials. Their income was considered to be a respectable and beneficial addition to their husbands' limited salaries. On the other hand, among high-status Javanese who had become officials of the Dutch colonial administration, it was considered "unseemly" for wives to be engaged in trade. After independence, middle- and upper-class women sought employment during periods of economic depression, temporarily at least, with no loss of status or respect.11

Ethnographers have also documented that contemporary Javanese women exercise control over daily income expenditures.12 Women are viewed as more rational than men in decisions on the allocation of family income. It has been suggested that Javanese men are considered to be unreliable and more willing to jeopardize the family's welfare for personal interests.13 The results of a recent study in urban Jakarta confirm that women are the preeminent managers of family finances.14 Fluctuations in the economic participation of upper-class Javanese women may influence some to deny their employment in deference to their husbands' status. In comparison, such motivations may be absent in Thai women.

Other cultural traditions may affect the attitudes and behaviors of employed Javanese women toward breastfeeding. As Chapter 5 mentions, humoral medicines and therapies are widely used in Semarang, including specific jamus (herbal drinks), which are believed to increase the quality and quantity of breastmilk. It is interesting to note that one-quarter of the employed women in the sample tried jamu and other traditional therapies when they experienced breastfeeding problems. Introduction of bottle formula was a last resort for these women. In comparison, traditional Thai recipes for tonics affecting women's reproductive processes are less commonly used today.15 In Bangkok, it appears that insufficient milk and other breastfeeding problems are resolved by immediately introducing the bottle.

Cultural factors are important in either facilitating or inhibiting breastfeeding generally. Higher-income women in Semarang do appear to be influenced by Western views of childrearing and feeding; however, many still use traditional midwives and believe in the efficacy of jamu, which may encourage them to continue breastfeeding in the face of competing ideas. In Thailand and Colombia, sociocultural factors appear to be inhibiting the continuation of breastfeeding under difficult conditions, such as employment outside of the home (Chapter 8).

In many cases, however, the conditions of work present insurmountable obstacles to the utilization of cultural methods to maintain breastfeeding. Specific attributes of labor force participation also may be important determinants of feeding patterns. The existence and enforcement of maternity benefits and maternity leaves, assurance of job security, type and location of child care, transportation time to and from work, breastfeeding breaks, and so forth may influence the decision and timing of a woman's return to outside employment and the patterns of infant feeding she chooses.

CONDITIONS OF EMPLOYMENT
Maternity Benefits and Return to Work

Maternity leaves and financial benefits can expand infant feeding options of working women. Legislation exists in Thailand, Colombia, Kenya, and Indonesia providing some form of benefits and/or leave. Only certain groups of formally employed women are covered, however, and enforcement is erratic. Pressure is felt by some women to return to their jobs at the end of maternity leave rather than leave the work force.

Bangkok women who work for public organizations are entitled to 45 consecutive days of paid maternity leave and an allowance of 50 bhat per month for each child up to two children, along with medical and dependents' benefits. Private sector workers receive 30 consecutive days of paid leave with job tenure guaranteed for that period only. Except for a few larger industries, where medical and dependents' benefits are given, there are no additional allowances provided. The Thai laws cover only women with regular salaries and not day laborers or self-employed women. In addition, women workers may be required to sign work contracts agreeing to waive their maternity rights in order to be hired.[16] Professional women in the civil service report that it would be difficult to advance or even maintain seniority if they took off more than their normal leave of 45 days.[17]

Kenya government employees are given two months maternity leave. Many private concerns in Kenya also follow this standard. Colombian labor legislation provides women in the formal labor economy a paid maternity leave of eight weeks. Similar labor legislation exists in Indonesia.

Data on maternity leave for the mothers in the study sample were available in two sites, Bangkok and Nairobi. At first glance, a seemingly paradoxical association between infant feeding patterns and paid maternity leaves is discerned. In Bangkok, women reporting maternity leaves are slightly <u>less</u> likely to initiate breastfeeding, more than <u>twice</u> as likely to have weaned by three months, and about three and a half times more likely to have weaned by six months as those employed mothers who report having <u>no</u> leave time. They are more than twice as likely to have introduced bottles by two months. An overwhelming 83 percent of mothers who had maternity leave were bottle feeding by two months postpartum. Similar to the Bangkok mothers, Nairobi women with paid maternity leave had shorter durations of breastfeeding than those without such leave. Women with no leave were less likely to initiate breastfeeding but, if they did, had longer durations.

These findings indicate that provision of maternity leave <u>alone</u> may not be adequate to assure breastfeeding. Without other support, a 30- to 60-day leave for women committed to return to work may not be sufficient to overcome other powerful influences promoting early weaning. The reasons for the apparent anomalies in the relationship between breastfeeding and maternity leave may lie in the characteristics of working women who receive leave as compared to those who do not. Women who receive maternity leave are more likely to be in clerical civil service and semi-professional jobs. These occupations are associated with cultural and ideological attitudes of upper-class women--characteristics, in themselves, which were associated with shortened breastfeeding durations. Women with no leave may hold jobs in the informal sector, such as day labor, market sellers, or domestics. These jobs may be compatible with bringing the child to work or with more flexible work hours. The lack of leave may, indeed, lead some of these women to leave the labor force after childbirth. In this case, with no secure job, they may not return to paid work as quickly as women <u>with</u> maternity leave.

The data from Bangkok permit examination of the effects of length of maternity leave for those women who <u>do</u> receive it. There is, in fact, a clear relationship between length of leave and probability of breastfeeding to at least three months of age: 22.3 percent of women with a leave of 0 to 30 days, 32 percent of those with 35- to 45-day leave, and 41.4 percent with a leave of between 46 to 60 days were still breastfeeding at three months. Correspondingly, 65 percent of mothers with under one month's leave, 22 percent with 35- to 45-day leaves, and 12.2 percent of women with a leave of two months' time had introduced a regular bottle by two months of age.

The positive influence of longer maternity leave on breastfeeding to at least three months in Bangkok suggests that longer leave would be beneficial, even unpaid leave without threat of termination might allow longer breastfeeding. Moreover, leave for groups of workers not now covered by national regulations would be an important improvement in the conditions of work. Allowance could also be given for annual leave to be added to maternity leave periods to extend the time mothers and infants can remain together. Enforcement of existing maternity leave provisions would assist some mothers to extend their period of breastfeeding.

In Colombia, in addition to a two-month maternity leave for workers in the formal economy, a 1967 labor law authorizes two 30-minute daily feeding periods for breastfeeding mothers. Of course, if the child remains at home or in a day care center in another part of the city, the legal right to a short breastfeeding break is irrelevant. According to the ethnographers, most Bogotá mothers use the legally allotted time to reduce the length of their workday by arriving later and leaving earlier. On-site creches or day care centers might overcome some of these hindrances to breastfeeding during the day, but new problems might be introduced by the need to commute with children. The ethnographic data indicate also that women fear their children will receive poor treatment at day care centers and do not utilize them for this reason.

Child Care, Work Hours, and Separation of Mother and Baby

> Earlier the milk did not drop and I fed with water for three days. I just began breast-feeding yesterday......I think I will breastfeed for one month and send the infant to Susin to be taken care of by my mother ...I cannot raise the baby myself because I work in shifts...six hours of work [then] twelve hours of recess and then another six hours of work...continuous like this (A 26-year-old

Bangkok textile worker originally from north-
eastern Thailand).

The type and location of child care arrangements and
the degree to which they facilitate contact between
mother and child also influence infant feeding behavior.
In all sites, most infants of mothers employed outside
the home remain in their home or at a relative's home.
In Bangkok, only 2 percent of women report bringing
children to the workplace. Larger numbers of Bogotá and
Nairobi women (15 percent and 11 percent) do take their
children to work with them, but they are still a small
minority of all employed women. This suggests that, for
these three urban cohorts, virtually all women who hold
jobs away from home are separated from their children
during working hours. In Semarang, a more substantial
proportion of women take children to work (25%), but,
still, most must leave children in the care of others.

Clearly, access to an infant during daytime working hours increases the potential for longer durations
of breastfeeding. The Bangkok sample shows that 64 percent of those with home jobs, 51 percent of those able
to return to see the child during the day, and 88 percent
of those who bring the child to work breastfeed to three
months. In comparison, only 24 percent of those who do
not see their children during working hours breastfeed
to three months of life. The differences hold for six
months of breastfeeding as well. Logically, the reverse
pattern is observed in regard to use of bottles by two
months: 43 percent of women with home jobs or who bring
the child to work use bottles by two months as compared
to 59 percent of women who see the child during the
workday and 80 percent of those who do not.

It is likely that the physical separation and scheduling problems associated with being at a work place
outside the home interfere profoundly with continuation
of breastfeeding for most employed women. For example,
most Bangkok women work five to seven days per week,
and they work long hours (56 percent work 8 to 9 hours
and an additional 20 percent work ten or more hours).
Among the majority of employed women who work outside
the home, 25 percent have travel time between home and
the place of employment of more than one hour per day.
This means that separation of mother and baby for ten
to twelve hours a day was not uncommon. In this regard,
only 14 percent of Bangkok women who travel more than
70 minutes to work breastfeed to six months, whereas
27 percent of the entire group of mothers who are employed outside the home do so.

In Bangkok, many of the lowest-paid factory workers live in slums that surround the factories. Although they live close to the place of employment, lunch breaks for these workers are only one half hour. Shortness of time may prevent the women from going home to breastfeed. Another feature of the Bangkok factory labor environment is that many women work a rotating shift, spending a week or so on day shift, then moving to an evening shift, and finally a night shift. This type of work schedule may stress the lactation process biologically, since the mothers' milk supply will have to adjust almost weekly to adapt to work shift changes.

Finally, difficulties in day care arrangements appear to lead some Bangkok mothers to cease working, change jobs, or continue breastfeeding at great difficulty to themselves. Women in Senanikhom and Central Plaza communities related that they gave up their jobs away from home as bricklayers or factory workers in favor of sewing or other piecework. Others slipped from the work site to return home in the morning or at lunchtime to breastfeed their children. As one mother from Senanikhom said "If they fire me I will have to leave . . . but what can be done? The baby is mine, the baby is more important than any other thing." On the other hand, many mothers stopped working for pay altogether even though it placed great financial constraints on their budgets. The ethnographic data indicate that poorer working women in Bangkok have the desire to breastfeed and would do so if there were structural supports available enabling them to breastfeed more easily.

As described in Chapter 3, the ethnography suggests that women in Bogotá employed away from home seldom successfully breastfeed their infants. Moreover, poor women who leave their infants in the care of young siblings cannot be assured that the babies are being fed. Although data are not available on transportation time for Bogotá working women, it is known that people living in the southern districts are disadvantaged because of the net deficit of jobs there.18 Those with jobs earn less than equally educated/skilled people in the northern districts. Thus, if a Bogotá woman living in a southern section takes a job closer to her home, it will be at a relatively lower wage.

In Semarang, as in the other cities, most mothers who work away from home must leave young infants with other caretakers for long periods of time, and the use of substitute milk becomes almost a necessity. Sixty-four percent of employed Semarang mothers with babies zero to six months of age use bottles compared with 22 percent of women with same-aged children who are not employed. On the other hand, in Indonesia, working hours are sometimes from 7:00 am to 1:00 pm which makes maintenance of breastfeeding somewhat easier.

FEMALE-HEADED HOUSEHOLDS

Recent research has underscored the phenomenon of female-headed households in developing countries.19 These are defined as households where women are the predominant income earners as compared with those where males are the "breadwinners." This situation can be a consequence of recent social and economic transformation, such as commercialization of agriculture; low-paying, insecure informal employment; migrancy; or familial stress under situations of impoverished city life. Short- and long-term migrancy can turn some male-headed households into de facto female-headed ones. Although this study did not have as a goal the collection of data on female-headed households, limited data were collected.

Only eight of the surveyed Bogotá women reported living in a household which included only themselves and their babies. In fact, the Colombian ethnographers identified 16 percent of ethnography case study interviewees as heads of households, suggesting that more women in the survey might be household heads as well. Three-quarters of survey mothers who were heads of households were in the poorest income categories compared with 40 percent of the women in households of larger size. Mothers in 63 percent of single-mother households were employed away from home compared to 25 percent of those in larger families. It appears that single-mother households in the Bogotá sample are also at great risk for introduction of bottles. The ethnography indicates that there may be an increasing tendency for Bogotá women to be the main financial support of their families. This phenomenon can be partially related to economic factors, such as rising male un- and under-employment, with inability to support a family and consequent abandonment of women and children.

The effect of employment on the 3 percent of the households which are headed by females in Bangkok is pronounced. Sixty percent of the employed mothers from female-headed households are in the lowest two income categories. Only one-quarter of the employed women in male-headed households are in these income groups. Seventy-three percent of the employed women in female-headed, low-income households introduced a bottle by two months compared with 50 percent of the employed mothers in lower-income, male-headed households.

There is a delicate relationship between family welfare and the ability to work for pay for poor women, especially those who are household heads. Child care and nutrition may be inadequate. If children become ill and mothers stay home to care for them, income is diminished for the entire family. Structural supports for single, employed mothers are needed or family survival is undermined.

CONCLUSION

This chapter has documented the various strategies of employed women to nourish and care for their infants. Overall, employed women tend to use bottles more than other mothers. This is the primary and predominant effect of work on infant feeding choices. In many sites, this early use of bottles and the physical separation of mother and child during the day dictate a relatively early end to breastfeeding as well. Clearly, however, working women from cultures where long breastfeeding is the norm still tend to breastfeed a substantial amount of time despite their employment. Women who are employed outside the home in Semarang and Nairobi breastfeed longer than women not engaged in paid labor in Bangkok and Bogotá, for example.

A critical insight in this regard is that, while mothers' employment (especially away from home and child) increases early bottle feeding and, in Bangkok and Bogotá, independently decreases the probability of longer breastfeeding, it cannot be responsible for the decision to wean early for most women. This is so because very few women work for pay during the first two months of their infants' lives. Most women who wean early are not employed, even though working for pay makes it more likely that an individual woman will wean early (Table 6.2).

A major public health concern is for poorer women with a constricted range of options available to them and especially for employed mothers who are also heads of households. These groups often suffer from the interaction of inadequate working conditions, low income, poor nutrition, and precarious family health and welfare. Under the conditions described, there may be high costs to the infant, to its mother and family, and to society for women to work at low wages. The data suggest that even when employed mothers, as in Bogotá, have control over their own income, this does not necessarily provide power in other spheres. Low-paying jobs, with no prestige and little or no security, do not offer increased status for women who hold them. Almost one-third of the Bogotá sample were domestic workers, for example.

This type of employment is easily viewed as an extension of household work, that is, considered of no social value. Similar attitudes may apply to other categories of female labor in other sites, especially work for pay in the home and street vending.

For women who must work for pay early in the infant's life, at the very least, convenient, quality child care alternatives with guaranteed frequent breastfeeding breaks need to be available. Before introducing child care alternatives for young infants, studies should be conducted to assess the attitudes of working mothers regarding location and utilization of child care facilities. Issues in need of clarification include various possible types of child care, their staffing, and financing.20 For example, working mothers in these samples used a variety of informal child care arrangements, rarely leaving their children with unrelated adults. This pattern is important and could be incorporated into policies for the establishment of day care facilities. Training programs and licensing procedures could be developed for some of the women who are relatives or who are known to the community and already providing child care. They, then, could be hired to continue providing services in centers or licensed homes.

Policies which would benefit mothers and their children include job training programs, supplementary income benefits, and other social services such as adequate paid maternity leave, breastfeeding breaks, a variety of options for child care, part-time employment, job sharing, and flexible hours. These benefits need also to be extended to workers in the informal sector, which predictably will continue to employ greater numbers of women in all four sites. Since legislation regarding maternity benefits always has the potential of discouraging employers from hiring women altogether, legislation must include adequate provision to prevent this from occurring. It is clear that many of the families in this study need a greater and more secure income, a goal which would be attained through more employment for both men and women. Finally, although by no means incidentally, an increase in services to employed women would recognize the social value of women's reproductive and childrearing contributions as well as their economic roles and could have a positive influence on women's equality and status.

NOTES

1. Michael Latham, The Decline of the Breast: An Examin-
    ation of Its Impact on Fertility and Health and
    Its Relation to Socioeconomic Status. Cornell Inter-
    national Nutrition Monograph Series, No. 10 (1982).

2. Penny Van Esterik, "The Cultural Context of
    Breastfeeding in Thailand," in Breastfeeding, Child
    Health and Child Spacing: Cross Cultural Perspec-
    tives, ed. V. Hull and M. Simpson (London: Croom
    Helm, 1985), pp. 139-61.

3. J. de Young, Village Life in Modern Thailand
    (Berkeley & Los Angeles: University of California
    Press, 1955), p. 24.

4. Data presented in this paragraph were taken from
    J. Knodel et al., "Thailand's Reproductive Revolu-
    tion: Rapid Fertility Decline in a Third World
    Setting," (Madison: University of Wisconsin Press,
    1987).

5. This discussion is based on M. Leon de Leal and
    C. D. Deere, "Rural Women in the Development of
    Capitalism of Colombian Agriculture," Signs 5, no.1
    (Autumn 1979): 60-77.

6. This is based on a WHO assessment of the GNP per
    capita in 1982 of US $390 for Kenya, $580 for Indo-
    nesia, $790 for Thailand, and $1,430 for Colombia.
    World Health Organization Development Reports, 1982,
    Geneva.

7. Margaret Jean Hay, "Luo Women and Economic Change
    during the Colonial Period," in Women in Africa,
    ed. N. Hafkin and E. Bay (California: Stanford Uni-
    versity Press 1976).

8. Kathleen A. Staudt, "Women Farmers and Inequities
    in Agricultural Services," in Women and Work in
    Africa, ed. E. G. Bay (Boulder, Co.: Westview Press
    1982), pp. 207-24.

9. Beatrice Whiting, "Changing Life Styles in Kenya,"
    in Daedalus (Spring 1977): pp. 211-26.

10. B. White, in "Population, Employment and Involution
    in Rural Java," Development & Change, 7 (1976),
    267-90.

11. H. Papneck and L. Schwede, "Earning and Spending in an Indonesia City: Family Strategies of Income Management," in A Home Divided: Women and Income in the Third World, ed. D. H. Dwyer and J. Bruce (forthcoming, Stanford University Press), p. 248. As the authors state, the periodic work experience of these women may explain the maintenance of high status, which might have come to be negatively evaluated if employment was permanent.

12. H. Geertz, The Javanese Family: a Study of Kinship and Socialization (Glencoe, Illinois: Free Press, 1961), p. 123.

13. Robert R. Jay, Javanese Villagers: Social Relations in Rural Modiokuto. (Cambridge: MIT Press, 1969), pp. 64, 92.

14. Papneck and Schwede, "Earning and Spending," p. 256.

15. A comprehensive discussion of the natural history of traditional and Western medicine in Thailand and Indonesia can be found in P. Van Esterik, "To Strengthen and Refresh: Herbal Therapy in Southeast Asia" (In Review: Social Science and Medicine).

16. Penny Van Esterik, "Infant Feeding Options for Bangkok Professional Women," in The Decline of the Breast. Cornell International Nutrition Monograph Series, No. 10 (1982), p. 68.

17. Ibid., p. 67

18. R. Mohan, "The People of Bogotá: Who They Are, What They Earn, Where They Live," World Bank Staff Working Paper No. 390 (Washington, D.C., May 1980).

19. Nadia Youssef and Carol Hetler, "Establishing the Economic Condition of Woman-Headed Households in the Third World: A New Approach," in Women and Poverty in the Third World, ed. M. Buvinic et al. (Baltimore: The Johns Hopkins University Press, 1983), p. 216.

20. Suzanne H. Woolsey, "Pied Piper Politics and the Child Care Debate," Daedalus (Spring 1977): 127-46.

7 The Influence of Health Services on Infant Feeding

Beverly Winikoff and Mary Ann Castle

What role do health service institutions and Western-trained professionals have in influencing women's infant feeding choices? What information, technical advice, and feeding supplies are provided to mothers with newborns during health care? What is the relationship between health care practitioners and the commercial marketing of infant formula? These were some of the motivating questions for undertaking the studies in Bangkok, Bogotá, Nairobi, and Semarang.

Data relating to feeding patterns and contact of mothers with Western-trained and traditional health practitioners have been presented in chapters 2 through 5. The present chapter utilizes these analyses and draws upon ethnographic material, data collected in hospitals, and interviews with physicians, health services administrators, social workers, pharmacists, and traditional birth attendants to explain similarities and interpret variations.

Most births in these four urban sites took place in an institutional setting. This ranged from virtually all births in Bangkok and Bogotá to 78 percent in Nairobi and 55 percent in Semarang. Rooming-in arrangements in hospitals ranged from 87 percent in Bogotá and 80 percent in Nairobi to 51 percent in Bangkok and 27 percent in Semarang. Taking into account the prevalence of home births and of rooming-in practices, the mothers in Bangkok (48%) and Semarang (40%) were still most likely to have been separated from their infants after birth. The type of birth attendant was recorded only in Nairobi and Semarang. Most Nairobi mothers (77%) were attended by physicians or trained nurse-midwives. Similarly bidans, Western-trained midwives, were the most frequently used attendants in Semarang (58%). Traditional birth attendants were used by 26 percent of the Semarang mothers and only 2 percent of the Nairobi women. In Nairobi, 13 percent of the women had family and friends in attendance; and 8 percent gave birth to their babies alone. Free formula samples were given to 12 percent of the women in Bangkok, 6 percent in Bogotá and Semarang, and 5 percent in Nairobi. Eighty-five percent of the Nairobi women reported they received some type of prenatal advice regarding infant care and feeding compared with approximately one-quarter of the mothers in the three other sites (Table 7.1).

Table 7.1 ASPECTS OF PERINATAL HEALTH CARE (PERCENT)

	BANGKOK	BOGOTÁ	NAIROBI	SEMARANG
Place of Infant Birth				
Hospital and				
maternity clinic	98	90	78	55
Home	2	10	22	45
Rooming-in				
(Hospital births)	51	87	80	27
Birth Attendant				
MD	--	--		14
Nurse-midwife	--	--	77*	58
Traditional birth				
attendant	--	--	2	26
Family, friends	--	--	13	2
Unattended	--	--	8	0
Receipt of				
Formula Sample	12	6	5	6
Prenatal Advice				
on Feeding	28	31	85	25

*M.D or nurse-midwife

BIVARIATE RELATIONSHIPS

Breastfeeding initiation rates in all four sites were high. There is only minor variation in initiation of breastfeeding according to location of birth, with highest rates for mothers who gave birth at home. Only in Bangkok is there as much as a 10 percent difference between initiation of breastfeeding in hospital-born children (86%) and in home births (96%). Thus, in these four cities there is not a problem of rejection of breastfeeding. Rather, the urgency uncovered by this study is the rising trend toward early supplementation with bottle formulas and the premature weaning of infants. The discussion below concentrates on aspects of health services that affect length of breastfeeding and timing of introduction of first bottles.

A preliminary investigation of the association of selected health service characteristics and infant feeding practices in all four sites is described in Tables 7.2 and 7.3. There is a clear trend at all four sites linking lower probability of breastfeeding for three months or more to hospital births. Higher percentages of women who give birth in hospitals than at home introduce an early bottle.

Public hospitals in Bangkok appear to have lower rates of breastfeeding and higher rates of bottle use than private hospitals. The populations served are also fundamentally different. For example, Huacheay is a private institution utilized by higher-educated, higher-income, Bangkok-born Chinese women compared with Rajvithi Hospital, which is a public institution more commonly favored by lower-income people. Inter-hospital variation is large in this city, as well. Aside from the fact that many of the hospitals are class and ethnically stratified, the institutions also have different policies regarding rooming-in and sample distribution. For example, two public hospitals, Rajvithi and Ramathibodi, have very different rates of rooming-in: 86 percent and 44 percent, respectively. Only 4 percent of mothers at Rajvithi received a sample compared to 12 percent at Ramathibodi. Forty percent of the mothers giving birth in Huacheay Hospital got such samples. Subtleties in these institution-specific hospital effects were not discernible from bivariate or, for that matter, multivariate analyses which grouped hospitals only as public or private.

In Bogotá, mothers of babies born in Social Security hospitals are more likely to introduce an early bottle and least likely to continue breastfeeding. This may be, in part, associated with the practice of providing four cans of milk per month for six months to employees covered by the benefits of the Institute of Social Security whose infants have a "medically recognized" nutritional need. This practice may predispose health workers and administrators at Social Security hospitals toward use of infant formula.

In Nairobi, there is a small negative relationship between hospital births and breastfeeding to at least

three months as compared with home births (Table 7.2).
There is, however, a clearer association between hospital births and introducing an early bottle (Table
7.3). Thirteen percent more women with hospital births
introduced a bottle by two months than did women giving
birth at home. Babies delivered by health workers were
more often fed infant formula (58%) than those delivered
by traditional midwives (50%) or family and friends,
or who were unattended (37%). Furthermore, in Nairobi,
mothers who deliver in a traditional pattern tend to
breastfeed exclusively for longer durations: 40 percent
of this traditional group were exclusively breastfeeding at three months compared with 18 percent of the
modern delivery group.

In Semarang, there is a clear negative relationship
between private hospital/clinic births and duration of
breastfeeding (Table 7.2). Women giving birth in maternity clinics consistently have the lowest percentage
still breastfeeding. Infants of these mothers also have
a much higher rate of bottle use at each monthly interval, with more than four times the number giving a
bottle at one month as compared with women who gave
birth at home. There is also a striking association
between less than optimal feeding patterns and physician-attended births. Women using traditional birth attendants have the highest prevalence of initiation and
duration of breastfeeding and are at lowest risk of
early introduction of bottles. Those who utilize licensed midwives fall between the two extremes but appear
to behave more like women who experience more traditional deliveries.

The hospital practices of separating the neonate
from its mother immediately after birth and keeping the
child in a nursery have been implicated in undermining
successful breastfeeding. In all four sites, having a
baby in a nursery is generally negatively associated
with breastfeeding duration and, even more strikingly,
is positively related to early bottle use. Thus, a
rooming-in procedure during the first days of life may
have a real impact on breastfeeding behavior for months
afterwards.

Formula use among hospital-born infants may be influenced by the practice of giving neonates feeds of
formula milk or glucose and by supplying free samples
to mothers either in the hospital or upon discharge.
For example, although 80 percent of the Nairobi women
delivering in health care facilities reported that the
baby stayed in the same room as the mother during the

Table 7.2   BREASTFEEDING TO AT LEAST THREE MONTHS BY
             HEALTH SERVICE CHARACTERISTICS

	BANGKOK	BOGOTÁ	NAIROBI	SEMARANG
Place of Infant Birth				
Private hospital		(59) 76.6		(300) 87.0
Public hospital	(780) 65.6	(140) 73.3		(163) 95.3
S.S. hospital	(171) 60.2	(64) 71.1		
Any hospital			(565) 94.8	
Home	(19) 78.9	(38) 80.9	(165) 98.6	(545) 94.3
Birth Attendant				
Trained midwife	--	--	--	(600) 92.7
TBA	--	--	--	(279) 95.2
MD	--	--	--	(124) 79.0
Other	--	--	--	(21)100.0
Location in Hospital:				
Rooming-in	(512) 65.8	(259) 75.3	(419) 94.8	(102) 96.2
Nursery	(461) 64.0	(40) 71.0	(112) 94.7	(332) 86.2
Receipt of Formula Sample:				
Yes	(125) 57.6	(23) 71.9	(27) 89.9	(46) 85.2
No	(849) 66.1	(281) 74.7	(676) 95.8	(979) 91.9

Table 7.3 EARLY INTRODUCTION OF BOTTLE BY HEALTH SERVICE CHARACTERISTICS*

	BANGKOK	BOGOTÁ	NAIROBI	SEMARANG
Place of Infant Birth				
Private hospital	(954) 46.4	(48) 47.1		(101) 32.5
Public hospital	(229) 58.1	(119) 45.4		(26) 15.9
Social Security hospital		(67) 54.4		
Any hospital			(210) 32.5	
Home	(28) 28.6	(29) 48.3	(41) 22.6	(62) 11.1
Birth Attendant				
Trained midwife				(113) 18.6
TBA				(21) 7.3
M.D.				(57) 41.0
Other				(3) 15.0
Location of Infant in Hospital				
Rooming-in	(602) 41.7	(220) 47.1	(205) 29.4	(17) 17.3
Nursery	(583) 53.0	(43) 56.6	(51) 37.8	(105) 29.5
Receipt of Formula Sample				
Yes	(150) 58.0	(24) 58.5	(15) 39.5	(12) 25.0
No	(1037) 45.7	(242) 47.6	(241) 30.2	(181) 18.0

*By 2 months in Bangkok, Bogotá, and Nairobi; by 4 months in Semarang

first day and night after birth, 38 percent of these infants were fed artificial foods (17 percent with formula; 21 percent with glucose solutions). In Semarang, there is a negative association between giving infants milk after birth in the hospital and breastfeeding through twelve months of life and a positive association with early introduction of bottles. Babies who are given sugar water in the first three days of life have patterns similar to those who receive milk: higher prevalence of bottle feeding and shorter breastfeeding than infants given no supplements.

Even though only a minority of women recalled receiving free formula samples, consistently in all sites, fewer mothers who received such samples continued to breastfeed their children at three months. More of these mothers initiated early bottle feeding than did those who were not given a sample in the hospital (Tables 7.2, 7.3).

LOGISTIC REGRESSIONS

In all sites, the study was able to identify certain aspects of mothers' contacts with the health services that were associated with shortened duration of breastfeeding or greater propensity to introduce early bottles, independent of all other background factors. Table 7.4 presents the adjusted risk odds ratios for various feeding outcomes. In Semarang, independent of all other factors (including income and educational status), a woman with a physician in attendance at childbirth is only half as likely to breastfeed to six months as a mother who used another birth attendant; and she is 1.5 times as likely to introduce a bottle by four months. In Nairobi, hospital birth is associated with a decreased tendency to breastfeed for six or nine months' duration. After controlling all background variables, a mother who gives birth in a hospital is only about half as likely to be breastfeeding at six months as a mother whose child is born elsewhere.

More in-hospital contact between Bangkok mother and baby is associated with a significantly increased chance of ever breastfeeding and a decreased chance of introducing bottles by two months. This is so for the entire sample and, separately, for employed mothers and those not working for pay. Women who do not work for pay outside the home and who receive a sample of infant formula are only 60 percent as likely to breastfeed to three months as those non-employed mothers not given a free sample.

Table 7.4   RELATIVE PROBABILITY OF CONTINUING
          BREASTFEEDING AND FOR INTRODUCTION OF
          EARLY BOTTLE BY HEALTH SERVICE CHARACTISTICS:
ADJUSTED RISK ODDS RATIOS AND 95% CONFIDENCE INTERVALS

	BREASTFED 3 MONTHS	BREASTFED 6 MONTHS	BOTTLE BY 2 MONTHS[*]
Bangkok			
Mother and Infant Contact in Hospital			.63 (.58, .82)
Free Samples to Mothers Not Employed Outside the Home	.60 (.35, 1.00)		
Bogotá			
Hospital Rooming-In for Mothers Not Employed		4.09 (1.36, 12.33)	
Nairobi			
Hospital Birth		.44 (.20, .86)	
Semarang			
Physician-Attended Birth		.50 (.30, .84)	1.644 (1.013, 2.669)

[*]4 months in Semarang

     Bogotá women who are not employed and who experience
rooming-in in the hospital are four times as likely to
be breastfeeding at six months as those who were separated
from their infants at birth. This underscores the important influence of rooming-in for women who are not employed in the formal sector (i.e., for most women). Here,
as in Bangkok, employed women may curtail breastfeeding
or introduce early bottles regardless of their birth
experiences because the fact of outside employment
itself has such a strong impact on certain infant feeding choices. The differential impact of health service
practices on mothers employed outside the home versus
mothers not so employed demonstrates that the interaction between health services, background factors, and
infant feeding behavior may be much more complex than
many conceptual frameworks suggest.

ADVICE, RECOMMENDATIONS, AND BRAND ENDORSEMENT
FROM HEALTH PERSONNEL

Additional supporting evidence of the influence
of health services on the feeding choices of mothers
is provided by qualitative data. In all four sites,
there is a tendency on the part of Western-trained
professionals to suggest the use of formula either as
a supplement or as a therapeutic response to breast
morbidity, insufficient milk, or illness of mother or
infant. A wide spectrum of trained health workers in
all sites display a striking degree of contradictory
information and lack of knowledge about lactation
management. Traditional birth attendants, on the other
hand, when confronted with breastfeeding difficulties,
generally suggest continued breastfeeding, increased
intake of food and liquid, massages-- and supplementation of the infant only as a last resort.

In Thai health facilities mothers may be referred
to social workers in municipal health centers if their
children are malnourished. These clients are generally
from the lowest-income families, and formula is given
to them free of charge. Apparently, some of the poorer
mothers residing in Bangkok slums sell the free formula
for cash at small stores, buying cheaper sweetened condensed milk for the infant and using the rest of the
money for daily living expenses. Thus, the infant receives the _worst_ possible source of nourishment through
the well-intentioned intervention of the health care
system.

The Bogotá ethnography indicates that many middle-
and low-middle-income women reported that, postnatally,
their physicians recommended specific milk. Some private
pediatricians recommended Figuestomil and Ferrimison
to be given right after the birth to enhance the baby's
appetite and some advised against night feeding because
it "caused indigestion." Women were directly influenced
in the introduction of early milk complements and weaning with formula. Chapter 3 describes how some Bogotá
mothers, for a variety of culturally conditioned
reasons, do not trust the quality of their milk--a perception reinforced, if not suggested, by health professionals. As one mother stated, "the milk is very light
or clear, it is not thick .... the doctor from La
Victoria told me that my milk is clear because it is
not good."

Bivariate analysis corroborates this association
between formula advice by health professionals and

shorter breastfeeding durations in Bogotá. Mothers who recall advice to use formula have a greater propensity to introduce a bottle by two months than those who recall discussing breastfeeding with health workers. This differential may reflect mothers' tendency to recall advice in confirmation of the feeding patterns they choose. On the other hand, it does appear from the ethnography that Bogotá women often accept professional opinions about their incapacity to nurse as well as recommendations to give up trying to breastfeed and to use various brands of milk.

Of the Nairobi mothers giving birth in hospitals, clinics or maternity homes, only 14 percent recalled being given any information on infant feeding at the health facility. Of those who did receive information, 52 percent report being told it is best to feed formula or cow's milk, 27 percent report being told it is best to breastfeed only, 9 percent report being told to feed both breastmilk and infant formula/cow's milk, and the remaining 12 percent report being told that neither type of feeding is best or could not recall the advice. Counting all those not told that exclusive breastfeeding is best, nearly three-fourths of those receiving any advice on infant feeding recall leaving the hospital either with wrong information or inadequate advice. Even more dramatically, in one site, junior hospital workers were observed selling bottles at 150 percent of cost to desperate mothers.

Extensive interviewing and participant observation were conducted at one Semarang health center. Women who complained of decreased breastmilk were told to increase their food intake and massage their breasts. Nonetheless, samples of milk powders were also distributed to mothers at the clinic. Instructions on how to prepare bottles and powdered foods were provided. Yet, the data show that less than half of all respondents boiled their babies' bottles before using them. The most malnourished children were among the poorest in the district, in whose houses there were problems of sewage disposal, clean water, and storage for prepared milk. Help and encouragement in breastfeeding might be more appropriate to the life conditions of these families than provision of formula: many cannot afford to continue to buy adequate supplies of formula or to prepare and store it safely.

Clinic policy was to advise women to stop breastfeeding children with diarrhea until after electrolyte solution treatment was completed. Interruptions in breastfeeding because of this policy may have given some women the idea that diarrhea is associated with breast-

milk. In any case, temporary cessation of breastfeeding
has been shown to be counterproductive in babies' re-
covery from illness. It also decreases milk supplies
dramatically, resulting in a higher probability of
"insufficient milk" and early weaning.

The doctors and <u>bidans</u> (Western, biomedically
<u>trained</u> midwives) in Semarang appear to be more favor-
able to the use of bottles than are the <u>dukuns</u> (traditional birth attendants) (Table 7.3). Since Indonesian
women of all classes rely on more than one kind of prac-
titioner, the integration of traditional and Western
advice by <u>dukuns</u> may soften the negative effects of
<u>bidan</u> and physician attitudes. (See Chapter 5 for a des-
cription of the responsibility and duties of the <u>dukun</u>
versus the <u>bidan</u>.)

THE MEDICAL CULTURE OF CHILDBIRTH

The "treatment" of a wide spectrum of breastfeeding
difficulties with infant formula supplementation can
be seen as a routine response by medical professionals
to patients' problems. This is consistent with the fact
that childbirth and infant feeding in the health care
facilities studied are organized on curative Western
medical models rather than traditional preventive practices. The extension of modern medicine into the traditionally female domain has begun to shape the very
definition of infant feeding into a clinical science.[1]

The description by the study anthropologist of
a maternity home in Nairobi demonstrates the alienating
nature of Westernized maternity care superimposed onto
a health system with gross shortages of equipment,
trained personnel, and facilities, and overburdened with
impoverished clients.

The particular maternity home observed admits
more cases per year than any other facility
in Africa--very likely the world. On a heavily
utilized day, 160 babies are born there. On
a slow day, less than 100. The observations
took place on a light day.

The facility is filthy. Outside the labor ward
ten women sit holding admission papers. Most
are in the second stage of labor. By the door
to the labor room, a curtained bed is used
to examine the women to determine priority.
Ones that are not in advanced stages of labor
are sent back to the antenatal clinic to wait.

When the birth is imminent they are ushered
into the labor ward where they are given the
next free bed. Beds are arranged around four
sides......with several delivery rooms in the
center. None of these rooms were in use. Instead, women were in various stages of giving
birth on the rubber-sheeted cots in the labor
wards. Midwives walked briskly between beds,
pulling off one set of rubber gloves and replacing them with a new set to catch the baby
or assist the next birth. Women moaned and
twisted on the beds, pulling up their skirts
in time for the birth. On a slow day, such
as the one observed, each woman had her own
cot. As the babies emerged they were given
immediately to their mothers. Cords were ban-
daged and mothers were returned to another
row of benches with a bundled baby in their
arms. They waited there until a ward assign-
ment was made.

In one of these wards, 94 mothers and their
newborns occupied about 60 beds. Two mothers
lay with their heads at opposite ends of one
bed and unwrapped their bundles. Here, when
they were strong enough, they could wash their
babies and examine and breastfeed them.
Mothers are kept 12-24 hours and released,
if they pay their fee on that day. I saw no
counseling or inquiries about breastfeeding
problems. In wards where mothers stay longer,
infant formula is distributed from the nursery
in feeding bottles. The sister-nurse in charge
here said they encourage mothers to breastfeed
before giving supplementary feeds. Pamphlets
from the Breastfeeding Information Group were
locked in a cupboard in a staff office. The
turnover is so high, nurses in some areas
barely speak with patients. Shortages of
staff, equipment, linen, drugs,... ...food
were all evident. A young......nurse was observed distributing a few slices of bread to
a ward of 78 postnatal mothers. Babies are
not bathed until six or more hours after delivery. I witnessed no support for new mothers
who have never breastfed before and nothing
to encourage a woman to establish lactation
other than the pleasure it might afford her
and her baby in such bleak surroundings.

It does not appear from the ethnographers that
either the Bangkok or Bogotá mothers giving birth in
modern facilities have traditional therapeutic measures

available to encourage breastfeeding in the face of difficulty. Women do not have support-helpers or time off
(postpartum rest from work in Colombia or "lying by the
fire" in Thailand).2 Faced with lack of support, and
seeing formula fed by health workers, what incentive
is there to breastfeed? How much less reason is there
to do so, if it is also suggested that the formula contents are more nutritious than breastmilk?

The clinical and technological approach to childbearing and feeding contributes to both physical and
psychic separation of mothers from infants in these
institutions. Birth becomes a medical event, separated
from life cycle processes, reinforcing reliance upon
medical supervision and "medicines" for infant nutrition. This is dramatically demonstrated in Kenya where
the same Swahili word is used to refer to medicine and
infant formula (Chapter 9). It is not surprising, then,
that one-third of the Nairobi infants were being fed
some complement of infant formula regardless of the cost
to the family or the perceived adequacy of breastmilk.

In general, individual bedside communication is
not a customary practice in Bangkok hospitals. Mothers
in Bangkok receive little information on breastfeeding,
either prenatally or immediately postpartum. Women who
state that they intend to breastfeed rarely receive advice or follow up. More information appeared to be given
on supplementary feeding. Moreover, patients often men-
tion that harsh tones and language are used by nurses
when they communicate information and advice. These descriptions are reminiscent of criticisms of the medical
practice in the West. Some problems are rooted in difficulties in communication between people of different
classes and cultural values. They reflect a lack of understanding by professionals of how information is best
offered to patients. Low income and poor mothers in
Bangkok and Nairobi state they will not approach physicians to ask about breastfeeding problems. They are con-
fused about answers to questions and embarrassed to demand clarifications even from female nurses or social
workers.

THE MARKETING ENVIRONMENT IN HOSPITALS

Mothers will be helped to breastfeed if professionals correct misguided knowledge about lactation management and also become more informed about communication
with patients. These strategies alone, however, cannot
change the tendency of hospitals to encourage artificial
feeding, in part, because of the continuing relationship

between the medical institutions and the industries producing infant foods. At all four sites, the marketing substudies identified important and extensive relationships between commercial marketers (detailers) and physicians, administrators, medically trained midwives, nurses, pharmacists, and social workers. Basically, these relationships are the result of attempts to increase the sales of infant formula products through their use in the health system and through the recommendations of health professionals. Chapter 8 elaborates the specific marketing techniques of infant food manufacturers and discusses how infant formula companies use both individual providers and institutions as promotion conduits for their products. The role of free formula supplies in influencing the behavior of staff, procedures and, ultimately, mothers is the result of effective marketing techniques which manage to stay within the bounds of ethical sales practices because of ambiguities in the WHO Code.

The following pages will utilize examples from the Bangkok ethnography in order to demonstrate the relationship between the health care institutions and company strategies. The ethnographers in Bangkok specifically chose hospitals and health care facilities as sites for the Phase II study. The marketing situation in Bangkok is highly competitive, with a large number of available products and aggressive promotion by some of the international formula manufacturers. Similar marketing strategies were observed at all sites, however, although the Bangkok environment was the most extreme. At all four sites, educational materials, posters, product samples, and free supplies to health facilities were given by company detailers. Gifts were occasionally given to health workers and hospitals, including pediatric equipment in Bogotá.

In Bangkok, contacts between company detailers and nurses were particularly congenial because many of the salespeople were once nurses themselves and maintained ties with their former colleagues and institutions. In the course of meeting with nurses in the hospital lunchroom and the nurses' dormitory, a group of detailers described their work:

> Every company's detailers are all here ......detailers know the nurses working in these hospitals. Milk detailers are assigned to specific zones or groups of hospitals......we are here to meet doctors and nurses...we cannot talk to mothers because the Ministry of Public Health prohibits us.

Now [that] the Ministry is campaigning for breastfeeding, they forbid us to make direct contact with mothers......[so] we find the way out by approaching through medical person-nel......Ordinarily, patients and mothers do believe the words of the medical doctors--once they know the brands of formula the hospitals use they tend to follow......which is helpful to us......we sell [at] a very special price to hospital staff like nurses and doctors. The price for these persons has to be lower than anywhere else......It's a kind of persuasion, or public relations. These people are of good help to us......Nurses often buy directly from detailers because they can get it cheap. They......order [formula] for relatives and friends.

All detailers are nurses with B.A. degrees. We used to work as nurses in these hospitals before......There is no rule of the hospital against the detailers. It is our right to contact doctors or nurses.

According to executives in industry, advertising agencies, and retailers, the hospitals and clinics have become sites for marketing and promotional activity. Direct marketing, such as the use of milk nurses, has been banned, although observations by research team members indicate that some nurses do represent companies in the hospital setting. Indirect promotion, through product samples or hospital supplies, is frequent and substantial. During the time of the field research, two Japanese companies reportedly increased their efforts to distribute free samples to mothers in hospitals. The other companies seemed to accept a system in which free supplies were turned over to hospital or clinic staff for use in the hospital. In a number of hospitals and clinics, infant formula was supplied as a discharge pack to mothers leaving the facility. Recently, an effort has been made to curtail distribution of formula samples in some Bangkok government hospitals. This has met with little opposition from industry, but the focus of market-ing activities seems to have shifted to distribution of information and free samples in well baby clinics.

It is instructive to examine the role of female health workers in an effort to assess their influence in changing the practices of the mothers in their care. A group of Bangkok hospital pharmacists, all female, were interviewed. They demonstrated varying and sometimes incorrect ideas about breastfeeding. Some had been contacted by sales representatives, and they sold formula to mothers at a 20 to 30 percent discount from market price.

In Bangkok, as in all sites, women nurses have the greatest contact with mothers. Nurses are mentioned as the major category of medical personnel responsible for helping with problems of breast morbidity and insufficient milk, although they receive no in-service training about breastfeeding. Every nurse interviewed on the Pediatrics and Obstetrics-Gynecology units had one or two direct contacts per month with the infant food company representative in the hospital. They also distribute discharge kits to mothers, including materials about infant formula. Bangkok nurses are in charge of the milk supply rooms and make direct purchases necessary for the hospitals. They determine how much infant formula they need for sales to patients. They can offer it directly for sale to mothers and make 5 to 6 percent commission per can. Nurses form friendships with patients and allow them to return to the hospital after discharge to purchase extra cans of formula at the discount price. The obvious profitability--and potential conflict of interest--for nurses who act as sellers of formula is clear.

Thus, female health workers do not challenge the medical/technical approach to reproduction. In fact, they reinforce and deepen it through their participation and acceptance of it for themselves. Nurses admitted that they faced great obstacles in breastfeeding their own infants. They were not allowed to return home for breastfeeding breaks. There were no staff nursery units at the hospitals. Maternity leaves were 45 days in government hospitals and 30 days in private ones. A majority of the nurses interviewed claimed they breastfed their own infants only between one and three days after birth. They were also aware that the use of infant formula in mixed regimes seemed to make babies less interested in breastfeeding. They reported breast engorgement and pain when they tried to breastfeed only occasionally, as after work. This group of women, then, could easily identify with the problems of their patients. Yet, from a professional point of view, they were surprisingly uneducated: they were unconvinced of the possibility of maintaining breastfeeding and ignorant of alternatives to the cessation of breastfeeding when problems arose. Nurses preferred to resolve their own infant feeding problems by using formula, which may have influenced greatly the attitudes and advice they imparted to mothers.

Female health professionals, by virtue of their own generally subordinate position to male physicians

and health care administrators, tend to accept the dominant obstetric model of childbirth and feeding. By virtue
of their biomedical training, they tend to deny the value
of traditional therapies in favor of "scientific" ones.
By virtue of their own inadequate conditions of work,
they cannot maintain breastfeeding, and by virtue of
the pervasive influence of formula companies and their
own benefits from sales of infant food, they emphasize
the value of infant formula over breastmilk.

The picture presented is gloomy, yet possibilities
for improvement exist. For example, contacts between
detailers and health care personnel which are detrimental can be stopped. Inducements to sell formula to new
mothers can be eliminated. Health officials can be shown
that their institutions are being stocked with formula,
bottles, and materials above and beyond need, and that
the supplies are used unnecessarily. Administrators,
policymakers, and health professionals can be alerted
to the effort to manipulate consumption by promotional
activities focused on health care providers. Female health
workers can be provided with work environments compatible with optimal feeding of their own infants. With
better information, these women professionals can become
a key factor in the restructuring of hospital routine.
Hospitals can better serve mothers by universal encouragement of exclusive breastfeeding without prelacteal
glucose or milk feeds and by reducing mother and infant
separation. Re-education programs for all levels of health
professionals can focus on lactation management and infant
nutrition, emphasizing cultural, ethnic, and class diver-
sities. Traditional beliefs that are beneficial to maternal and infant health can be incorporated into preventive
care programs, and traditional birth attendants can be
utilized in education, training, and support for breastfeeding women. These suggestions can lessen the institutional and professional discouragements to breastfeeding and lead to the establishment of more humane medical
services for all women and children.

NOTES

1.   For a discussion of the history of the medicalization of reproduction in the West see A. Oakley, <u>Women Confined: Towards a Sociology of Childbirth</u>, (New York: Schocken Books 1980).

2.   This viewpoint is discussed by Penny Van Esterik in "The Cultural Context of Breastfeeding in Rural Thailand," in <u>Breastfeeding, Child Health and Child Spacing: Cross-Cultural Perspectives</u>, ed. V. Hull and M. Simpson (London: Crown Helm, 1985), pp. 139-61.

8 The Influence of Marketing on Infant Feeding

James E. Post and Robert A. Smith

Of the many policy questions relating to infant feeding in the developing nations, none have provoked as much controversy as those surrounding the marketing of infant formula. For more than a decade, beginning with the first industry-sponsored codes of conduct (1975) and highlighted by the World Health Organization's International Code of Marketing of Breastmilk Substitutes (1981), the cutting edge of policy action has been directed to marketing practices. The regulation of marketing behavior has been advocated by health professionals since the early 1970s and is the principal outcome of the WHO Code. The aim of the Code is to:

> contribute to the safe and adequate nutrition of infants, by the protection and promotion of breastfeeding, and by ensuring the proper use of breastmilk substitutes, when these are necessary on the basis of adequate information and through <u>appropriate marketing and distribution.</u> (Article 1) (emphasis added)

"Appropriate marketing and distribution" is defined to mean no advertising, promotion, or direct contact between manufacturers and sellers of breastmilk substitutes and mothers of infants (Article 5). Rather, appropriate marketing is to occur in the context of legitimate manufacturer and distributor contact with health workers and health care institutions. In other words, the WHO Code envisioned that the focus of the marketing system would shift from mothers and the general public to health workers and the health care system.

To implement effectively the letter and spirit of the Code requires an understanding of the specific circumstances of the "marketing system" in each nation. Although the Code's provisions are generally applicable to all nations, it is readily acknowledged that immense differences exist from country to country. This chapter presents a comparative analysis of the marketing systems in Bangkok, Bogotá, Nairobi, and Semarang. Since no base-line studies of the infant foods markets existed in any of these cities prior to the consortium project, this chapter represents one of the first opportunities to present a descriptive comparison of the infant foods market. In addition, the influence of marketing promotion on consumer behavior is assessed in several ways.

Bangkok, Bogotá, Nairobi, and Semarang are distinc-tive environments for the purchase and sale of infant food products. Bangkok is by far the most competitive environment, with many sellers of infant foods and more manufacturers represented than at any other site. Nairobi, by comparison, represents a market that is substantially dominated by one manufacturer whose share of the infant foods market overwhelms that of all other competitors combined. The countervailing forces of competition which exist in Bangkok are missing in Nairobi, but are offset in part by a larger government presence that includes price controls and a relatively stricter influence on marketing behavior. Bogotá and Semarang differ signifi-cantly from both Bangkok and Nairobi. Bogotá represents a large market in which two infant formula manufacturers compete in substantial ways, but are also much affected by government price regulations. Semarang is a unique market in several respects, affected by a dominant company but one which also happens to be Indonesian-owned. Thus, there is a government interest in the success of the domestic infant formula manufacturer which is unparalleled in any of the other markets.

These structural characteristics derive from many sources, some related to geographic and climatological factors that affect the ability of a country to support a dairy industry, others related to deliberate policy actions by governments to promote or constrain economic growth along specific paths. These background variables are of current and historical importance because they form the policy setting in which business and governmental decisions are made. Without an appreciation of such matters, there can be no complete understanding of the marketing system upon which policy interventions can be based.

Figure 8.1 presents a framework of variables that have been systematically studied in each of the four field sites. The nine boxes in the left portion of the figure represent "supply-side" factors related to the amount of infant formula and other infant foods available for sale in a specific market. The variables to the right side of the figure are related to the demand for infant formula among individual consumers and segments of the consumer market. In each of the study sites, descriptive data were collected and organized to provide a profile of how each factor affected others. The cross-sectional survey of mothers, in turn, permitted an analysis of the influence of various factors on maternal preferences and attitudes.

Many factors influence the market practices of companies that manufacture and sell infant foods. Market practices are a reflection of basic industry policy decisions regarding the production, distribution, and promotional strategies used to reach potential purchasers. These policy decisions are themselves influenced by a variety of factors, ranging from competitor's actions to government policies and programs. In the four markets or sites studied, it was found that government policies and programs on such matters as taxation, labor, industry development, and public health all had an influence on the policy decisions and behavior of the manufacturers.

MARKETING TRENDS

The marketing of infant foods, especially infant formula, has changed in a number of important ways since 1981. Data collected in this study highlighted five important trends:

1.   increased amount of price competition;

2.   increased product availability, with infant formulas being readily available in every category of retail outlet used by consumers;

3.   discontinuance of consumer-oriented mass media advertising;

4.   extensive promotion of commercial infant foods to health care workers and, through them, to consumers; and,

5.   continued distribution of infant formula samples to mothers, directly or indirectly, many of whom live in a high-risk environment.

Each of these trends was evident in the four communities studied (Table 8.1.). Local conditions do mediate the extent to which these trends are affecting the operation of the infant foods market.

Figure 8.1   RELATIONSHIP OF MARKET FACTORS

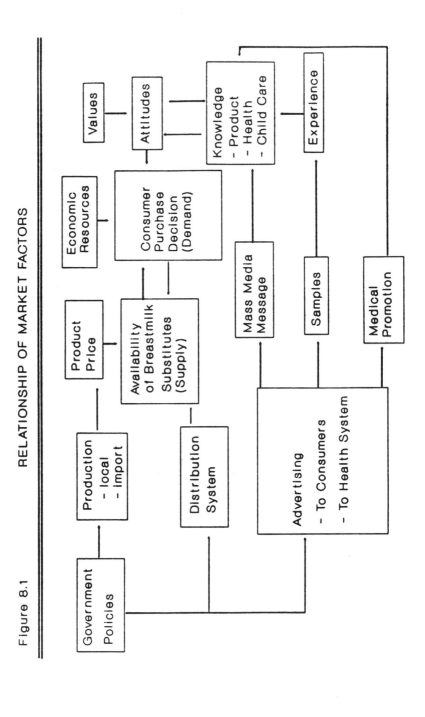

Table 8.1   COMPARATIVE MARKET CHARACTERISTICS

	BANGKOK	BOGOTÁ	NAIROBI	SEMARANG
Price Competition	Substantial	Limited	Limited	Moderate
Product Availability	Very High	Medium	Medium	High
Mass Media	Some	None	None	Very Little
Medical Promotion	Intense	Intense	Intense	Intense
Product Sampling	Substantial	Low	Low	Low

Pricing

Price competition among various brands of commercial infant foods was evident in each of the communities studied. Such competition is not inconsistent with the WHO Code. The Code provides that practices such as discount coupons, premiums, special sales, loss leaders, and tie-in sales are not to be used to induce sales at the retail level. Article 5.3 further states that "This provision should not restrict the establishment of pricing policies and practices intended to provide products at lower prices on a long term basis." In general terms, the industry has maintained that the Code does not prevent the continuation of a normal trade price structure, including the meeting of competitive prices.

The degree of price competition manifested in the four countries studied varies with the competitive structure of the local market. There is very little price competition in Kenya where one company dominates the market. In Thailand and Indonesia, where there are many competitors, pricing is predictably aggressive.

Data from the retail audits conducted in each site indicate certain "clustering" of infant foods around key price levels. For the most part, the products at various price points are of the same quality (e.g., humanized formulas; full protein formulas; full cream milk). The product groups compete against one another as breast-milk substitutes and the brands compete within each group. However, occasional peculiarities in this pattern suggest competitors sometimes try to reshape the normal trade price structure in each market.

Availability

Infant formula products are widely available in each of the communities studied. Retail audits, conducted in each city by local marketing research firms or experts, included brands, types of products, prices, sizes, and point-of-sale promotion. On a comparative basis, several key findings stand out. As seen in Table 8.2, infant formula products and other commercial infant foods are widely available in each location. Sellers reach most of the population by distributing their products through the retail outlets most frequently used by consumers to purchase food products. In none of these communities was infant formula restricted to distribution through pharmacies or drug stores. It should also be noted that commercial infant foods are readily available in retail outlets regarded as "most convenient" by consumers. This includes supermarkets and general provision stores, as well as neighborhood shops and markets. The distribution pattern in each city indicates an effort by manufacturers and distributors to place these products within easy reach of potential consumers.

The retail audits disclose no geographic segmentation by distributors. There has been no evidence of an effort to restrict availability to those areas of cities frequented by high-income users or those with fewer "risk characteristics."

Finally, we have noted that the leading brand in each market tends to have the highest degree of presence, or "penetration," in the highest volume outlets. This is significant because such exposure, or "visual presence" as it is called in the advertising business, serves as a form of product advertising. In the context of the WHO Code's call for elimination of mass media promotion, companies have had a clear incentive to expand rather than reduce the number of outlets carrying their products.

Table 8.2   AVAILABILITY OF INFANT FORMULA
             BY TYPE OF OUTLET

	Percentage Carrying	
Bangkok	Any Formula	Leading Brand
Large Provision Stores	76	47
Medium Provision Store	76	62
Small Provision Stores	63	44
Chemists/Drug Stores	38	13
Medicine Shops	40	40
Bogotá		
Supermarkets	93	
Chain		92
Other		94
Drug Stores	87	
Chain		100
Other		74
Shops	52	
General		49
Other		43
Nairobi		
Self Service	100	90
Shops	92	
Large		87
Medium		90
Small		80
Drug Stores	100	--
Market Stalls	100	96
Semarang		
Supermarkets	100	100
Retail Stores/Shops	100	100
Drugstores	100	100

Media Advertising

The infant foods industry has largely abandoned consumer-oriented media advertising as a promotional tool. The WHO Code contains numerous provisions that attempt to foreclose direct promotion to consumers. The data collected in this study indicate that each of the national governments has acted to halt radio and television advertising of infant foods. The regulatory efforts have been carried out in conjunction with government media programs to promote breastfeeding.

In Colombia and Indonesia, the national governments acted to restrict mass media promotion in advance of the 1981 World Health Assembly's approval of the Code. In Kenya and Thailand, the national governments have used the Code as a basis for drafting specific rules to restrict mass media promotion. This research disclosed only a few isolated violations of these laws.

Analysis of consumer response indicates that consumers in all four cities have a high recall of past mass media (television, radio, and print) advertising. There is a strong suggestion that the messages of past promotions still linger in the minds of consumers. In Bogotá and Semarang, for example, more than one-half of the women surveyed reported advertising recall. In both cities, women with higher family income were more likely to recall advertising than women with less income. In Semarang, women between the ages of 20 and 34 showed a higher recall level as well.

In Nairobi, 68 percent recalled infant formula advertising on radio or television. Women in their twenties showed the highest recall. There was also a positive association with the level of education.

In Bangkok, 83 percent recalled mass marketing advertising. Women with higher income and educational attainment were significantly more likely to recall promotional advertising. The overall awareness of advertising was higher in Bangkok than in any other of the study sites.

Medical Promotion

As direct promotion to consumers has declined, infant formula manufacturers and distributors have increased promotion and contact with health workers. Promotion through the health sector is a direct consequence of the Code. Because more babies are being born in hospitals, and health workers are an important source of advice and counsel to mothers, this is a particularly critical trend.

Article 6.2 of the Code states that "No facility of a health care system should be used for the purpose of promoting infant formula or other products within the scope of this Code. This Code does not, however, preclude the dissemination of information to health professionals." Within the framework of this general language, the Code attempts to restrict, define, or structure the parameters within which commercial marketing should occur in the health care system.

An extensive discussion of promotion through the health sector is contained in Chapter 7. However, it is important to note that the WHO Code allows for manufacturers to provide "educational information" to health workers and health care institutions for eventual distribution to mothers. In each community, we found company-produced booklets, pamphlets, and other printed materials. These materials varied in quality and the degree of conformance with Code requirements for accuracy and non-idealization of bottle feeding.

In addition to printed materials, manufacturers in each community continue to provide travel and research funds, equipment, and other forms of assistance to health workers and health institutions.

Samples

The fifth significant marketing trend observed is the continued effort of infant formula sellers to place product samples in the hands of new mothers. It is widely accepted among marketers that the most effective way to encourage consumer adoption of a product is to place it in the hands of consumers. This accounts for endless free samples of toothpaste and deodorant in the United States and continued efforts by infant formula companies to distribute samples of their products in developing nations.

The WHO Code specifically addresses the widespread distribution of samples. Article 5.2 of the Code states "Manufacturers and distributors should not provide, directly or indirectly, to pregnant women, mothers or members of their families, samples of products within the scope of this Code." Samples may, however, be provided to health workers "when necessary for professional evaluation or research at the institutional level" (Article 7.4).

Product samples are ostensibly provided for two purposes to encourage both brand awareness and brand use. Overall, the rate of sampling in these four urban areas is not particularly high. Bangkok mothers had the highest reported rate of receiving samples (12%), followed by Bogotá (6%), Nairobi (5%), and Semarang (4%).

In two of four sites, interesting patterns emerge when these rates are examined by the place of infant's birth. In Bangkok, nearly one out of every three mothers who delivered in a private hospital reported receiving a free formula sample at the hospital. In Semarang, where the overall rate of sampling is lower than in Bangkok, the pattern of distribution is much broader and involves a variety of health care workers. Approximately one-half of the mothers who reported receiving a sample delivered their babies at home, or in a midwife's home, and were attended to by dukuns (traditional midwives) or bidans (government-trained midwives). This pattern suggests that formula companies view these birth attendants as promotional conduits and do not focus promotional contacts on hospitals alone. Of additional interest in Semarang is that the rate of sampling to mothers of children older than twelve months at the time of the interview was 7 percent, suggesting a small decline in this practice since the Indonesian government endorsed the WHO Code.

The efforts of WHO and public action groups to reduce the distribution of product samples have met with mixed success since 1981. There has been a reduction of direct sampling to mothers in compliance with the provisions of Article 5.2. This field research discovered very little that suggests manufacturers are using the "professional evaluation or research" clause of Article 7.4 to justify continued sampling. What has occurred, however, is the continued and even expanded provision of free supplies to health care institutions. In each of the field sites, the provision of free supplies for use in health care institutions was accepted and practiced. In each case, however, aggregate supplies being provided were in excess of the needs of newborns in the institutions. Thus, the health workers were encouraged to share these supplies with mothers. In fact, the free supplies become product samples. This is a pattern that appears to be occurring in many nations.1

CONSUMER BEHAVIOR

In the model presented in Figure 8.1, consumer behavior is hypothesized to be influenced both directly and indirectly by product promotion. Various practices are expected to cause, or to be associated with, consumer decisions to bottlefeed, and to purchase a particular brand. The data analyzed in this study permit a number of conclusions to be drawn about the influence of promotional activity--especially samples--on consumer behavior, attitudes, and brand awareness. Given the different cultural settings and promotional approaches in each site, these conclusions are best presented by city.

Bangkok

Within the highly competitive Bangkok market, it was not surprising to see relatively high rates of sampling. Approximately 12 percent of the mothers surveyed reported receiving a free sample of infant formula, and the primary source of that sample was the hospital where the baby was born (96%).

Women with higher income and education and women who had worked prior to having their baby were significantly more likely to receive a sample of infant formula on discharge. There was also a positive association with age, with women under the age of 20 being least likely to receive a sample (4.9%) and women above the age of 30 most likely (16.7%). The most dramatic difference in the proportion of those receiving and not receiving free samples can be seen in the comparison between those delivering in public versus private hospitals. Fewer than one in ten women who had their baby in a public hospital left with a sample of infant formula, whereas nearly one in three who delivered in a private hospital reported receiving a sample.

The product sampling practices of sellers in Bangkok produce mixed results. Women who never breastfed are only slightly more likely to have received a sample than women who do breastfeed (12.7% vs. 11.9%), a difference that is not statistically significant. This observation casts doubt on the hypothesis that women who receive free samples are those who could not breastfeed, and therefore were appropriate recipients. There is also no difference in likelihood of having received a sample between those women who did and did not introduce bottle feeding by the end of the first month (13.1% vs. 11.1%). However, women who bottlefed by the end of the second month were significantly more likely to have received a sample than those who did not (14.2% vs. 10.0% p<.05). Similarly, women who did not breastfeed for three months were significantly more likely to have received samples than those who did (15.4% vs. 10.6%, p<.05). Given the generally short weaning interval

observed in Bangkok, it is not surprising that an increase in bottle feeding is followed by a drop in the rate of breastfeeding.

Product sampling does have a significant effect on brand awareness, however. Women who received a sample recalled a greater number of brands than women who did not receive a sample. In Bangkok, virtually every woman who received a sample could name the brand and tell our interviewers whether or not it was available in the local market. Of those who received a free sample, 79 percent reported having used it to feed their baby. Perhaps more important from a commercial standpoint, 44 percent of those who have purchased infant formula have purchased the brand they received as a sample, and 31 percent of those who have purchased formula are currently using the brand they received as a sample. This confirms the general proposition that experience with a product, however obtained, is a key predictor of future product use.

The commercial sophistication of consumers in Bangkok extends to their awareness and attitudes toward infant foods. Approximately 83 percent of the respondents recalled mass market advertising of commercial infant foods. Although such mass advertising last occurred several years before the survey, women with higher income and educational attainment retained a high degree of recall, as did women who were employed prior to giving birth. This high degree of promotional awareness is reinforced by an equally high degree of brand awareness. On an unaided recall of brands, 97 percent of respondents were able to name at least one brand of infant formula and more than 90 percent could name two or more brands. As was the case for recall of advertising and receiving a free sample, mothers with higher income and education were able to name more brands, and a higher proportion of all brands, than mothers with lower income and education. Receipt of a free sample of infant formula also had a very high statistical association with greater brand recall.

Consumer attitudes have also been influenced by the commercial marketing of infant foods. It was interesting to note that mothers in Bangkok overwhelmingly agreed that breastfeeding is superior to bottle feeding, and yet there were noteworthy differences in the response to statements regarding attitudes toward bottle feeding. Respondents were asked whether or not they agreed with the statements, "Formula feeding is less trouble than breastfeeding," and "Using formula milk is modern." Overall, 32 percent agreed that feeding with formula milks is less trouble than breastfeeding and

69 percent agreed that it is modern. Women who agreed with both statements were significantly more likely to have higher incomes, although more educated women were less likely to argue that formula feeding is modern. Women who worked prior to delivery were not more likely to agree with either statement, and the receipt of a free sample of infant formula does not seem to have any measurable influence on these attitudes. This indicates that any differences in behavior between employed and other mothers--or those who received samples and those who did not--may not be due to different attitudes toward infant feeding, but may be related to different experiences, such as the need to work or the receipt of the sample.

Bangkok has a population that is highly aware of commercial infant foods and of specific brands. The overall rate of sampling, while significant, is not extraordinarily high, but does have a number of clear effects. Women who received samples are able to recall the brand and report its availability in local markets. Perhaps most important, those who received a free sample and are using formula to feed their babies report having purchased the sample brand at least once. Thus, placement of the product in the hands of a mother has its intended effects: product use and purchase.

As product samples remain available to mothers-- directly as samples in violation of the WHO Code, or indirectly as "free supplies" to health care institutions which subsequently pass them on to mothers--they seem likely to continue having this "use and purchase" effect. Coupled with broad product distribution in retail outlets, high product visibility in individual stores and shops, and continuing advice from health workers to use a particular brand (a greater percentage of respondents reported brand recommendation than reported receiving a free sample), consumer demand for commercial infant foods in Bangkok will continue to expand.

Bogotá

The direct influence of promotional activities is best seen through product sampling, where the presence of the product in the hands of the consumer is most likely to result in use and, more often than not, adoption. In Bogotá, however, only 6.2 percent of the women interviewed reported receiving a free sample of infant formula. There appears to be no pattern of distribution by income, years of schooling, age, or parity. However, women who were employed at the time of the interview were more likely to report receiving a sample than women who were not in the labor force. In hospitals where rooming-in was not practiced, receipt of a sample was more likely, and delivery in a Social Security hospital was significantly associated with receipt of a free sample. These associations may be explained by the facts that (1) employed women may be more likely to be covered by the Social Security medical system and (2) the Social Security hospitals do not generally offer rooming-in arrangements for mothers and babies.

Even though the number of women reporting receipt of a free sample was small, we sought to determine whether or not a free sample of infant formula had an effect on infant feeding patterns. Regression analysis did not show any independent effect of receiving a free sample with the duration of breastfeeding or the early introduction of bottle feeding.

Approximately one-half of the women in the Bogotá sample recalled mass market advertising of commercial infant foods. Women with higher educational attainment are more likely to report recall of advertising as are women with higher family incomes. In Bogotá, there were no significant differences between primiparous and multiparous women in this regard, nor were comparisons by age revealing of any pattern. An important aspect of infant foods marketing in Bogotá was the practice of physician endorsement of formula brands. One in four women reported that they used a particular brand of formula on recommendation of a physician. The higher a woman's family income and education, the more likely she was to receive this kind of endorsement. Delivery in a private hospital was also strongly associated with brand endorsement by a physician. In addition, women who received a free sample of infant formula were more likely to report this kind of endorsement than those who did not receive a free sample. This strongly suggests that product endorsement by the physician and receipt of a free sample occurred simultaneously or in a manner that creates a clear, unified message for the mother.

There is a broad availability of commercial infant foods in Bogotá, and mothers make decisions amidst a mix of price, quality, and advice factors. The available infant formulas and cereals are produced by multinational companies, while flours, starches, and other foods that are being fed to infants are produced locally. Distribution networks for all these foods are highly developed and extensive so that the full spectrum of products is usually present in most outlets selling any infant foods. Only drug stores have a restricted list of food products for sale. Among the common problems facing consumers are labels in English not Spanish, misstatements of nutritional value, and misrepresentation of a product's suitability as an infant food. There is also a problem of quality and mislabelling among certain locally produced food products.

The price competition among infant formulas and cereals is limited, in large measure because the market is shared by only two companies. Price competition among other products (such as non-formula milks, grains, and starches) which are used as substitutes is more evident, a situation which exacerbates problems of quality and mislabelling. In this climate of greater competition, there is little incentive to improve quality and increase production costs since prices cannot be raised accordingly. Meanwhile, consumers face difficult choices when their incomes are limited.

The promotion of commercial infant foods through mass market advertising has virtually disappeared in Bogotá and has led producers to promote their products through expanded regular contacts with the health sector. Company representatives regularly visit health care facilities, talk with health workers, and distribute product information for future dissemination to mothers. Brand endorsement by health workers is routine, and health workers understand that one outcome of this endorsement is brand loyalty. A more subtle type of promotion, but one that is important under advertising restrictions, is product visibility. The extensive visibility of brands and the many different types of infant foods contributes to a positive image of these foods. Within this competitive framework, the distribution of free samples is limited, but targeted through Social Security hospitals.

A distinctive feature in Bogotá is the extent to which mothers use many different foods, and combinations of foods, to feed their babies. Both these patterns are the result of cultural beliefs and economic conditions that constrain the ability to purchase higher quality infant foods. These conditions mean that brand endorsement by physicians must be considered in the light of two possible explanations: the physicians are expressing their own loyalty to a particular company, and/or they want to be sure the first breastmilk substitute is appropriate for infant feeding.

Nairobi

Overall, the provision of free samples does not appear to be a significant market practice in Nairobi. Only 4 percent of the women surveyed reported receiving a free sample of infant formula. However, 90 percent of these women reported that the sample they did receive was provided at a hospital or clinic. While the distribution of samples was not widespread, there did appear to be significant differences between those who did and did not receive a free sample. Specifically, higher education, age, previous employment, multiparity, and not reporting rooming-in were significantly associated with the receipt of a free sample. Women who delivered in a clinic or hospital were also more likely to report receiving a free sample than those who delivered outside that setting. Several hospitals were singled out for the frequency of their involvement with free sample distribution.

The effect of promotional samples to mothers on infant feeding patterns has not been a central policy issue in Nairobi. The small number of women receiving samples strongly suggests that this practice is not among the primary influences that affect the overall pattern of infant feeding, nor is it a key element of the marketing strategies of the infant formula companies. Curiously, although women who delivered in private hospitals were more likely to receive a free sample than women who delivered in public hospitals, receipt of a sample in that setting was not associated with bottle introduction by the end of the first month. Women who received a sample in a public hospital were, however, significantly more likely to introduce the bottle by the end of the first month than those who did not receive a sample. Because the number of women who delivered in public hospitals and reported receiving samples is so small, however, we can only speculate on the meaning of this particular association.

Sixty-eight percent of the women surveyed in Nairobi recalled infant formula advertising on radio or television. There were some demographic differences in advertising recall. Women with higher education were more likely to recall this form of promotion than women with fewer years of education, and women who were in the labor force prior to having their infants were also more likely to recall advertising. As in other cities, women in their twenties were more likely to recall these messages than either younger or older women.

The women in Nairobi also showed a relatively higher degree of brand awareness. There are eight brands of infant formula available in the Nairobi market, and, on average, women could name at least two of these brands without interviewer prompting. When read a list of brands, recognition jumped to nearly 60 percent. Given that some of the available brands are minor brands, not widely available, the true consumer awareness is closer to 70 to 75 percent of the generally available set of brands.

Education is positively associated with brand awareness, as is parity, previous labor force participation, and receipt of a free sample of infant formula. Further, the same association between the respondent's age and recall of advertising exists for brand awareness. Women in their twenties are able to recognize more brands than either younger or older women.

Nairobi women have a generally positive attitude toward bottle feeding and infant formula in particular. Nairobi women appear to have a strong investment in the belief that infant formula is a <u>necessary</u> supplement to breastfeeding during the earliest months of a child's life. When asked to indicate their agreement or disagreement with the statement "A child will be healthier if it receives infant formula in addition to breastmilk in the first three months of life," 85 percent of those surveyed agreed! This attitude appears to be held uniformly, with no significant differences among women on the basis of age, previous labor force participation, place of delivery, or parity. Women with more than ten years of education are less likely to agree with the statement than women with fewer years of education, but it is not clear that this represents a stronger commitment to breastfeeding.

The stated belief in the nutritional importance of infant formula probably represents a conviction that formula is a necessary <u>supplement</u> to breastfeeding. When asked how many months breastfeeding alone is adequate to feed an infant, the median age was three months. When asked the appropriate age to wean an infant, however, the median age reported was eighteen months. This suggests that consumers perceive an important role for infant formula as a supplement during that period of time between exclusive breastfeeding and termination of lactation.

There are other indications that women in Nairobi have a strong commitment to bottle feeding. When asked if infants should be breastfed when they are hungry regardless of where the mother and baby are, 79 percent of the mothers responded affirmatively, but 77 percent also indicated that bottle feeding was more appropriate.

And, when asked "If you had more money would you prefer to bottlefeed instead of breastfeed your baby?," 32 percent indicated that they would.

The fact that one-third of those interviewed admit that financial constraints influence their feeding decisions raises interesting questions for a population that has a strong propensity to use formula supplementation. A significantly greater percentage of those not feeding any commercial milks, or only using cow's milk, than those currently using formula would prefer to bottlefeed exclusively if money were no object. Not only does this highlight the appeal of bottle feeding, but points to the existence of a significant number of women who were actively price conscious regarding their infant feeding regimens.

A final bit of supporting evidence for this combination of price and value awareness was seen in the response to questions regarding the reasons for feeding particular brands of cow's milk or infant formula. Among those currently feeding cow's milk, the dominant reason given was price (35%), followed by availability. For infant formula, the primary reasons were the mother's preference for that particular brand (29%), followed by the baby's preference (25%).

Overall, the analysis of consumer behavior among women in Nairobi reveals little variation in a highly positive orientation toward commercial infant foods. The lack of competition pressures, coupled with government restrictions and WHO Code compliance, have muted the competitive aggressiveness the industry displays in other settings. There is very little sampling, but that which we did observe was disproportionately in private hospitals. This suggests that some suppliers are taking advantage of ambiguities in the Code, although being selective in their targets. The fact that women who delivered in private hospitals are more likely to report brand endorsement from health care workers and receipt of literature suggests that the industry in Nairobi is concentrating its promotional activities on private institutions.

Semarang

The provision of samples to new mothers was not particularly extensive in Semarang. Only 5 percent of the mothers surveyed reported receiving a free sample of infant formula. Even though overall sample distribution was not extensive, there were some differences in the likelihood of receiving a sample. Women who reported monthly income above 61,000 rupiah (approximately US $98) were significantly more likely to report receiving a free sample than women who reported monthly family income below that level. Approximately 8 percent of the women in this income group reported receiving a free sample. This group accounts for nearly one-half (48%) of all women who reported receiving samples but only 4 percent of the entire sample.

Women who received a free sample were less likely, but not significantly less likely, to be breastfeeding at three, six, nine, and twelve months than women who did not receive a sample. There are clear differences in introduction of regular bottles by the first and second months, and by the third and fourth months women who received samples were statistically significantly more likely to have begun bottle feeding. By the end of the third and fourth months, the proportion bottle feeding is twice as great among those who received a sample than among those who did not receive a sample.

To examine the independent effects of receiving a free sample on infant feeding outcomes, a stepwise logistic regression model was fit for bottle introduction at the end of the first, second, third, and fourth months. Receipt of a sample was not significantly associated with infant feeding outcomes. After controlling for income, schooling, labor force participation, and health services variables, the effect of receiving a sample disappears. In this model, delivery in a private maternity home and a physician attendant at delivery are both significantly associated with early bottle introduction (Chapter 7). The bivariate relationship between receiving a sample and infant feeding outcomes is, therefore, best explained by the association between receiving a free sample and both the birth setting and maternal characteristics, which are, in turn, associated with infant feeding outcomes.

In short, this analysis suggests that the receipt of a free sample does not have an independent effect on early bottle feeding in Semarang. What is significant from a policy point of view, however, is that midwives frequently distribute samples with the knowledge that one effect is a high probability that the brand eventually used will be the brand received as a sample.

The indirect effects of commercial promotion in Semarang are found in three specific areas: advertising recall, brand awareness, and consumer attitudes. The patterns of advertising recall in Semarang were in the expected directions. More than one-half of the women

surveyed recalled infant formula advertising, a significant number in view of the absence of such media promotion during the several years prior to the WHO Code
adoption. Advertising recall was significantly higher
for women with higher levels of either income or education. As expected, women in the prime childbearing ages
of 20 to 34 are more likely to recall advertising than
women under the age of 20 and women 35 years of age or
older.

Brand awareness shows a pattern similar to that
of advertising recall. In Semarang, there is a significant linear relationship between the mean number of
brands recalled and both monthly family income and years
of schooling. As with advertising recall, awareness is
generally lower for the youngest age group, increases
steadily, and then falls off for older women. There is
no difference by parity, and the differences noted by
the type of birth attendant are, for the most part, explained by differences in income.

In contrast to several other sites, we observed
that there was a relatively low rate of awareness of
the total number of available milk products. The highest recognition was only 40 percent of the nineteen
brands generally available in the market.

The Semarang survey contained a few items with
which to gauge consumer attitudes toward commercial
infant foods. Respondents overwhelmingly (97%) agreed
that breastmilk is better than bottle milk. Two additional items help define the degree of orientation toward bottle feeding in Semarang. Twenty-seven percent
of the sample agreed with the statement "Bottle feeding is an upper-class symbol." But there is a significant inverse relationship between both years of
schooling and family income, and agreement with that
statement. This strongly suggests that lower-income
women do have some desire to emulate upper-class
behavior, and that bottle feeding is perceived as one
available path of doing so. Women currently employed
were also significantly less likely to agree, although
the magnitude of that difference was not particularly
great (29% vs. 21%).

Among the other indicators of consumer attitudes,
none provided a strong sign of support for bottle feeding. All together, it is clear that women in Semarang
are not predominantly oriented toward bottle feeding.
Even among women currently in the labor force, a group
that is expected to be more favorably oriented toward
bottle feeding, the proportion expressing a favorable

attitude on any given item was never more than 25 percent.

The continued orientation toward breastfeeding in
Semarang may have been most strikingly illustrated with
the responses to a question about the feeding advice
the respondent would give her daughter or a neighbor
about infant feeding. Only 8.5 percent said they would
recommend supplementary bottle feeding, and then "only
if necessary." Semarang remains largely a traditional
society with a population that is still oriented toward
breastfeeding. In sum, this remains the most influential
factor in consumer behavior.

In terms of their purchasing behavior the people
of Semarang appear to be very sensitive to price fluctuations. Disposable income determines which product
a mother will purchase at any given time. Because there
seems to be a weak understanding of distinct product
groups within the broad infant foods category, reduced
income may lead a mother to search for the lowest price
item. This can lead to the use of a humanized formula
one week, a full cream milk the next, and a formulated
milk the third.

The majority of women interviewed do not reveal
any predisposition to bottlefeed, nor do they have positive attitudes toward bottle feeding. Recall of advertising and awareness of available products is associated
with socioeconomic variables, as would be expected, but
the overall interest in commercial infant foods is not
particularly high. On the other hand, there is a variety
of different formula milks available, and promotional
samples of formula are being distributed to mothers in
every birth setting and by both traditional and modern
birth attendants. Thus, producers and distributors of
commercial infant foods have not overlooked any potential point of contact in either the retail or health
care settings.

CONCLUSION

If we can conceive of infant formula promotion in
the Third World in terms of "push" and "pull" strategy,
it is clear that the promotional patterns observed in
these four sites have changed in response to the mount-
ing criticism that preceded the World Health Organization Code, and in the response to the recommendations
of the Code itself. Prior to the Code, mass marketing
techniques were an effective pull strategy, a way to
reach potential consumers directly. Since the passage
of the Code, companies have responded by trying to push

their products through the health care system and have had few ways other than greater availability, and hence product visibility, to attract consumers toward their products. With this in mind, one can see why courting the loyalty of health care workers, and their endorsement of a company's products, is perhaps a more important, although less visible, strategy of promotion.

Although sampling rates were not very high in the four study sites, it appears the practice works. It also appears that there is some discrimination in the targeting of mothers who are to receive samples. Women of higher education, income, and labor force participation are the target audience, although the evidence also suggests that others receive these products and have a desire to emulate the behavior of higher-status women. Sampling is only one of a number of visible tactics that have a modest impact at face value, but when taken together produce a synergistic effect that results in a very strong company presence. These practices, in concert with one another, comprise a total marketing strategy. Thus, the low rates of sampling should not be interpreted as evidence that overall promotional activity has declined. Rather, infant formula companies have met their marketing needs through a liberal interpretation of WHO Code provisions, especially those dealing with health care promotion. In each of the sites studied, their continued sales success seems assured.

In every site, it appears that higher levels of income, education, and employment experience are correlated with knowledge, brand awareness, and receipt of product samples. The commercial marketing of infant feeding products is a highly interactive system. The consumer is neither wholly reactive and passive, nor wholly independent in making product choice judgments. The marketing experts in the infant food companies recognize this interactive system, and act to influence consumers both directly and indirectly. The results from the four study sites confirm their success.

NOTE

1.   See Nestle Infant Formula Audit Commission, Quarterly Reports 1984-1986.

9 The Cultural Context of Infant Feeding

Penny Van Esterik

Ethnographic description and analysis expand to fill the space available. A set of observations on traditional medicines may merit an exegesis of thirty pages. A conversation can become the subject of twenty pages of discourse analysis. In short, while survey data retain or even increase their impact when condensed, often in tabular form, ethnographic data must be expanded and given context rather than summarized. For this reason, instead of merely condensing the community ethnographies in the four countries, this chapter develops a framework for the analysis of the cultural context of infant feeding. The meaning of cultural context is illustrated as are the reasons for its importance and how it can be linked to social action and policy decisions concerning maternal and infant health.

Over the last decade, nutritionists, medical specialists, and health planners have come to recognize the importance of "cultural factors" in the design and implementation of programs related to maternal and child health. "Cultural factors" in these circumstances may not be very clearly defined or explain much, but there appears to be a need to acknowledge them in passing. They may be identified as residual factors, particularly when other factors fail to account for the variations under examination, and they are certainly implicated when programs fail to accomplish their objectives.

"Culture" is often blamed for generating attitudes and beliefs which are seen by development planners as obstacles which must be overcome by education. Particularly common in the literature on maternal and child health is the argument that culture restricts the consumption of certain foods and dictates the consumption of others. Numerous authors have criticized both the facts and the interpretation of the "traditional cultural

factors" influencing food choices.1 But this approach
to cultural determinants of behavior still persists in
recent literature reviews for policymakers concerned
with maternal and infant nutrition.2

Many of the problems in integrating different methods
of data collection stem from difficulties in operational-
izing the concept of culture. These problems stem in
large part from the wide range of non-overlapping and,
occasionally, contradictory definitions of culture. Major
disagreements center around a narrow or a broad definition
of the term. In this project, both perspectives contributed to our understanding of the cultural context of
infant feeding. This broad understanding of culture can
be used to produce shorthand sketches contrasting, for
example, Kenyan and Colombian designs for living or ways
of life, and may include relevant historical information
(e.g., colonial experience) as well as behavior, such
as method of carrying infants, preparing food, and so
on.

Narrower definitions of culture emphasize the cognitive dimension--the ideas, values, and beliefs underlying behavior. In an influential definition, Goodenough
wrote that "a society's culture consists of whatever
it is one has to know or believe in order to operate
in a manner acceptable to its members."3 This definition
emphasizes models for interpreting behavior and rules
or principles underlying behavior, rather than the behavior itself. This approach to culture was used in this
project to draw attention to some dimensions of the conceptual structures and logical systems underlying mothers'
decisions concerning infant feeding.

USING THE CONCEPT OF CULTURE

Defining culture and stating that cultural factors
are important for understanding infant feeding decisions
does not alter the fact that the concept is very difficult
to use. It is clear that we are unlikely to be able to
look for narrowly defined or easily measured cultural
variables or indices to capture the variations within
or between cultural systems.

Yet, there is in the literature clear agreement
that maternal attitudes toward breast and bottle feeding
are culturally conditioned and, indeed, influence infant
feeding decisions. The problem is how to collect and
interpret this information. The most widely accepted
method in health and nutrition research is the construc-

tion of knowledge, attitude, and belief questions which can be administered through household surveys. In spite of the well-known limitations of this method, there are few alternative methods accepted as valid in the fields of nutrition and health.

Underlying much of the literature on the determinants of infant feeding practices is a nagging unaddressed question. Can we, given our current research methods, distinguish between mothers who want to breastfeed and cannot, and mothers who do not want to breastfeed and do not? Both categories of women may fail to initiate breastfeeding or breastfeed for only a short period of time. We assume the former group have the knowledge and attitudes to support breastfeeding but are unable to: they are constrained in some way--by inappropriate medical practices, excessive promotion of breastmilk substitutes, or lack of social support, for example. We assume the latter group do not want to breastfeed for a number of reasons and therefore do not initiate breastfeeding or breastfeed for only a short length of time.

The difference between these two categories of women lies not only in their demographic characteristics but also in their heads--the ideas, beliefs, and assumptions about infant feeding that make up the cognitive and affective dimensions of human behavior. Studies of the determinants of infant feeding practices often include these factors under the variables of maternal knowledge and attitudes or cultural factors. Studies that do not emphasize these factors acknowledge their possible importance.

Knowledge and attitudes regarding infant feeding can be studied in a number of different ways. Most common in nutrition and public health research is the use of a single context questionnaire where respondents are asked if, or to what extent, they agree or disagree with a statement. Scores on these knowledge and attitude questions may then be related to actual infant feeding practices of the mother. There are a number of problems with this approach, however, which researchers must address. Infant feeding in general and breastfeeding in particular are very personal and emotionally charged subjects. For this reason, it is difficult to obtain reliable, valid information on mothers' attitudes, beliefs, and knowledge through survey methods. Since the interviewers usually have had no previous contact with the respondents, it is difficult for them to evaluate how the interview setting affects mothers' responses.

Interviewers' biases may encourage mothers to predict
what the interviewer wants to hear and answer accordingly.
This problem is complicated by respondents' desire to
be polite to strangers (as in Thailand) or their hesitancy
to speak frankly in front of authority figures perceived
as possessing more power. In addition, standardized knowledge and attitude statements about infant feeding often
reflect verbal cliches or key images developed through
health education or breastfeeding promotion campaigns.
The problem of phrasing culturally appropriate questions
or statements without biasing the response is particularly
difficult in this study, where the survey was administered
in seven languages (Indonesian, Jaluo, Javanese, Kikuyu,
Kiswahili, Spanish, and Thai) in four sites. As a result,
questions from one survey are not directly comparable
to those from other sites although the general topic
areas may overlap.

There are also serious conceptual problems in relating knowledge, attitude, and belief to actual practice.
The links between knowledge and belief, belief and attitude, and attitude and practice are both poorly understood and ambiguous. Not only can we not demonstrate
a causal relationship between attitude and behavior,
but we often cannot even predict the direction or order
of the relationship. Behavior may well change before
attitude changes, not after. For example, breastfeeding
promotion campaigns, based on linear reasoning linking
knowledge to belief, attitude, and practice, often aim
to increase correct knowledge about the importance of
breastfeeding. In our study, the survey results confirm
that women in all four sites have a high level of knowledge about the benefits of breastfeeding, regardless
of their infant feeding practices.4 It is thus not surprising that breastfeeding promotion campaigns based
on improving knowledge, attitude, and belief about the
benefits of breastfeeding have not, by themselves, proved
to be an effective means for changing infant feeding
patterns.

This approach to knowledge and attitudes, based
on social psychological methods and theories, does not
reflect the way anthropologists approach human behavior.
Nor does it do justice to the complexity and flexibility
of human decision making, including changes which affect
patterns of infant feeding. For example, women may weigh
such factors as preference for dresses zippered up the
back, avoiding sexual intercourse, or thwarting their
mothers-in-law in the complex calculus of infant feeding
decisions. Even an apparently straightforward interpretation of behavior may generate erroneous assumptions

about cultural attitudes. For example, the conclusion that the use of Western-style blouses indicates a desire for modesty and a negative attitude toward exposure of the breast may be unjustified: in areas of the world where the evil eye can poison breastmilk, blouses may, in fact, be worn to protect the breasts and breastmilk from danger.

Moreover, people have the capacity to tolerate an amazing degree of inconsistency between what they say they "believe," what they do believe, and what they do. It is the capacity of mothers to tolerate inconsistency, to hold contradictory beliefs and attitudes about infant feeding, and to interpret options that reinforces the need for means of data collection and analysis beyond traditional knowledge and attitude assessment. This broader background information is referred to here as the "cultural context" of infant feeding decisions. This context may be thought of as an additional level of analysis which integrates social, cultural, and biological factors. Such an additional level of analysis is necessary for the interpretation of attitude data. Survey responses alone seldom provide the data necessary for such contextual interpretation.

For example, knowing that most of the Nairobi women surveyed agree that breastfeeding makes breasts sag, without accompanying knowledge of how sagging breasts relate to women's body image and self image in Kenya, may easily result in misinterpretation of this information or distortion of its meaning. Body image, beliefs about breast size, and beauty are embedded in culture specific systems of gender ideology. How are women valued in each society? (Chapter 3) This leads us to ask "How are women's productive and reproductive roles integrated?" "How do integration strategies differ according to class?" Although these issues are not directly explored in either the survey or the ethnography, they are part of the context necessary for the interpretation of research results.

It is unrealistic to expect a research project on infant feeding practices in four countries to produce this total background context; however, the ethnographic component provided useful insights which are interspersed in the theme (Chapters 6, 7, and 8). The ethnographic component offered additional means for evaluating mothers' answers and opportunity for gathering clues about how women think about infant feeding. These clues include unsolicited comments, overheard conversations, evaluations of other mothers' behavior, retrospective exegesis on past and present infant feeding experiences, observed mother-child interaction, and other shreds and patches accumulated in the process of ethnographic field work. Case studies of a limited number of households in each community provided an overview of how infant feeding decisions fit in with other life decisions.

To make use of this data, the concept of style is instructive. The concept of "infant feeding style" grew out of the experience of trying to integrate information on cultural context into the study of infant feeding in the four sites. While the survey data could be compared across the four cities, the content of community ethnographies and case studies was more culturally specific and difficult to compare. The first attempt at defining the infant feeding style in urban Kenya has been published and a comparison of Thai and Indonesian styles is underway.5

INFANT FEEDING STYLE AND STRUCTURE

The conceptual model emerging from this approach to ethnographic data defines culture as the interaction between style and structure. Style refers to the manner of expression characteristic of an individual, a period of time, and a place. The concept of infant feeding style is used to communicate fundamental cultural assumptions underlying infant feeding decisions. It refers to the manner of feeding infants in particular communities, and includes both the way the task is accomplished, shared images of the appropriate way to feed an infant, and the values, attitudes, and beliefs associated with that behavior. Infant feeding style includes the style of interaction between mothers and infants, eating style (how does the infant feeding pattern fit with the household meal pattern?), breastfeeding style (how is breastfeeding accomplished?), and feeding "in style," reflect-ing the fact that infant feeding choices are part of dynamic, changing trends and fashions.

To understand differences in breastfeeding style in the four countries, it may be useful to distinguish between breastfeeding as a process and breastmilk as a product. Process or product interpretations may be emphasized in different contexts. For example, breastfeeding style in Bangkok and Bogotá reflected a dominant product interpretation, while in Kenya a process interpretation was closer to the way mothers perceived breastfeeding. In Semarang, both product and process interpretations were common (Chapters 2, 3, 4, and 5).

Both personal and shared styles of infant feeding interact with organizational and institutional structures, such as health care institutions and marketing systems. The Chapters on health care institutions and marketing systems (Chapters 7, 8) as determinants of infant feeding demonstrate how important these structures are in influencing mothers' infant feeding choices. The interaction between style and structure should allow us to predict how infant feeding choices might be affected by different policy options.

Talking about Infant Feeding

Style emerges through the process of interpreting the varied clues ethnographers produce. One of the most useful clues for understanding style is language. Through an examination of how women in the four sites talked about infant feeding, we can suggest media messages and strategies of lactation management which would be most compatible with the infant feeding style in each country. Since project ethnographers work in the local language, their reports emerge first in a local language (Indonesian, Spanish, or Thai, for example) and are then translated literally and conceptually into English. With care, the process of translation can provide insight into the conceptual structure and classification systems of the local language. Primary ethnographic data was collected in Indonesian, Javanese, Jaluo, Kikuyu, Kiswahili, Spanish, and Thai. A detailed examination of this topic would require extensive competence in each language and inclusion of a sociolinguistic component to the research design. However, a limited knowledge of some of the languages is enough to suggest that there are important differences in the way infant feeding is discussed in each language.

What are some of the insights that can be gained from examining how mothers talk about infant feeding? To what extent does the language used reflect cultural principles underlying infant feeding?

Colombian mothers used a number of terms to describe childhood illnesses, including:

acidosis   vomiting, diarrhea, dehydration, caused
             by food
barrigones   children with large stomachs, attributed
             to worms
descuaje   diarrhea and stomach pain, cured by massage

Mothers' approaches to curing childhood illnesses focus around the concepts of <u>resfrio</u>, "coldness" in the stomach caused by eating cold foods, and <u>recaida</u>, a "relapse" while recuperating. The emphasis on balancing hot and cold foods, particularly at the first sign of illness is reflected in the special recipes prepared for infants and children:

<u>caldo caballuno</u>	soup prepared with garlic, salt, onion, and coriander
<u>changua</u>	soup prepared with garlic, salt, onion, coriander, milk, egg, and bread
<u>tetero-agua de panela</u>	feeding bottle containing milk with food and brown sugar

Clearly, in Bogotá, mothers do not idealize the convenient, fast way to feed an infant. Instead, they stressed the time they spent on preparing complex food mixtures for their children as if more time was equated with greater care and love. The more elaborate and time consuming the infant meals, the better for the infant. Homemade foods were considered more dependable.

The descriptive terms alert the researcher to the humoral system guiding mothers' treatments for infant illness and explain the elaborate preparation of the contents of the feeding bottles. This style of infant feeding is more compatible with infant formula use than with breastfeeding, and the practices of the health care system in Bogotá further reinforce this use of feeding bottles.

In Thailand, where milk is not a popular adult drink, milk products are classified and discussed in a way which makes it difficult to identify the nutritional content of the milk (humanized, full cream, skimmed, etc.). Mothers refer to breastmilk substitutes as bottled milk (<u>nom khuat</u>), powdered milk (<u>nom pong</u>), canned milk (<u>nom krapong</u>), or mixed milk (<u>nom pasom</u>). This is further complicated by the fact that one of the most common brands of milk, Bear Brand, makes sweetened condensed milk, full cream powdered milk, and infant formula. Knowledge of the brand name alone does not always help mothers obtain humanized milk for their infants. However, one brand of infant formula so dominated the market in Thailand that it has been used as a classifier for infant formula. "Lactogen" is both a particular <u>brand</u> of infant formula and a general <u>classifier</u> for humanized milks. For example, in Thai, the following conversation is possible:

> Question: What kind of Lactogen do you give your baby?
> Answer: I give my baby Similac kind of Lactogen.

This observation raises interesting theoretical questions for linguists and consumer researchers concerning the use of brand names (particularly in languages using noun classifiers). It also raises practical questions about the construction of media messages related to infant feeding.

A second set of terms which tells us something about Thai concepts of child development is the identification of kinds of babies--babies that are fussy and irritable (<u>ngor ngae, khii oon</u>), sickly babies (<u>khii rog</u>), babies that grow quickly (<u>tow waj</u>), babies that anger easily and cry until they get their way (<u>khii moho</u>), and ador-able smiling babies that do not cry (<u>naarak</u>).

The ideal baby seems to be one that is easy to raise (<u>liang ngai</u>). A maternal task, then, is to discover what kind of baby she has, rather than try to shape an infant into a certain pattern of behavior. She will seek a way of feeding her infant which will be suitable for the kind of infant she has; when she has established that fit, her infant will be easy to raise. This is a primary goal, and media messages concerning infant feeding can build on the idea of "easy to raise." A similar campaign in Bogotá would not work, since it would not fit with the style of infant feeding there.

In Kenya, a country where milk is recognized as an important food for adults and children, milk products are thought of very differently than in Thailand where the availability of milk products is very recent. The category "milk" includes cow, goat, sheep, and human milk, according to Luo and Kikuyu informants. Fresh milk products are viewed as ordinary foods and are a valued part of family meals for many Kenyans. Infant formula, on the other hand, is viewed more as a "superfood" or a food with special properties. The Swahili term <u>dawa</u> is applied to traditional and Western medicines, charms and amulets, and products like infant formula, tonic drinks, and glucose drinks.6 The semantic content of the term <u>dawa</u> is not lost on advertisers who now use the term in their advertisements for infant formula.

The process of translation of Indonesian and Javanese ethnographies uncovered several cultural concepts
which help explain infant feeding patterns in Semarang.
Two terms in particular are elaborated in discussions
with mothers. The first, jamu, refers to a category of
herbal medicinal drinks that are particularly important
to women before and after childbirth. The properties
and ingredients of jamu for Javanese mothers go far beyond its use for increasing breastmilk production. The
tonics are a means of restoring a mother's strength so
that she can maintain control over her own and her children's health.

Similarly, Semarang mothers were concerned about
insufficient milk, and they distinguished between:

tidak cukup	not enough milk
tidak keluar	milk doesn't come out
kosong	empty breast
kempeng	to suck on an empty breast (Java-nese)

Each term connotes a different set of meanings.
But their elaboration in conjunction with the term jamu
suggests not preoccupation with a problem, but the importance of breastfeeding. Unlike Bangkok mothers,
Semarang mothers have at their disposal means for solving transitory problems like fluctuations in milk supply,
and confidence that jamu and massage will be effective.

Another phrase, jajan pasar, children's food purchased in the market, alerted the researchers to the
important category of "snack" foods for infants and
children, and the importance of food vendors who provide a wide variety of ready-made porridge (bubur) suitable for infants and children of different ages. This
clue concerning eating style has implications for the
development and promotion of local weaning porridges
and snacks to counter the growing market for expensive
imported commercial cereals such as Cerelac and Nestum.

From Talk to Action

Infant feeding style is important for predicting
changes in infant feeding practices, for understanding
how lactation is managed, and for evaluating culturally appropriate strategies for improving infant health.
Lactation management issues include solving individual
mothers' breastfeeding problems (such as perceived insufficient milk) and also developing approaches to

broader issues such as rejection of colostrum, uses of
wet-nursing and milk banks, and caring for sick infants.
Approaches to the last three issues are discussed below:

Colostrum. Semantic clues in the specific languages
of the study assist in the construction of survey questions and aid in the interpretation of study results.
They also point out alternate and even contradictory
interpretations of key concepts within a single community. For example, colostrum is a term derived from
Western biomedical theory. Understanding mothers' attitudes to this product may explain why some Indonesian
and Thai mothers either throw the product away or delay
initiating breastfeeding. Mothers from Bangkok and Semarang described this early milk as a thick, impure product which clogged the passages and blocked the "pure"
breastmilk. Just as dried glue clogs the passage of
clearly flowing glue from a tube, so the thick residues
which clog the passage of clean breastmilk have to be
cleaned out and thrown away to encourage the flow of
colostrum and breastmilk. If this interpretation is
correct, however, the amount thrown away may be minimal,
and the act of squeezing out the first few drops may
be best thought of as a cleansing ritual. But some
Semarang mothers also describe colostrum as thin and
watery, causing the infant to have a swollen stomach.
This latter interpretation may explain why lactating
women are reluctant to drink too much water. In both
cases, women are comparing colostrum to the product seen
after the "let down" reflex has released a free-flowing
supply of mature milk.

Because of the negative attitudes in some cultures
concerning colostrum, it may be appropriate to encourage the view of colostrum not as a useful product but
simply as part of the process of breastfeeding. This
would have implication for early breastfeeding immediately after birth and possibly, by extension, at every
feed when the first few drops of impure milk are thrown
away. A message such as "The sooner you breastfeed, the
better the milk" is compatible with early breastfeeding regardless of whether the cultural interpretation
is a "product" or "process" orientation.

Wet-Nursing and Milk Banks. In all four countries,
wet-nursing was viewed as a form of emergency "insur-
ance" or short-term care designed to help a mother
through difficult times or to save an infant whose
mother had died. Wet-nursing in preparation for adoption (as in Oceania) or as part of the "farming out"
of an infant to another person's care (as in European

55

upper classes in the past) is uncommon in these countries. It is, therefore, not surprising that wet-nursing has a fairly negative image, since the wet nurse must not usurp the role of the mother. The negative image of wet-nursing and the restrictions surrounding it act to strengthen and reinforce the bonds between mother and infant.

Although the mothers in Semarang claimed never to have observed a mother breastfeeding an infant other than her own, they felt that it could be done if the natural mother's milk does not flow and she does not want to use breastmilk substitutes. If someone else breastfed an infant, the mother would be less confident and concerned that her relation to the infant would be less close. In the rural outskirts of the city, women cited Moslem restrictions on wet-nursing and felt that they would only breastfeed another infant if the natural mother had died. They expressed concern over contagious diseases and whether another women's breastmilk would "agree" with the child.

Among the Javanese and Thai mothers of Chinese ancestry, breastmilk can be shared between infants of the same sex, but not the opposite sex. Thai rural mothers permit their newborns to be breastfed by a woman, often related, who is locally widely recognized as a "good nurturer." This establishes a good habit for the breast-fed infant.7

The Nairobi study noted cases of grandmothers breastfeeding their own and their daughters' infants. While this is acceptable, there is concern if an infant is given milk from a woman of another lineage or from ano-ther ethnic group altogether. This has implications for the establishment of milk banks both in Nairobi and other places where breastmilk is interpreted as a conduit for ancestral essence or power.

Caring for Sick Infants. Mothers interpret the health of their infants by reference to their models of health and illness. The alternate explanatory models for most mothers in this study included Western biomedical theories of disease causation, humoral theories balancing hot and cold properties, and a number of folk and popular theories used for self-treatment.

From these models, mothers select treatments that fit with their past experiences concerning infant feeding. In countries like Thailand where Western drugs are widely available, they are integrated into mothers' strategies for keeping their infants healthy. In addition to glucose mixtures, tonics, and appetite stimulants, the use of laxatives and suppositories is common, particularly for infants receiving infant formula. The reasoning underlying this treatment is quite understandable. The hard, dry stools produced by a formula-fed infant are interpreted as indicators of constipation, particularly by mothers more used to the softer stools of a breastfed infant.

Less easily explained is the logic behind the decision to stop breastfeeding a sick infant. This detrimental practice denies important fluid and nutrients to infants when they need them most. But the reasons behind this treatment differ. One interpretation compatible with observations in Nairobi and Semarang is that the infant is already so full of liquids that they are "leaking out" and, naturally, should be withheld. An alternative interpretation more common in Bangkok and Bogotá is that the breastmilk itself has caused the illness and therefore must be removed. Mothers blame themselves for "spoiling" their breastmilk, either by eating foods which do not agree with their infants, or by emotional upsets such as anxiety or fright. This second interpretation is derived from the humoral theory of disease causation.

Once again, health promotion campaigns concerning management of infant illness will be more effective if health planners know which mode of interpretation underlies most mothers' decisions. Or they may design messages compatible with both interpretations, a strategy which might be particularly effective in Semarang where both interpretations co-exist. This can only be done, however, after examining the models of disease causation mothers use to treat infant illness.

CONCLUSION

This chapter argues that the cultural context of infant feeding can be understood as the relation between style and structure. These concepts capture the kind of information which best complements survey data. Style is important because it emphasizes intracultural variability in motivational, cognitive, and behavioral dimensions and provides culturally appropriate definitions for key variables like work, food, breastfeeding, and so forth. Knowledge and attitude surveys can suggest how generalizable aspects of infant feeding style are and how features of style are transmitted. (Is there a difference in attitudes based on age, for example?)

It is commonly assumed that policymakers need numbers to evaluate policy options and that ethnographic observations are illustrative anecdotes. This research project demonstrates that the linkage between ethnographic data and policy can be much more direct. Because ethnographic description is both holistic and richly contextualized, it is easy for policymakers to picture the real life conditions of the families their policies will affect. Some products of ethnographic field work, such as community sketches and mothers' life histories, are avail-able much faster than survey data, which require substantial processing.

Finally, it is the cultural context underlying infant feeding decisions from which solutions to infant feeding problems must come. The same "culture" which some policymakers view as an "obstacle" to development must ultimately provide solutions assembled from available options, ideas, and strategies already in the cultural repertoire. In this case, the task of the policymaker is to choose options and implementation strategies which are most compatible with the infant feeding style in each country. For example, strategies which fit with Bogotá mothers' preference for complexity in infant feeding regimes and Bangkok mothers' concern for having infants that are easy to raise will likely be more successful than strategies developed in ignorance of the infant feeding style in each country.

Knowledge of style without consideration of structural constraints or supports would, however, be equally unproductive. Structural constraints, such as the powerful influence of the health care system in Nairobi, and structural supports, such as the system of local food vendors selling porridge in the streets of Semarang, must also be fitted into policy decisions to suggest new directions to improve infant feeding practices in developing countries.

NOTES

1.   C. Laderman, "Symbolic and Empirical Reality: A
     New Approach to the Analysis of Food Avoidances,"
     American Ethnologist 8, No. 3 (1981): pp. 468-93.
     M.C. Latham, "Nutrition and Culture," Nutrition
     and National Policy, ed. B. Winikoff (Cambridge:
     MIT Press, 1978).

2.   S. Hamilton, B. Popkin, and D. Spicer, Women and
     Nutrition in Third World Countries. (New York:
     Praeger, 1984).

3.   W. H. Goodenough, "Cultural Anthropology and Lin-
     guistics," in Report of the Seventh Annual Round
     Table Meeting on Linguistics and Language Study.
     P. Garvin, ed. (Washington, D.C.:   Georgetown
     University, 1957), p. 167.

4.   V. H. Laukaran and P. Van Esterik, "Maternal Know-
     ledge and Attitudes Towards Breastfeeding and Breast-
     milk Substitutes," in The Determinants of Infant
     Feeding Practices: Preliminary Results of a Four
     Country Study.   Research Consortium for Infant
     Feeding Study, Working Paper No. 19 (New York:
     The Population Council, 1984).

5.   P. Van Esterik and T. Elliot, "Infant Feeding and
     Style in Urban Kenya," Ecology of Food and Nutrition
     18, No. 3 (1986): 183-95.

6.   P. Van Esterik and T. Elliot, "Infant Feeding and
     Style in Urban Kenya"

7.   P. Van Esterik, "Commentary: An Anthropological
     Perspective on Infant Feeding in Oceania," in Infant
     Care and Feeding in the South Pacific. ed. L.
     Marshall (New York: Gordon and Breach, 1985).

10 Breastfeeding Practices and Postpartum Amenorrhea

Lily W. Lee

Postpartum amenorrhea is an important component of birth intervals and is one of the most important natural contraceptive mechanisms. In much of the developing world, the use of contraceptive methods is infrequent and breastfeeding remains an important means of delaying pregnancy.

Many previous studies have demonstrated that populations with longer durations of breastfeeding have longer lengths of postpartum amenorrhea. Corsini collected data from 30 national samples and estimated a linear model describing the relationship between breastfeeding and amenorrhea.[1] The mean length of amenorrhea among women with no breastfeeding was estimated to be 1.33 months, and each additional month of breastfeeding was expected to increase the length of amenorrhea by 0.56 months. Bongaarts and Potter drew data from 26 national sub-samples and found that the relationship between breastfeeding and amenorrhea could be adequately described by a monotonic increasing and non-linear function.[2]

For individuals, the duration of the postpartum amenorrhea appears to be largely a function of a woman's breastfeeding practices. It has been widely hypothesized that the basic link between breastfeeding and postpartum amenorrhea is the frequency and intensity of breastfeeding. In a study conducted in an urban area of Zaire, serum prolactin--a hormone necessary for the production of milk and believed to be related to the interruption of follicular development and ovulation--was measured from samples collected within 22 months postpartum. Prolactin level was found to decline rapidly in mothers who were breastfeeding less than four times per day. Among mothers breastfeeding more than six times per day, serum prolactin did not decline significantly during

Feeding Infants in Four Societies

the first twelve months postpartum.3 Another study done among Guatemalan and Hungarian breastfeeding women found that, for the first twelve months, higher frequency of breastfeeding was associated with higher probability of remaining amenorrheic.4 None of the women ovulated during full breastfeeding (no supplementation), but within sixteen weeks of introducing supplementary food, ovarian follicular development had returned in twenty mothers and ovulation occurred in fourteen of them.

The Infant Feeding Study provides valuable data for assessing the relationship between breastfeeding and amenorrhea. Detailed information was obtained on the feeding practices of breastfeeding mothers, including the frequency of breastfeeding and the type and timing of supplementation used. This chapter shows that the length of postpartum amenorrhea is positively correlated with the length of breastfeeding; furthermore, the probability of resuming menstruation in a given postpartum period is highly correlated with the frequency and pattern of breastfeeding.

Certain cases were excluded from our examination of the relationship between breastfeeding and amenorrhea because of obvious misreporting or potentially misleading information. Cases of obvious misreporting included situations where the reported lengths of amenorrhea or breastfeeding were longer than the current number of months postpartum (current age of index child). Potentially misleading information was excluded in situations where (1) the woman was pregnant prior to resumption of first menses; and (2) the woman had initiated the use of hormonal contraceptives that would either initiate or delay the onset of menses. A listing of the number of cases excluded due to these reasons is presented in Table 10.1.

LENGTH OF BREASTFEEDING AND AMENORRHEA

In the four urban centers in which the sample survey was conducted, the level of modernization and the erosion of traditional breastfeeding practices varied considerably. Shorter breastfeeding durations were recorded in Bangkok and Bogotá than in Semarang and Nairobi. Median durations of breastfeeding and amenorrhea were estimated using the cohort life table method employing information from all the women in the samples (Table 10.2). Women in Bangkok and Bogotá had very similar breastfeeding and amenorrhea profiles: the median duration of breastfeeding was 7.00 months in Bangkok and 7.86 months in Bogotá. Median length of amenorrhea

Table 10.1   CASES EXCLUDED FROM ANALYSIS

	Bangkok	Bogotá	Nairobi	Semarang
Total women interviewed	1,422	711	980	1,358
Number of cases excluded	47	49	82	104
Reasons: Amenorrhea length> Postpartum month	14	8	26	27
Breastfeeding length> Postpartum month	0	41	9	9
Pregnant prior to first menses	6	--	24	16
Hormonal contraceptives prior to first menses	27	--	23	52

Table 10.2   MEDIAN DURATION OF BREASTFEEDING AND
POSTPARTUM AMENORRHEA (IN MONTHS)

	Median Breastfeeding	Median Amenorrhea
Bangkok	7.00	2.88
Bogotá	7.86	3.28
Nairobi	16.22	6.87
Semarang	>24.00	10.00

was 2.88 months and 3.28 months respectively. Median breastfeeding lengths in Nairobi and Semarang were 16.22 months and >24 months. Correspondingly, the estimated median lengths of amenorrhea were longer for these two sites: 6.87 months in Nairobi and 10.00 months in Semarang. The strong positive relationship between the length of breastfeeding and the length of amenorrhea in a population is once again supported by these four samples.

A more detailed sub-group analysis further exemplifies this positive relationship. By focusing on women who had weaned their child at the time of the interview, exact durations of breastfeeding and of amenorrhea could be known. Median duration of amenorrhea was then estimated for each of the known breastfeeding durations. The pattern of positive relationship is unmistakable: women who breastfed longer also had a longer duration of amenorrhea. This was evident in all four samples (Table 10.3, Figure 10.1).

Table 10.3   MEDIAN DURATION OF AMENORRHEA BY KNOWN
DURATION OF BREASTFEEDING

Duration of Breastfeeding (months)	Bangkok	Bogotá	Nairobi	Semarang
0 - 3	2.05	2.52	3.87	4.36
4 - 7	3.25	3.50	4.93	7.78
8 - 11	7.50	6.00	6.52	10.69
12 - 15	--	--	9.30	11.75
16 - 19	--	--	--	12.63

FREQUENCY OF BREASTFEEDING

It is interesting to note, however, that for a given length of breastfeeding, the duration of amenorrhea varied quite substantially across the four sites. Bangkok, Bogotá, and Nairobi had similar relationships between breastfeeding and amenorrhea lengths, but Semarang had longer durations of amenorrhea at any given length of breastfeeding.

This differential effect of breastfeeding on duration of amenorrhea may, perhaps, be explained by the difference in breastfeeding practices in these four samples. Among women who were currently breastfeeding, the mean frequency of breastfeeding per day differed among the four samples. Bogotá women had the lowest frequency of breastfeeding in each postpartum interval, while Semarang women had the highest (Table 10.4, Figure 10.2). During the first four months postpartum, Semarang women breastfed an average of 10.6 times a day, while Bogotá women only breastfed an average of 6.9 times.

Figure 10.1 MEDIAN DURATION OF AMENORRHEA BY KNOWN LENGTH OF BREASTFEEDING

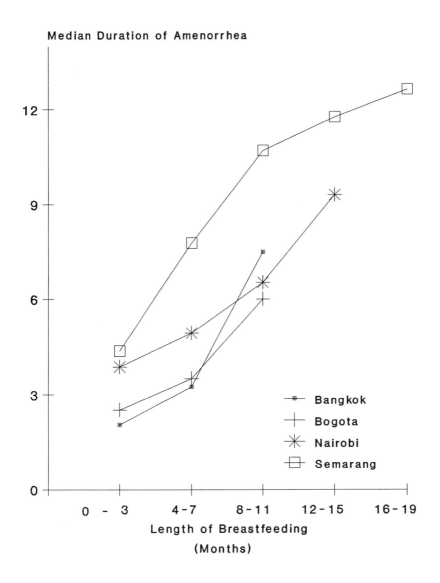

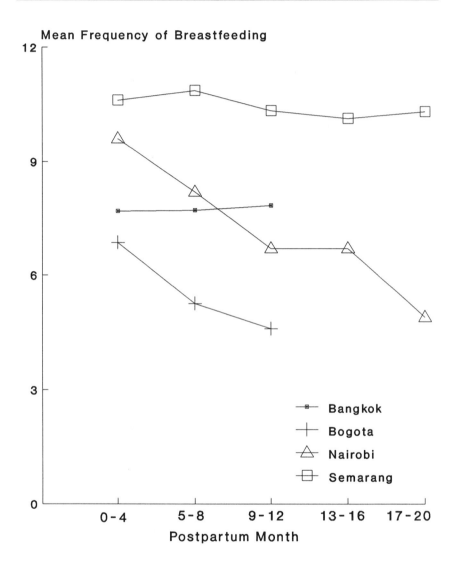

Figure 10.2 MEAN FREQUENCIES OF BREASTFEEDING

Mean Frequency of Breastfeeding

Bangkok
Bogota
Nairobi
Semarang

Postpartum Month

Table 10.4   MEAN FREQUENCY OF BREASTFEEDING

Postpartum Months	Bangkok	Bogotá	Nairobi	Semarang
0 - 4	7.96	6.86	9.60	10.60
5 - 8	7.71	5.25	8.20	10.86
9 - 12	7.84	4.60	6.70	10.33
13 - 16	--	--	6.70	10.12
17 - 20	--	--	4.90	10.30

This difference in breastfeeding frequency correlated well with the difference in amenorrhea length: women with higher mean frequency of breastfeeding tended to have longer mean duration of amenorrhea for a given length of breastfeeding.

If frequency of breastfeeding does indeed play a role in determining the duration of amenorrhea, one should be able to observe a higher proportion of women remaining amenorrheic among women with higher frequency of breastfeeding. Currently breastfeeding women were divided into two groups: those with mean frequency of five times or less per day and those with mean frequency of six times or more per day. The proportion still amenorrheic was calculated for these two categories at each month postpartum. The results are presented in Table 10.5 and Figure 10.3. The proportion remaining amenorrheic was higher in the higher breastfeeding frequency group in most postpartum periods in all four samples. This consistent pattern lends support to the theory that frequency of nipple stimulation is a major factor in delaying the onset of postpartum ovulation.

PATTERNS OF BREASTFEEDING

Supplementation of breastfeeding with other sources of food also appears to have an effect on the onset of menstruation. The more supplementation was given to a child, the less the frequency and intensity of breastfeeding. Three patterns of breastfeeding are identified: exclusive breastfeeding, breastfeeding with food supplements, and breastfeeding with food and milk supplement. The proportion amenorrheic among these groups, along with those not breastfeeding at each postpartum period, is presented in Table 10.6. The proportions amenorrheic

Figure 10.3   PROPORTION AMENORRHEIC BY POSTPARTUM MONTH
                AND CURRENT FREQUENCY OF BREASTFEEDING

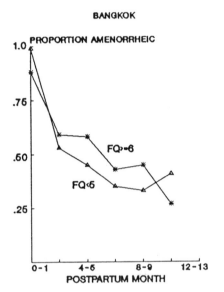

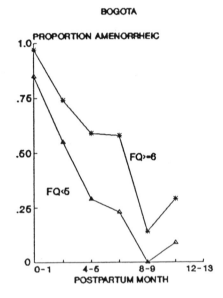

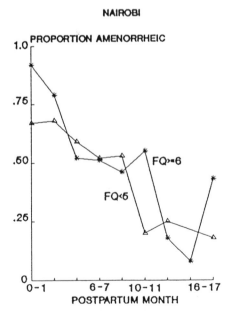

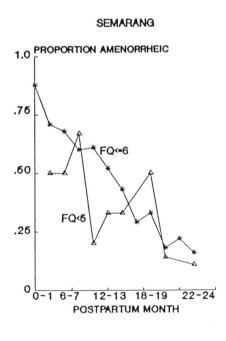

Table 10.5   PROPORTION OF WOMEN STILL AMENORRHEIC BY CURRENT FREQUENCY OF BREASTFEEDING AMONG CURRENTLY BREASTFEEDING WOMEN

Postpartum Months	Bangkok		Bogotá		Nairobi		Semarang	
	FQ<5	FQ>6	FQ<5	FQ>6	FQ<5	FQ>6	FQ<5	FQ>6
0-1	1.0	.88	.85	.97	.67	.92	--	.88
2-3	.53	.59	.55	.74	.68	.79	.50	.71
4-5	.45	.58	.29	.59	.59	.52	.50	.68
6-7	.35	.43	.23	.58	.52	.51	.67	.60
8-9	.33	.45	.00	.14	.53	.46	.20	.61
10-11	.41	.27	.09	.29	.20	.55	.33	.52
12-13	--	--	--	--	.25	.18	.33	.43
14-15	--	--	--	--	--	.08	--	.29
16-17	--	--	--	--	.18	.43	.50	.33
18-19	--	--	--	--	--	--	.14	.18
20-21	--	--	--	--	--	--	--	.22
22-24	--	--	--	--	--	--	.11	.16

at each postpartum month for the "full breastfeeding" and "no breastfeeding" groups are graphed in Figure 10.4.

Two interesting patterns are evident in Table 10.6 and Figure 10.4. First, for each breastfeeding pattern, the proportion remaining amenorrheic decreases with increasing postpartum month, suggesting an internal mechanism of increasing probability of return to fertility with time postpartum. Second, for each postpartum period, the proportion amenorrheic is always highest in the exclusively breastfeeding group (BF ONLY) and lowest in the non-breastfeeders (NO BF). Furthermore, the exclusively breastfeeding group also tends to have the highest proportion amenorrheic among the three categories of breastfeeding women. (There are some minor exceptions to the above observations. These exceptions are largely a function of very small group sizes constituting that particular proportion.)

Figure 10.4   PROPORTION AMENORRHEIC AMONG FULL
BREASTFEEDERS AND NON-BREASTFEEDERS

■ Full Breastfeeders   ▨ Non-Breastfeeders

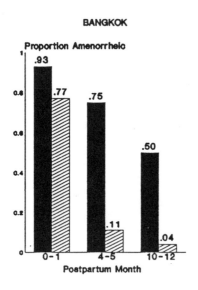

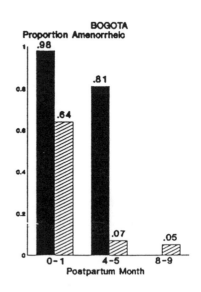

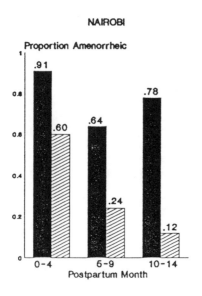

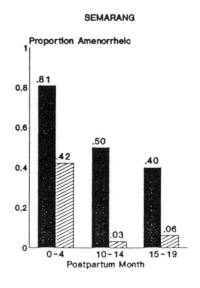

Table 10.6   PROPORTION AMENORRHEIC BY FEEDING
PATTERN AND MONTH POSTPARTUM

	BF ONLY	BF+FOOD	BF+FD+MK	NO BF
Bangkok				
0 - 1	.93	.83	.88	.77
2 - 3	.64	.64	.43	.13
4 - 5	.75	.53	.52	.11
6 - 7	.86	.39	.31	.05
8 - 9	.57	.47	.23	.08
10 -12	.50	.29	.30	.04
Bogotá				
0 - 1	.98	.89	.96	.64
2 - 3	1.00	.71	.56	.13
4 - 5	.81	.44	.36	.07
6 - 7	1.00	.42	.33	.04
8 - 9	--	.22	--	.05
10 -12	--	.57	--	.02
Nairobi				
0 - 4	.91	.64	.68	.60
5 - 9	.64	.52	.49	.24
10 -14	.78	.41	.32	.12
15 -19	--	.13	.25	.14
Semarang				
0 - 4	.81	.78	.51	.42
5 - 9	.67	.67	.35	.11
10 -14	.50	.42	.46	.03
15 -19	.40	.29	.31	.06
20 -24	--	.19	.19	.10

CONCLUSION

The results of this analysis once again support
the positive relationship between length of breastfeeding and length of amenorrhea. Furthermore, it provides
evidence that frequency and pattern of breastfeeding
are important determinants of a woman's risk of resuming menstruation. Detailed longitudinal breastfeeding
histories of postpartum women are needed to understand
how actual breastfeeding practices affect the risk of
resuming menstruation. This information would be helpful in formulating well-defined, individual-based guidelines for determining when contraceptive use should be
initiated among postpartum women. This can be very im-

portant in the parts of the developing world where mothers are practicing patterns of infant feeding which feature heavy reliance on supplementation and reduction in frequency and duration of breastfeeding. In order to provide safe, effective, acceptable, and appropriate postpartum contraception, health care workers need to be equipped with guidelines that take into account the estimated risk of resuming ovulation given a woman's current breastfeeding practices.

NOTES

1. C. Corsini, "Is the fertility reducing effect of lactation really substantial?" in Natural Fertility, ed. Leridon and J. Menken, IUSSP Proceedings, 1979, pp. 197-215.

2. J. Bongaarts, and R. Potter, Fertility, Biology and Behavior: An Analysis of the Proximate Determinants. New York: Academic Press, 1983.

3. P. Delvoye, M. Demaegd, and J. Delonge-Desnoeck, "The influence of nursing and of previous lactation experience on serum prolactin in lactating mothers. Journal of Biosocial Sciences, 9 (1979): pp. 447-51, 1977.

4. WHO, Contemporary Patterns of Breastfeeding (Geneva: World Health Organization, 1981), p. 59.

11 The Influence of Infant Feeding Practices on Morbidity and Child Growth

Beverly Winikoff and Virginia H. Laukaran

The consensus among health professionals on the superiority of breastfeeding is based on scientific data regarding the immunological properties of breast-milk as well as on field studies comparing morbidity in breastfed and bottlefed infants.1 While assessment of the health impact of infant feeding practices was not the primary purpose of the infant feeding studies reported here, they were designed to permit the analysis of correlations between feeding methods and morbidity and growth on a cross-sectional basis.2 It was decided to include questions on infant morbidity in the weeks prior to the survey to permit a descriptive analysis of morbidity for infants with different feeding patterns. Anthropometric data were also collected in order to correlate growth with feeding patterns. The major questions that we wanted to ask were:

o   Are some infant feeding choices associated with greater risk of poor health status?

o   Can such associations be demonstrated convincingly in representative samples such as the ones available in this data set?

The questionnaire for each city included items on whether or not the child had been ill (experienced a respiratory infection during, or had diarrhea) in the last two weeks (four weeks in Indonesia). In each site, local terms were used to describe respiratory infections and diarrhea. The Indonesian research team used a four-week recall for morbidity rather than two-weeks as for the other sites. It has been shown previously that recall of morbidity declines over time with proportionally more events reported during a one-week than a two-week recall period. Thus, there is a loss of events when a longer recall period is used. The results reported here are thus not directly comparable across the four sites, but can describe for each site the extent to which infant feeding practices and other background variables are independently associated with morbidity (Table 11.1). Child growth was measured in each site using portable Salter scales.3

The sample examined included infants in their third through tenth month of life, in other words, from two through nine completed months of life. This was done for several reasons. In the first place, morbidity in very early infancy might be a reflection of congenital problems or conditions at birth whereas infectious disease morbidity has a lower prevalence in the very early weeks of life. In the second place, choosing infants slightly older than the first two months would allow for a greater range of feeding patterns and therefore, would enable discovery of differences in the outcomes of different feeding patterns. Infants older than the tenth month of life were not included because prior research suggests that feeding patterns have a diminishing effect on morbidity outcome as the infant nears its first birthday.

Table 11.2 demonstrates the variability in the feeding patterns in the four sites. There is a considerable amount of current breastfeeding in all sites, although in Nairobi and Semarang subsamples breastfeeding is much more prevalent than in Bangkok and Bogotá. Bottles are commonly used in all sites, but in Semarang less so than in any of the other sites. Semarang is also remarkable for a high incidence of exclusive breastfeeding whereas the incidence in Bogotá is very low. There is very little use of bottle feeding as an exclusive method of feeding in Nairobi or Semarang. Use of early bottles is more common in Bangkok and Bogotá than in Nairobi and Semarang. Breastfeeding for at least three months is almost universal in Nairobi and Semarang unlike Bangkok and Bogotá.

MORBIDITY AND INFANT FEEDING

After examination of cross-tabulations to choose relevant variables, multiple logistic regression analysis was performed to examine the relationship of infant feeding to child morbidity. The data on infant feeding and morbidity were used along with other associated background variables. The background variables which were entered in the regression included: the age of the mother, the mother's education, the mother's birthplace (Bangkok, Bogotá, and Semarang), the socioeconomic status of the family (which in three of the four sites was represented by income and in the fourth site, Nairobi, was represented by a compound variable which described sources of water and electric power), refrigeration (Bogotá only), the birth order of the child, and the exact age of the child in months (Bangkok, Bogotá, and Nairobi). For each site, the background variables were slightly different because of differences in characteristics of the populations and in the social and demographic variables that were included in each survey.

The feeding factors explored for association with these outcomes represented both present feeding patterns and history of feeding. Of interest was whether the child was breastfed at present, whether it was bottlefed at present, was it exclusively breastfeeding or exclusively bottle feeding. In addition, some historical variables were tested: Was the child breastfed at least three months? Was a regular bottle introduced by the end of two months of age?

The dependent variables for these analyses were occurrence of diarrhea or respiratory conditions during the weeks prior to the survey. Separate models were tested for respiratory and diarrheal disease since the mechanisms for health effects of infant feeding may differ for the two types of illness.

A first analysis looked at the relationships between the background variables and the outcome variables of recent diarrhea and recent upper respiratory infection without any reference to feeding. There were no significant associations found in any of the sites between the background variables and upper respiratory infection. Similarly, in both Bangkok and Semarang, no associations were found with diarrhea. In Bogotá and Nairobi, however, the older the child the more likely the report of recent diarrhea. In Bogotá, possession of a refrigerator was associated with less diarrhea. Paradoxically, higher income was associated with greater likelihood of recent diarrhea in Bogotá. Perhaps this reflects a consequence of the greater propensity for higher-income women to work for pay away from home leaving children with potentially inadequate caretakers.

In the next stage of the analysis, a variable representing current breastfeeding and another variable representing current bottle feeding were added to the predictor variables. Several of the feeding variables were found to be significantly related to the outcome even after controlling for other possibly confounding factors (Table 11.3). In Nairobi, for example, breastfeeding is associated with less than half the risk of recent URI as not breastfeeding (RÔR, .48). In Bogotá, bottle

Table 11.1   REPORTED DIARRHEA AND UPPER RESPIRATORY ILLNESS IN PAST TWO WEEKS IN CHILDREN AGED 2-9 MONTHS (PERCENTAGES)

	Bogotá		Bangkok		Nairobi		Semarang*	
	Diarrhea	URI	Diarrhea	URI	Diarrhea	URI	Diarrhea	URI
	9	22	7	24	15	17	31	60

*In last 4 weeks

Table 11.2   INFANT FEEDING PATTERNS IN FOUR SITES (Percentages)

	Any Breast-feeding	Any Bottle-feeding	Exclusively Breastfed	Exclusively Bottlefed	Bottle by 2 Months	Breastfed 3 Months
Bangkok (n=879)	51	61	37	47	46	68
Bogotá (n=456)	53	77	17	42	49	77
Nairobi (n=448)	87	60	36	10	28	95
Semarang (n=374)	82	36	62	16	19	93

Table 11.3 SUMMARY OF SIGNIFICANT ASSOCIATIONS BETWEEN
CURRENT BREASTFEEDING, CURRENT BOTTLE FEEDING,
BACKGROUND VARIABLES, AND MORBIDITY IN
LOGISTIC REGRESSION ANALYSIS

	Diarrhea	URI
Bangkok	Income (-) p=.05	0
Bogotá	Breast (-) p=.00 Bottle (-) p=.03 Income (+) p=.04 Refrigerator (-) p=.05	Bottle (+) p=.04
Nairobi	Age Child (+) p=.05 Water/SES (-) p=.02	Breast (-) p=.05
Semarang	Bottle (+) p=.04	0

feeding is significantly related to increased probability
of recent URI.

The diarrhea associations are somewhat more complicated. In Semarang, any bottle use is associated with
increased diarrhea (RÔR, 1.91). In Bangkok, when bottle
feeding is a control variable, higher income is negatively
associated with diarrheal disease, as expected. The same
background variables remain significant in the Nairobi
analysis even after the additions of feeding variables.
In Bogotá, however, there were some peculiar associations.
Possession of a refrigerator appears to protect against
diarrheal disease, and higher income appears, paradoxically, to increase the probability of diarrheal disease.
Breastfeeding is associated strongly with decreased probability of diarrhea. Oddly, bottle feeding (once breastfeeding is controlled) also appears to decrease diarrheal
disease, suggesting that mixed feeding, in this group,
is associated with the least diarrhea.

In the next analysis, exclusive uses of bottle or
breast as the source of milk were included as independent
variables, replacing the other feeding variables. In
Nairobi, exclusive bottle feeding was positively associated with the probability of diarrheal disease, but the
p value fell just short of significance (p=.056). In
no other site were the exclusive feeding variables significantly associated with morbidity outcomes. In fact,

the labels "exclusive breastfeeding" and "exclusive bottle feeding" must be used with caution in these analyses. Because of the extensive early food supplementation found in these sites, virtually no children in the age range chosen for this analysis were solely milkfed. The entire "exclusive breastfed" group, therefore, can be assumed also to have had food in the diet. In addition, since many mothers, especially in Semarang and Nairobi, continued to breastfeed substantially even after adding bottles, a protective effect of breastfeeding may also have existed in the "not exclusively breastfed" group.

In a final analysis, feeding history was examined in relation to morbidity. Two variables were chosen: breastfed three months, which describes whether breastfeeding lasted at least three months or not, and bottle by two months, which records whether the child was fed with a bottle on a regular basis by the age of two months or not. Using these variables, the analysis demonstrates that in Bangkok, upper respiratory infection is more probable in those children bottlefed before two months. The paradoxical effect of income on diarrhea persists in Bogotá, and better water supply and higher socioeconomic status are again highly associated with lower probability of diarrhea in Nairobi.

A summary of the results of all these analyses is given in Table 11.4. The feeding variables are significantly associated with morbidity outcomes in all sites and for both diseases but with no strong consistent pattern. Interestingly, the association is as frequent for upper respiratory infection as for the more intuitively linked diarrheal disease. For upper respiratory disease, three of the four variables significantly associated in any analyses are feeding variables. For diarrhea, the feeding variables appear also, but so do a number of other background variables.

CHILD GROWTH AND INFANT FEEDING

The information on child growth included in the study was analyzed to determine if the pattern of feeding could be correlated with the adequacy of growth. The National Center for Health Statistics (NCHS) reference standard for growth was used for all sites in the analysis given here. As has been described previously, the age data for Semarang were collected in a manner that is not consistent with the other countries and makes comparisons of weight-for-age difficult to interpret in terms of the adequacy of growth and for comparisons with the other sites. For this reason, weight-for-height was used for initial comparisons describing the four sites.

Table 11.4   SUMMARY OF SIGNIFICANT ASSOCIATIONS
             BETWEEN ALL FEEDING/BACKGROUND VARIABLES,
             AND MORBIDITY IN LOGISTIC REGRESSION ANALYSIS

	Diarrhea	URI
Bangkok	Income (-)	Bottle by 2 months(+)
Bogotá	Breast (-) Birth order(+) Bottle (-) Age child(+) Refrigerator(-) Income(+)	Bottle(+) Mother's age(-)
Nairobi	Water/SES(-) Age of child(+) [Exclusive bottle (+)]	Breast(-)
Semarang	Bottle feeding(+)	0

Table 11.5   DISTRIBUTION OF WEIGHTS-FOR-HEIGHT
             PERCENT OF NATIONAL CENTER FOR HEALTH
             STATISTICS STANDARD

	Bangkok	Bogotá	Nairobi	Semarang
<80	3	2	5	4
80- 89	10	5	9	18
90- 99	28	19	21	35
100-109	32	37	26	28
110-119	18	24	18	10
120+	10	14	22	5

The percent of the population with weight-for-height less
than 90 percent of the NCHS standard ranged from 7 percent
in Bogota to 22 percent in Semarang (Table 11.5).

Table 11.6   PERCENTAGE DISTRIBUTION OF Z SCORES OF
              WEIGHT-FOR-AGE, FEMALES, BANGKOK

		Age in Months				
Z-score	0-2	3-5	6-8	9-12	Total %	(n)
< -2.0	0	0.6	2.4	10.1	3.3	(21)
-1.99 to 0	29.6	33.9	67.6	67.3	51.2	(313)
.01 to 1.99	60.2	60.3	28.2	22.1	41.4	(253)
> 2	10.2	5.2	1.8	0.0	3.9	(24)
Total (%)	100.0	100.0	100.0	99.5	99.8	(611)
(n)	(108)	(174)	(170)	(159)		

The percentile of the NCHS standard weight for age was calculated for each child in Bangkok and the corresponding Z-score was calculated for each centile. Examination of the Z-score distribution by age (Tables 11.6, 11.7) reveals that, up to the end of the fifth month, the percentage more than two standard deviations below the mean was very small, 1 percent or less. The percentage more than two standard deviations below the mean increased progressively in babies in the 6-8 month and 9-12 month groups for both sexes. The proportion in each age group with Z-scores in the range of 0 to -1.99 was about a third up to the fifth month of life and increased substantially to over 60 percent among those six to twelve months of age. When Bangkok infants were classified as currently receiving breastmilk or other milks and the mean weight was plotted for each group by age interval, no differences were observed in weight by feeding pattern.

A similar analysis was carried out on the data from Semarang. Each infant was classified according to whether breastfeeding was continued for at least three or nine months. Comparisons were made of the mean weight by the age of the child for those who were breastfed up to three months or were not and for those who were breastfed nine months or were not. No differences were seen in the growth of those with longer or shorter periods of breastfeeding

Table 11.7 PERCENTAGE DISTRIBUTION OF Z SCORES OF WEIGHT-FOR-AGE, MALES, BANGKOK

	Age in Months				
Z-score	0-2	3-5	6-8	9-12	Total % (n)
< -2.0	1.0	0.9	5.4	13.0	5.4 (37)
-1.99 to 0	28.7	37.7	62.4	65.3	50.7 (350)
.01 to 1.99	63.4	59.4	31.2	20.5	41.8 (289)
> 2	6.9	1.9	1.0	1.2	2.1 (15)
Total (%)	100.0	100.0	100.0	100.0	100.0 (691)
(n)	(101)	(212)	(202)	(176)	

regardless of the infant's age at the time of the interview. There was no difference in the results of the analysis for three or nine months of breastfeeding (Table 11.8).

To examine this issue in another way, the percent of babies whose weight was less than the tenth percentile weight-for-age was calculated where possible (Bangkok, Bogotá, and Nairobi): currently bottlefed and currently breastfed babies were examined separately. In Bangkok and Bogotá, slightly more than 10 percent of the children had weights less than the tenth percentile, regardless of feeding pattern. Less than ten percent of the Nairobi children fell below the tenth percentile whether bottlefed or not. On the other hand, fully 29 percent of those not currently breastfeeding were below the tenth percentile in weight-for-age (Table 11.9).

A regression analysis (not shown), employing the same independent variables as the morbidity analysis, demonstrated that in Nairobi breastfeeding was significantly associated with not being below the tenth percentile in weight-for-age. There were no significant predictors of being less than tenth percentile weight for age in Bangkok and Bogotá.

Table 11.8   MEAN WEIGHT-FOR-AGE (KG.) BY BREASTFEEDING
AT 3 MONTHS AND 9 MONTHS, SEMARANG

Current Age	Breastfed 3 months		Breastfed 9 months	
	Yes	No	Yes	No
3 mos.	5.8	5.13	--	--
4 mos.	6.35	5.45	--	--
5 mos.	6.86	7.06	--	--
6 mos.	6.89	7.29	--	--
7 mos.	7.17	7.05	--	--
8 mos.	7.47	7.50	--	--
9 mos.	8.04	7.65	8.01	8.10
10 mos.	7.76	7.00	7.77	7.23
11 mos.	8.09	9.45	8.21	8.11
12 mos.	8.25	8.40	8.23	8.39
13 mos.	--	--	7.71	8.94
14 mos.	--	--	8.34	9.34
15 mos.	--	--	9.09	9.95

Table 11.9   PERCENTAGE OF INFANTS WITH WEIGHT-FOR-AGE
LESS THAN TENTH PERCENTILE BY CURRENT
FEEDING METHOD

	Any Breastfeeding		Any Bottle Feeding	
	Yes	No	Yes	No
Bangkok	12	14	14	12
Bogotá	11	12	11	12
Nairobi	8	29	9	9

CONCLUSION

Analyses have revealed evidence for a protective
effect of breastfeeding on morbidity. It is noteworthy
that upper respiratory infection appears to be at least
as, if not more, affected by feeding patterns as diarrheal
disease. Another interesting point is that, in Bangkok,
higher income confers no health advantage on the whole:

the background variables alone show no relationship to diarrhea. When bottle feeding and breastfeeding are entered as variables, however, low income does become a predictor of diarrheal disease. This can be taken to mean that the expected health advantage of higher income only shows up when feeding pattern is controlled, that is, upper-income women are more likely to be using suboptimal methods of feeding and, in effect, dissipating their income advantage for health.

It is striking that in none of these analyses does maternal education appear to be significantly associated with better health outcome. Since these sites are completely separate and have different educational and morbidity patterns, there is no clear reason why maternal education has no predictive significance in any site. One mechanism may be that, among these urban populations, information transmission and literacy are high enough to improve infant health for most of the population. Thus, beyond a modest level of education, further increase in schooling may make little difference in health outcome.

There seem to be essentially no perceptible effects of feeding patterns on growth in these data. This may occur because growth effects are, in fact, the result of an accumulation of morbidity effects. Thus, impacts of feeding patterns on morbidity may be discernable before an aggregate effect on growth is observable, especially in the early months of life. It also may be that even children who are normal in weight-for-age do suffer some excess morbidity if they are not fed optimally. This need not be of sufficient frequency or severity to have a measurable effect on growth.

Children in Nairobi do appear to be at a significant growth disadvantage if not breastfed. It is not clear whether those children who are not breastfeeding are, in some fundamental way, different from the rest of the cohort or whether the deficiency in weight is truly a result of lack of breastfeeding. It is possible, of course, that Nairobi is different from the other sites in this regard. It is plausible that it is more detrimental not to be breastfed in Nairobi than in Bangkok, Bogotá, or Semarang. This would be consistent with the very large differences in the determinants of morbidity shown in the other analyses: for example, in Semarang, only one significant association appeared in eight separate analyses of diarrhea and upper respiratory infection, whereas in Bogotá eight different variables were significantly associated with morbidity in the same exact analyses.

It is obvious, therefore, that although something is known of the effects of family background, and feeding patterns on morbidity in the aggregate, the interaction of these factors is different in each site. Certainly, no analysis of the determinants of morbidity should be considered complete without attention to feeding practices. Not only are feeding patterns important in understanding the determinants of morbidity, but it may significantly modify our understanding of how other important variables, such as income and education, interact to affect morbidity patterns.

NOTES

1. Task Force on the Assessment of the Scientific Evidence Relating to Infant-Feeding Practices and Infant Health. Pediatrics. Vol. 74, No. 4, October 1984 Supplement.

2. Cross-sectional studies have been criticized because breastfed babies who are experiencing health problems may be selectively changed to infant formula and thus the results may be biased in favor of breastfed infants. This problem, if it does occur, would be no more serious for cross-sectional designs than for other types of studies. More significantly, cross-sectional designs, such as those used here, cannot reveal the temporal dimensions of the relationships among their variables, and any associations that are observed may or may not be causal.

3. Salter scales for weighing were obtained from UNICEF. The methods were those recommended by D. B. Jelliffe and E. F. P. Jelliffe, Human Milk in the Modern World. (London: Oxford University Press, 1978). Interviewers were trained by senior investigators with experience in field anthropometry. The scales were standardized and calibrated regularly under the direction of survey supervisors. Recumbent length was measured using portable measuring boards (infantometers) designed for this purpose. The same brand was used in each site.

12 Summary

Beverly Winikoff

It would not be difficult to emphasize in summary the usual conclusion of comparative multi-site studies: that each place is different and that, to be useful, policies and programs must conform to the realities of each location. On the other hand, an opportunity exists here to discover important similarities among these sites. Some of these similarities may be obvious (but also easily overlooked) such as the large preponderance of women who <u>do</u> breastfeed and the generally positive attitudes of mothers toward nursing. Even with regard to the details of nursing and supplementation some notable similarities can be observed.

The assumption of regional similarities in culture and outlook usually leads to grouping countries geographically for descriptive purposes. The data from this study, however, demonstrate that striking parallels can be found across regions and important differences exist within the one region (Southeast Asia) in which there were two study sites. A typology of feeding patterns based on the information gathered by the Infant Feeding Study would group Bangkok and Bogotá (with shorter breastfeeding, more early bottles, shorter weaning periods, and less exclusive breastfeeding) on the one hand, and Nairobi and Semarang on the other. Although obviously culturally, historically, and geographically quite different, Bangkok and Bogotá mothers choose feeding patterns more similar to each other than to those chosen in Nairobi and Semarang. Thus, many of the influences on overall patterns of feeding are probably due to variables which are superimposed on culture and traditional norms for child care.

This study has identified several of these issues, including the effect of modern medical practices and of the adaptation of women to modern labor force conditions, as well as the availability of alternative infant feeding products. All of these factors are important conditioning elements which act on mothers to alter traditional patterns of feeding children, producing the feeding patterns discovered in these four sites in the early 1980s. Although not designed for the purpose, the studies have also been able to demonstrate certain other relationships which have been proven by other studies. In the first place, the relationship between feeding practices and postpartum ammenorrhea is obvious in these populations. Not only the fact of breastfeeding but the frequency of feeding and the extent of supplementation have effects on the timing of a woman's return to fertility after childbirth. With regard to child health, evidence in this study reinforces the clear conclusion in the medical literature that too early supplementation, lack of breastfeeding, and contamination of infant foods causes increased morbidity. Although neither fertility nor morbidity issues were the subject of this study (and the samples studied were not ideal for gaining information on these topics), the data do contain observable effects demonstrated elsewhere in the medical literature.

Perhaps the most striking fact about infant feeding is the high level of initiation of lactation among all these urban women (Table 12.1). For each sample, 90 percent or more of women began breastfeeding after childbirth. For all major subgroups of women, initiation of lactation was almost equal, although there is a general tendency for more urbanized, upper-income women to be less likely to begin breastfeeding. A special subgroup of women, those whose babies had medical

Table 12.1   SAMPLE CHARACTERISTICS BY SITE

Percent	Bangkok	Bogotá	Nairobi	Semarang
Ever Breastfed	90	97	97	95
Primiparous	43	38	26	25
>5 Children	3	3	11	12
No Schooling	5	2	18	14
Born in City	43	36	22	54[*]
Working for Pay	35	25[**]	16	25
Institutional Birth	98	90	78	44
Breastfed 6 Months	54	56	86	86
Breastfed 9 Months	48	48	31	18
Bottle by 2 Months	48	48	31	18

[*]Includes a recently incorporated rural area
[**]Outside the home only

problems immediately after birth, appear to be at particular risk of not initiating breastfeeding at all. Yet,
even among these women, most do begin breastfeeding.

The second obvious and important feeding pattern,
observable in all four sites, is the high rate of very
early supplementation of breastfeeding. The acceptability of other milks in contrast to foods for use as early
supplements varies among the sites, but both sorts of
supplements are quite common in all groups. In Bangkok
and Bogotá, bottle feeding appears to be used in a
manner more similar to its use in modernized western
cultures: as a substitute for breastfeeding. Mothers
in Nairobi seem quite comfortable using milks of all
kinds as supplements to breastfeeding and appear to view
the use of such products as part of the introduction
of children to a wide array of adult foods. The bottle
appears to be compatible with continued breastfeeding
and not necessarily a substitute for it. The women in
Semarang seem less disposed to use supplementary milks
than the mothers in the other sites, but they very often add semi-solid foods to infants' diets. Although
in all sites early bottle feeding tends to predict
shorter than average breastfeeding, the mothers in
Bangkok and Bogotá appear to wean much more quickly once
bottle feeding is introduced. For these mothers, maintenance of partial breastfeeding along with bottle
feeding seems to be more problematic.

Aside from the overall findings of high initiation of lactation and early supplementation, the
specifics of feeding patterns varied markedly among the
groups. For each of these four samples the median durations of breastfeeding were quite different. Again,
Bangkok and Bogotá mothers evidence relatively shorter
durations (6.01 and 6.91 months) while mothers in
Nairobi and Semarang tend to breastfeed quite a bit
longer (16.2 and 20.4 months). Breastfeeding duration
is also reflected in the percentage of women who
breastfed for six months or more. Based on children who
had already attained at least six months of age, the
propensity for prolonged breastfeeding is markedly different in the sites. Again Bangkok and Bogotá for one
cluster; Semarang and Nairobi the other. Slightly more
than half of Bangkok and Bogotá women with children
older than six months have breastfed for that long or
longer, whereas in Nairobi and Semarang over 85 percent
of mothers with children six months or older have
breastfed at least as long as six months. Similar differences are noted when nine months of breastfeeding
is assessed: in Bogotá, about 35 percent of mothers with
children over nine months have breastfed that long and
in Bangkok, 48 percent, whereas 77 percent of Nairobi

mothers and 79 percent of Semarang mothers with children over nine months have breastfed for at least nine months.

Early supplementation with bottles is also different among the four sites, and in a similar pattern. Only 18 percent of mothers in Semarang and 31 percent of mothers in Nairobi have introduced bottles by two months. In Bangkok and Bogotá, however, the percentage is approximately 50 percent at two months. By four months, less than one-quarter of Semarang mothers have introduced bottles to the diets of their infants whereas 60 percent of Bangkok mothers and 73 percent of Bogotá mothers have done so.

The socioeconomic composition of the four study groups of mothers varies (Table 12.1). This is in part because of the different sampling strategies and in part because of the very different nature of the populations studied. The data indicate substantially higher fertility among women in the Nairobi and Semarang samples than among women in the Bangkok or Bogotá groups. In the former sites, there were many more women of parity 6 or greater (Semarang, 12%; Nairobi, 11%; Bangkok, 3%; and Bogotá, 3%). Many more mothers were primiparous in Bangkok (43%) and Bogotá (38%) than in Nairobi (26%) and Semarang (25%). Similarly, there were educational differences among the samples. No education whatever was reported much more frequently among the Nairobi and Semarang mothers than among the Bangkok and Bogotá women. Less than 5 percent of women both in Bangkok and Bogotá reported no education whereas 18 percent of those in Nairobi and 14 percent of those in Semarang reported no schooling. These differences cannot be accounted for solely by differences in whether or not the high-est income groups were included in the sample since the Bogotá and Nairobi groups were truncated and excluded upper income women whereas the Bangkok and Semarang groups did not.

In Nairobi, the overwhelming majority of mothers were not born in the city. This tendency was also true in Bogotá and in Bangkok but not quite as strongly. In Semarang, slightly more than half the mothers reported city birth, but, as described earlier, about one-third of the sample were really from a rural district which was recently incorporated in an urban area. Mothers born there also reported birth in the city although they are essentially rural women.

Surprisingly, most births in three of the four sites took place in institutional settings. This ranged from virtually all births in Bangkok and Bogotá (98%

and 90%) to 78 percent of the births in Nairobi and just under half of the births in Semarang. The tendency of mothers to report current work for pay was also very different in the four sites. The least propensity to work was evidenced by the women in Nairobi: only 16 percent overall reported working in any sort of income-earning capacity. Bangkok mothers reported the most work. Thirty-five percent were earning income and about 25 percent were doing so outside the home. About one-quarter of Bogotá women also worked outside the home. In Semarang, about 25 percent were working for pay--in or outside the home--when interviewed. It should be remembered, however, that the cohort of women in Semarang and Nairobi had, on average, substantially older children.

Very few of the socioeconomic variables have significant associations with the probability of initiating breastfeeding, although in Thailand, both Bangkok birth and older age of the mother predicted a lower likelihood of ever breastfeeding. A shorter duration of breastfeeding is consistently correlated with high income in Bogotá, Bangkok, and Semarang, but not in Nairobi. Having an urban-born mother reduces the likelihood of longer breastfeeding in Bogotá, Bangkok, and Nairobi. Early bottles are associated with higher income in Bangkok, Nairobi, and Semarang. This is not the case in Bogotá, however, and in Bogotá there is a paradoxical relationship which may help to explain the lack of association with income: more educated women are less likely to introduce early bottles than women with less education. For the other three sites, education seems to have no independent effect on the probability of introduction of early milk bottles.

The effect of work for pay on mothers' feeding behaviors is a topic of much interest and relatively little factual information. It is interesting to note that among these four sites, work does not have a consistently significant independent association with shorter breastfeeding duration in two sites (Semarang and Nairobi) while it is very strongly associated with curtailed breastfeeding in the other two (Bogotá and Bangkok). In Semarang, work is associated with a tendency to use bottle feeding earlier in the life of the child, but, in Nairobi, even this association is not present. In the two sites in which work was an important determinant of duration of breastfeeding, it was overwhelmingly associated with truncated breastfeeding and early introduction of the bottle.

In these two sites, Bangkok and Bogotá, it was discovered that employed women and women not working for pay responded quite differently to the effects of other influences. It appeared that working women were so strongly pushed toward early introduction of bottles and curtailment of breastfeeding that very few of the other socioeconomic or health services variables had any effect on breastfeeding duration. Women who did not work outside the home in Bangkok and in Bogotá appeared more sensitive to the interplay of various other factors which could influence their feeding choices. In particular, they seemed much more sensitive to the effects of health services' practices on feeding chores.

In all sites, the study was able to identify certain aspects of mothers' contacts with the health services that were associated with shortened duration of breastfeeding or greater propensity to introduce early bottles, independent of all other background and employment factors. In Bogotá, for women who did not work, the practice of rooming-in was associated with greater breastfeeding durations, even controlling for all associated background socioeconomic variables. In Bangkok, more in-hospital contact between mother and baby was associated with a significantly increased chance of ever breastfeeding and a decreased chance of introducing bottles by two months. This was so for the entire sample and for working as well as non-working mothers analyzed separately. For mothers who were not employed outside the home, receiving a sample of infant formula in the hospital was associated with lower likelihood of breastfeeding for at least three months. In Nairobi, hospital birth was associated with a decreased tendency to breastfeed for six or nine months duration, even after controlling for socioeconomic status, education, parity, and urban birth of mothers. In Semarang, independent of all other factors, having a birth attended by a physician was associated with shortened breastfeeding and earlier introduction of bottles.

The ways in which health service practices are translated into earlier supplementation and greater use of bottle feeding have been discussed in each of the site reports. It is an important finding of this work, however, that in each site one can identify significant negative practices associated with modern Western health care in terms of their effects on infant feeding patterns. It appears, in general, that contact with more technology and more Western-type maternity services is associated with less breastfeeding and earlier introduction of bottle milk. On the other hand, increased contact between mother and baby seems to override, to some extent, the propensity for modern medical care to result in less breastfeeding and more supplementation.

One of the reasons for the strong association between health service practices and shortened breastfeeding may be the relationship documented between the health services and the sellers of commercial infant foods. It appears that a strong commitment to marketing through the health system has been made by sellers of infant formula. All four marketing sub-studies identified relationships between commercial marketers and the health services, specifically with physicians but also (and perhaps more ominously) with traditional midwives and pharmacists. These were interpreted as attempts to increase the sales of infant formula products through their use in the health system and through the recommendation of health professionals. Many of these activities of the sellers of infant formulas and other infant feeding products are permitted under the standards established by the WHO International Code of Marketing of Breastmilk Substitutes.

There was a high level of government awareness of the existence and provisions of the International Code in all four countries. In each case, government appears to have taken steps to implement the Code, especially with reference to its provisions restricting media advertisement directly to mothers. The marketing of formulas and other infant products through the health services, however, has seemed to constitute a successful method of circumventing the prohibition of media advertising. In the first place, media advertising in the past appears to have left its mark in at least three of the four sites, with extremely high recall of formula advertising even though such advertisements had not been in the media for many years. Only in Semarang was the market "young" enough that many mothers had not felt the effects of formula advertising. In all four sites, however, the ability of sellers of infant products to reach mothers through the health services and health professionals was manifest.

The attitudes of mothers toward breastfeeding appeared to be shaped by a variety of factors including, but not limited to, the quantifiable background variables and the mothers' experiences in the labor force, their contacts with the health service, and their exposure to sellers of infant feeding products. Beyond all these influences, the cultural context through which mothers interpret their experiences has a great bearing on their attitudes about infant feeding and specifically about breastfeeding. It was noted that in each of the four sites mothers seemed to have quite different orientation toward the meaning of breast and bottle feeding and the benefits and/or disadvantages of each for their infants.

In all four sites, women expressed positive feelings about breastfeeding and the certainty that it was the most beneficial way to feed young babies. Beyond this initial endorsement of breastfeeding by mothers and the intellectual assessment of breastmilk as the best food, some of the women were clearly ambivalent about breastfeeding and others were also positive about bottle feeding. In Bogotá, women tended to be unsure of their ability to produce "good" breastmilk and seemed to have the notion that they needed to "help" their breastmilk with something else. They were constantly afraid of having spoiled, contaminated, or otherwise hurt the quality of their milk by their own daily activities or by having been under stress, having eaten the wrong food, or having been sick. This led to the concern with a need to add other sources of food to keep the child healthy. Similar issues were evident in the ways these women chose to bottlefeed. They were constantly looking for better mixtures to put in bottles, adding herbs and other food to increase nutritive and health qualities. The cultural context thus provided a ready environment for the introduction of bottle milks as a new solution to problems of infant nutrition.

Bangkok mothers appeared generally positively oriented toward breastfeeding and, in fact, were extremely committed breastfeeders. They also, however, had extremely positive attitudes toward bottle feeding, viewing bottle milk as modern, healthful, and likely to increase the robustness of their babies. They viewed the addition of milk almost as one might a tonic and often expressed the sentiment that a baby fed breastmilk plus other bottled milk would probably enjoy the best health status.

Mothers in Semarang seemed the most traditional breastfeeders, with the least exposure to bottle feeding practices or messages. Their attitudes to breastfeeding were quite positive, and they had surprisingly little information or opinion on bottle feeding. Many women saw bottles as an unnecessary modern "invention" and could not understand why they were needed. In the two Southeast Asian sites, where milk is not a common element in the adult diet, it seemed more difficult for mothers to distinguish between infant formula and other milks and, in some ways, less natural to introduce these milks into the child's diet.

The market environment was dominated by one or two major sellers in Bogotá and Nairobi. The most extremely competitive marketing situation was Bangkok where there were many brands of formula and other milk, all competing for the attention of consumers with easily altered purchasing habits and a great deal of sophistication about consumer issues. In Semarang, the penetration of consumer demand for infant milks was much lower, and mothers seemed to respond to price more than quality of the different types of milks.

Examination of the available information on the factors influencing mothers' infant feeding decisions suggests that urbanization and high socioeconomic status may create disincentives to traditional patterns of breastfeeding. On the other hand, several influences were identified which are susceptible to change and which, therefore, have become the major focus of recommendations for policy to improve infant feeding practices.

It seems, from many perspectives, that the most appropriate places for intervention are the health services themselves. This is true, in part, because it can be demonstrated in all sites that health services have an influence on mothers' decisions about infant feeding. It is also true, apparently, that infant feeding product marketing is becoming increasingly common through the health services. It is thus imperative that medical professionals be well informed about infant feeding and the implications of different choices for the health of mothers and babies. Health workers need to be able to evaluate the information and suggestions given to them by the marketers of infant feeding products. In addition, an informed health professional will be more likely to develop and carry out policies within health institutions which will support breastfeeding mothers. One of the most serious issues identified in this study is the lack of information and support from health professionals (particularly physicians) for mothers who are breastfeeding.

Finally, employed women, although they are a distinct minority in each of these cities, have particularly serious problems in maintaining appropriate infant feeding patterns. Suggestions need to be developed and experimental programs created which would test different ways of helping mothers who must return to their jobs early in the lives of their infants. Among other things, maternity leave and day care, as well as income and/or food supplements, are suggested as ways to help groups of mothers. For mothers who must be separated from infants for long periods of the day, strategies for managing mixed breast and bottle feeding, when necessary, should be taught both to health advisers and to mothers. Although maintenance of breastfeeding after supplementary milks have been introduced is relatively common in two of the cultures studied, it appears to be much less possible for mothers in the other two places. How mothers can learn to continue breastfeeding even after adding bottle milks is an area which requires further exploration.

One of the most common concerns of mothers, identified in each of these study sites, is the perception of insufficient milk. Further studies are needed of the biological/psychological/sociological issues involved in the insufficient milk syndrome. From the data collected in this study, it appears that a good deal of milk "insufficiency" may be a result (and not a cause) of early supplementation of babies. Mothers often misperceive the adequacy of their milk supply and add unnecessary supplemental milk. This then decreases the amount of milk produced because of decreased demand from the baby. The extent to which health professional advice is responsible for suggesting or confirming mothers' suspicions of insufficient milk needs further assessment. In addition, more work is needed to define the instances of true, biological milk insufficiency and to learn more about the cause, cure, and, if possible, prevention.

This work suggests that women have very positive attitudes toward breastfeeding and, in fact, do initiate breastfeeding to an extraordinary extent. How to help mothers to maintain breastfeeding (and to breastfeed exclusively for as long as appropriate) seems to be the central problem identified by the feeding patterns described in the study. From an examination of the pattern of influences on mothers, several suggestions can be made. There appear to be many influences which act similarly on women in all four sites. On the other hand, there are important differences in some of the interactions and some of the feeding patterns identified. Understanding some of the consistencies among all four sites, such as maternal commitment to breastfeeding and the influence of health services, as well as the differences, such as the effect of employment outside the home and the acceptability of continuing to breastfeed and bottlefeed at the same time, will make possible the development of reasonable policy to assist women in these and other settings. Societal factors identified as important determinants of infant feeding patterns act upon infants only through their impact on the women who care for them. In the end, after all, it is the choices of mothers which determine how infants will be fed.

Bibliography

B˜agenholm, G. B. Kristiansson, and A. A. Nasher.
"Child Feeding Habits in the People's Democratic
Republic of Yemen. II. Supplementary Foods and
Weaning Patterns," Journal of Tropical Pediatrics
1987;33(5):278-83.

Baer, E. C. "Breastfeeding: Ultimately Appropriate,"
World Education Reports. No. 19, 1976.

Barros, F. C., C. G. Victora, and J. P. Vaughan.
"Breastfeeding and Socioeconomic Status in Southern
Brazil," Acta Paediatr Scand 1986;75(4):558-62.

Berg, A. The Nutrition Factor. Washington:
Brookings Institution, 1973.

Bergevin, Y., C. Dougherty, and M. S. Kramer.
"Infant Formula Samples Shorten the Duration of
Breastfeeding," Lancet 1983;1(8334):1148-51.

Bongaarts, J. and R. Potter. Fertility, Biology and
Behavior: An Analysis of the Proximate Determinants.
New York: Academic Press, 1983.

Breast Feeding Versus Bottle Feeding. A Brief for
Policy Makers in Developing Countries," Nursing
Journal of India 1984;75(2):32-3.

Campbell, C. E. "Nestle and Breast vs. Bottle
Feeding: Mainstream and Marxist Perspectives," Int
Journal of Health Services 1984;14(4):547-67.

Carballo, M.   "Social and Behavioral Aspects of
Breast Feeding," Journal of Biosocial Science
(1977);Supplement 4:57-68.

Chavalittamrong, B. and P. Jirapinyo.   "The Weight of
Thai Infants Exclusively Breast-fed and Formula-fed
From Birth to Four Months," Journal of the Thai
Medical Association 1987;70(5):247-51.

Chetley, A.   "Marketing Breastmilk Substitutes,"
Letters to the Editor, Lancet 1980:7-8.

Corsini, C. "Is the fertility reducing effect of
lactation really substantial?" in Natural Fertility,
ed. Leridon and J. Menken, (eds.) IUSSP Proceedings,
1979, pp. 197-215.

Cresecio, E., and M. S. Herbert.   "Morbidity and
Nutritional Status of Breastfed and Bottlefed
Filipino Infants," Fertility Determinants Resource
Notes 1980;15.

David, C. B. and P. H. David.   "Bottle-feeding and
Malnutrition in a Developing Country: The 'Bottle-
starved' Baby," Journal of Tropical Paediatrics
1984;30(3):159-64.

De Young, J.   Village Life in Modern Thailand.
Berkeley & Los Angeles: University of California
Press, 1955.

Delgado, H., J. Delonge-Desnoeck, and C. Robyn.
"Serum-Prolactation in Long-Lasting Lactation
Amenorrhea," Lancet (1976);2:288-89.

Delvoye, P.   M. Demaegd, and J. Delonge-Desnoeck.
"The influence of nursing and of previous lactation
experience on serum prolactin in lactating mothers.
Journal of Biosocial Sciences, 9 (1979):447-51, 1977.

Doyal, L. and I. Pennell.   The Political Economy of
Health.   Boston: South End Pr., 1981.

Engle, P.   Child Care Strategies of Working and Non-
Working Women in Rural and Urban Guatemala.   (Cal
Poly State University, San Luis Obispo, California,
September 30, 1987). Unpublished paper.

Fildes, V. "Neonatal Feeding Practices and Infant
Mortality During the 18th Century," Journal of
Biosocial Science (1980);12:313-24.

Forman, M. R. "Review of Research on the Factors Associated with Choice and Duration of Infant Feeding in Less-developed Countries," Pediatrics 1984;74(4 Pt 2):667-94.

Geertz, H. The Javanese Family: a Study of Kinship and Socialization. Glencoe, Illinois: Free Press, 1961.

Goodenough, W. H. "Cultural Anthropology and Linguistics," Report of the Seventh Annual Round Table Meeting on Linguistics and Language Study. P. Garvin, ed. Washington, D.C.: Georgetown University, 1957.

Greiner, T., P. Van Esterik, and M. C. Latham. "The Insufficient Milk Syndrome: An Alternative Explanation," Medical Anthropology 1981;5.
Greiner, T. The Promotion of Bottle Feeding by Multinational Corporations. Cornell International Nutrition Monograph Series, No. 2, 1975.

Greiner, T. "Influence of Infant Food Advertising on Infant Feeding Practices in St. Vincent," International Journal of Health Services 1982;12:53-75.

Greiner, T., S. Almroth, and M. C. Latham. The Economic Value of Breastfeeding - Ghana and the Ivory Coast. Cornell International Nutrition Monograph Series No. 6, 1979.

Gussler, J.D. and L. H. Briesemeister. "The Insufficient Milk Syndrome: A Biocultural Explanation," Medical Anthropology 1980;4:4-24.

Gussler, J. D., M. A. Wao-Lun, and N. M. Smith (eds). International Breastfeeding Compendium 3rd Ed. Ohio: Ross Labs, 1984.

Guthrie, G. M. "Infant Formula Samples and Breast Feeding Among Philippine Urban Poor," Social Science and Medicine. 1985;20:713.

Haaga, J. G. "Evidence of a Reversal of the Breastfeeding Decline in Peninsular Malaysia," American Journal of Public Health 1986; 76(3):245-51.

Habicht, J-P., J. DaVanzo and W.P. Butz. Does Breastfeeding Really Save Lives? - or are Apparent Benefits Due to Biases? American Journal of Epidemiology 1985;123(2):279-90.

Habicht, J-P. and K.M. Rasmussen (1985). Model for
Analysis of the Relationship Between Breastfeeding
Data and Postpartum Anovulation Data. In J. Dobbing
(ed.), Maternal Nutrition and Lactational
Infertility. Raven Press: New York, 1985.

Hamilton, S., B. Popkin, and D. Spicer. Women and
Nutrition in Third World Countries. New York:
Praeger, 1984.

Harfouche, J. K. Breast-feeding Patterns: A Review
of Studies in the Eastern Mediterranean Region.
Alexandria, Egypt: World Health Organization.
Regional Office for the Eastern Mediterranean, 1982

Hay, Margaret Jean. "Luo Women and Economic Change
during the Colonial Period," in Women in Africa, N.
Hafkin and E. Bay,(ed) California: Stanford
University Press 1976.

Helsing, Elisabet and Savage F. King. Breastfeeding
in Practice: A Manual for Health Workers. London:
Oxford University Press, 1982.

Hendrickse, R. G. "Some Thoughts about Infant
Feeding," Annals of Tropical Paediatrics
1983;3(4):163-8.

Holland, B. "Breast-feeding and Infectious
Diarrhea," JAMA 1987;257(24):3361-2.

Howie, P. W. and A. S. McNeilly. "Breastfeeding and
Postpartum Ovulation," IPPF Medical Bulletin. 1982
16(2):1-3.

Huffman, S. L. "Determinants of Breastfeeding in
Developing Countries: Overview and Policy
Implications," Studies in Family Planning.
1984;15:170-83.

Hull, V. J. "Breast-feeding and Fertility: The
Sociocultural Context," International Journal of
Gynecology and Obstetrics 1987;25 Suppl:77-109.

Hull, V. "Women Doctors and Family Health Care: Some
Lessons from Rural Java," Studies in Family Planning
10, 11/12,(1979): 315-25.

Hull, V. and M. Simpson (eds). Breastfeeding, Child
Health and Child Spacing: Cross-Cultural
Perspectives. London: Croom Helm Ltd., 1985.

Isenalumhe, A. E. and O. Oviawe. "Prelacteal Feeds and Breast-feeding Problems," Indian Journal of Pediatrics 1987;54(1)"89-96.

Jain, A. K. "Demographic Aspects of Lactation and Postpartum Amenorrhea," Demography India (1970);7:255-71.

Jain, A. and J. Bongaarts. "Breastfeeding: Patterns Correlates and Fertility Effects," Studies in Family Planning 12(3), 1981.

Jason, J. M., P. Nieburg, and J. S. Marks. "Mortality and Infectious Disease Associated with Infant-feeding Practices in Developing Countries," Pediatrics 1984;74(4 Pt 2):702-27.

Jay, Robert R. Javanese Villagers: Social Relations in Rural Modiokuto. Cambridge: MIT Press, 1969.

Jelliffe D. B. and E. F. P. Jelliffe. Human Milk in the Modern World. London: Oxford University Press, 1978.

Joseph, S. C. "The Anatomy of the Infant Formula Controversey," American Journal of Diseases of Children. 1981;135(10):889-92.

King, J. and A. Ashworth. "Historical Review of the Changing Pattern of Infant Feeding in Developing Countries: the Case of Malaysia, the Caribbean, Nigeria, and Zaire," Social Science and Medicine 1987;25(12):1307-20.

Kleinman, A. Patients and Healers in the Context of Culture. Berkeley: University of California Press, 1980.

Knodel, J., et al. "Thailand's Reproductive Revolution: Rapid Fertility Decline in a Third World Setting," Madison: University of Wisconsin Press, 1987.

Knodel, J. and N. Debavalya. "Breastfeeding in Thailand: Trends and Differentials 1969-1979," Studies in Family Planning 1980;2:355-77.

Konner, M. and C. Worthman. "Nursing Frequency, Gonadal Function and Birth Spacing among !Kung Hunter-Gatherers," Science 1980;207:788.

242 Bibliography

Laderman, C. "Symbolic and Empirical Reality: A New Approach to the Analysis of Food Avoidances," American Ethnologist 8, No. 3 (1981): pp. 468-93.

Lakhani, S. "Practical Therapeutics: Present Day Hospital Practices Influencing Breastfeeding in Nairobi, Kenya," East African Medical Journal 198461(2):163-8.

Latham, M. C. "Infant Feeding in National and International Perspective - Decline in Human Lactation," Annals of New York Academy of Science. Reprint (1977);300:197-209.
Latham, M. C. "International Perspectives on Weaning Foods: Economic and Other Implications," Academic Press, 1979.

Latham, M. C., T. C. Elliott, B. Winikoff, J. Kekovole, and P. Van Esterik. "Infant feeding in urban Kenya: A pattern of early triple nipple feeding," Journal of Tropical Pediatrics 32(1986): 276-80.

Latham, M. C. "Nutrition and Culture," in Nutrition and National Policy, ed. B. Winikoff. Cambridge: MIT Press, 1978.

Latham, M. C. The Decline of the Breast: An Examination of Its Impact on Fertility and Health and Its Relation to Socioeconomic Status. Cornell International Nutrition Monograph Series, No. 10 (1982).

Laukaran, V. H. and B. Winikoff. "Contraceptive Use, Amenorrhea, and Breastfeeding in Postpartum Women," Studies in Family Planning. 1985;16:293-301.

Leon de Leal M. and C. D. Deere. "Rural Women in the Development of Capitalism of Colombian Agriculture," Signs 5, no.1 (Autumn 1979): 60-77.

Lesthaeghe, R. J. and J. Page. "The Postpartum Non-Susceptible Period," Population Studies (1980);34:143-169.

Manderson, L. "Bottlefeeding and Ideology in Colonial Malaya: The Production of Change," International Journal of Health Services. 1982;12:597-525.

Martorell, R. and C. O'Gara. Breastfeeding, Infant Health, and Socioeconomic Status. Medical Anthropology (1985);9:213-232.

Mata, L. J. The Children of Santa Maria. Cambridge, Mass: The MIT Press, 1978.

Meldrum, B. and C. Di Domenico. "Production and Reproduction. Women and Breastfeeding: Some Nigerian Examples," Social Science and Medicine 1982;16(13):1247-51.

Millman, S. "Breastfeeding and Contraception: Why the Inverse Assocation?" Studies in Family Planning 1985;16(2):61-75.

Mintz, S. W. Sweetness and Power. New York: Viking, Penguin, 1985.

Morse, J. M. "Infant Feeding in the Third World: A Critique of the Literature," Ans. Advances in Nursing Science 1982;5(1):77-88.

Mosley, W. H. (ed) Nutrition and Human Reproduction New York: Plenum Press, 1978.

Nag, M. "The Impact of Sociocultural Factors on Breastfeeding and Sexual Behavior," in Rodolfo A. Bulatao and Ronald D. Lee (eds.), Determinants of Fertility in Developing Countries. Vol. 1: Supply and Demand for Children, New York: Academic Press, 1983.

Nestlé Infant Formula Audit Commission, Quarterly Reports 1984-1986.

Notzon, F. "Trends in Infant Feeding in Developing Countries," Pediatrics 1984;(4 Pt 2):648-66.

Oakley, A. Women Confined: Towards a Sociology of Childbirth. New York: Schocken Books 1980.

Oni, G. A. "Contraceptive Use and Breastfeeding: Their Inverse Relationship and Policy Concern," East African Medical Journal 1986;63(8):522-30.

Oni, G. A. "Effects of Women's Education on Postpartum Practices and Fertility in Urban Nigeria," Studies in Family Planning 1985;16(6 Pt 1):321-31.

Papneck, H. and L. Schwede, "Earning and Spending in an Indonesia City: Family Strategies of Income Management," in A Home Divided: Women and Income in the Third World, ed. D. H. Dwyer and J. Bruce (forthcoming, Stanford University Press).

Pelto, G. H. Infant Feeding in Developing Countries-
-Beliefs and Motivations. Nutrition Foundation
Monograph Series, for International Symposium on
Infant, Childhood Feeding, Michigan State University,
1978.

Popkin, B. M., R. E. Bilsborrow, and M. E. Yamamoto.
Breastfeeding Practices in Low Income Countries:
Patterns and Determinants. Carolina Population
Center Paper, No. 11, Chapel Hill: University of
North Carolina, 1979.

Popkin, B. and S. De Jesus. Determinants of
Breastfeeding Behavior Among Rural Filipino
Households. Philippines: University of the
Philippines, 1976.

Post, J. and E. Baer. "Analyzing Complex Policy
Problems: Social Performance of the International
Infant Formula Industry," in Research in Corporate
Social Performance and Policy: A Research Annual ed.
Preston L. E. Vol. 2. Greenwich, Connecticut: Jai
Press, 1980.

Post, J. and E. Baer. "Codes of Marketing for
Breastmilk Substitutes," The Review 1980;25:52-61.

Potts, M. and S. Thapa, eds. Breast feeding and
Fertility. Cambridge, England: Galton Foundation,
1985.

Raphael, D. The Tender Gift: Breastfeeding. New
York: Schocken Books, 1976.

Report of the Task Force on the Assessment of the
Scientific Evidence Relating to Infant Feeding
Practices and Infant Health, Pediatrics Oct.
1984;74:4, Part 2:579-83.

Riordan, J. and B. A. Countryman. "Basics of
Breastfeeding. Part I. Infant Feeding Patterns Past
and Present," Jogn Nursing 1980;9(4):207-10.

Salokoski, M. [From Breast Feeding to Bottle Feeding.
An Example of the Dubious Benefits of the West in
Developing Countries] Katilolehti 1983;88(7-8):197-
206.

Seward, J. F. and M. K. Serdula. "Infant Feeding and
Infant Growth," Pediatrics 1984;74(4 Pt 2)):728-62.

Short, R. V. "Breast Feeding," Scientific American. 1984;250:35-41.

Simopoulos A. P. and G. D. Grave. "Factors Associated with the Choice and Duration of Infant Feeding Practice," Pediatrics 1984;74(4 Pt 2):603-14.

Simpson, M., H. Makil and L. Makil. "Infant Feeding among Urban Filipino Women," Fertility Determinants; Resource Notes The Population Council Jan. 1985;4.

Smart, C. and B. Smart. Women, Sexuality and Social Control. London: Routledge and Kegan Paul, 1978.

Smith, D. P. "Breastfeeding, Contraception, and Birth Intervals in Developing Countries," Studies in Family Planning 1985;16(3):154-63.

Smith, D. P. and B. Ferry. Breastfeeding Differentials. London: World Fertility Survey, 1983.

Solimano, G. and M.F. Rea. Rethinking Infant Nutrition Policies Under Changing Socio-Economic Conditions. Sao Paulo Project, 1980.

Staudt, Kathleen A. "Women Farmers and Inequities in Agricultural Services," in Women and Work in Africa, ed. E. G. Bay Boulder, Co.: Westview Press 1982.

Task Force on the Assessment of the Scientific Evidence Relating to Infant-Feeding Practices and Infant Health. Pediatrics. Vol. 74, No. 4, October 1984 Supplement.

Van Esterik, P. Beyond the Breast-Bottle Controversy. Rutgers: Rutgers University Press, (forthcoming).

Van Esterik. P. "The Cultural Context of Breastfeeding in Rural Thailand," Breastfeeding, Child Health and Child Spacing: Cross-Cultural Perspectives, ed. V. Hull and M. Simpson London: Crown Helm, 1985.

Van Esterik, P. and T. Elliott. "Infant Feeding and Style in Urban Kenya," Ecology of Food and Nutrition 18, No. 3 (1986): 183-95.

Van Esterik, P. and T. Greiner. "Breastfeeding and Women's Work: Constraints and Opportunities," Studies in Family Planning 1981: 182-95.

Van Esterik, P. Sweetened Condensed Soma: Dietary Innovation in Southeast Asia. Unpublished paper, 1979.

Van Ginneken, J. K. "Impact of Prolonged Breastfeeding on Birth Intervals and on Post-Partum Amenorrhea," in Nutrition and Human Reproduction. ed. W. H. Mosley. New York: Plenum Press, 1978.

Van Steinbergen, W. M., J. A. Kusin, C. D. With, E. Lacko, and A. A. J. Jansen "Lactation performance of mothers with contrasting nutritional status in rural Kenya," Acta Paediatr. Scand.72 (1983, 805-10). Viteri, F. E. et al. [Maternal and Infant Nutrition in Developing Countries] Boletin de la Oficina Sanitaria Panamericana. 1985;98(6):558-98.

Wharton, B. A. "Food for the Weanling: The Next Priority in Infant Nutrition," Acta Paediatr Scand [Suppl] 1986;323:96-102.

Whitehead, R. G. and A. A. Paul. "Growth Charts and the Assessment of Infant Feeding Practices in the Western World and in Developing Countries," Early Human Development 1984;9(3):187-207.

Whiting, Beatrice. "Changing Life Styles in Kenya," in Daedalus (Spring 1977): pp. 211-26.

Winikoff, B. "The Obstetricians Opportunity - Translating Breast-Is-Best From Theory to Practice," American Journal of Obstetrics and Gynecology 1980;138:105-17.

Winikoff, Beverly, et al. The Infant Feeding Study: Bangkok Site Report; The Infant Feeding Study: Bogotá Site Report; The Infant Feeding Study: Nairobi Site Report; The Infant Feeding Study: Semarang Site Report. New York: The Population Council, 1986.

World Health Organization. Contemporary Patterns of Breastfeeding. Report on WHO Collaborative study on Breastfeeding. World Health Organization, Geneva, 1981.

World Health Organization. "The prevalence and duration of breast-feeding: A critical review of available information," WHO Statistics Quarterly 2(1982): 192-216.

World Health Organization. "The dynamics of breast-feeding," WHO Chronicle 37, no. 1 (1983): 6-10.

Index

Abbott, 55
Amenorrhea, lactational, 18,75,89,97,203-14;
  and length of breastfeeding, 204-09,228;
  and frequency of breastfeeding, 206-07,228;
  and patterns of breastfeeding, 209-13

Bangkok, Thailand, 4,15-41,215-26,228-34;
  commercial marketing of infant formula in,
    166,169,172,174,175;
  hospital practices in, 147-49,153-61;
  maternal employment in, 121-31
Bidan. See Traditional birth attendant
Bogota, Colombia, 43-66,215-26,228-34;
  commercial marketing of infant formula in,
    166,172,174,177,179;
  hospital practices in, 147-49,154-58;
  maternal employment in, 121-31
Birth attendants. See specific type
Breastfeeding:
  advice on, See specific type of health care
    professional;
  attitude towards, 19,75,76,101,106,176,181-184,
    188-91,227,233,234;
  duration of, 18,25,46,52,70,71,76,85,97,229;
  and influence of health institutions' practices,
    149,150,153,156;
  and postpartum amenorrhea, 204-06;
  exclusive, 18,46,71,83,99,209-13;
  frequency of, 46,75,97,99,206-09;
  immunological properties of, 216;
  initiation of, 18,25,46,52,71,97,228;
  and modesty, 75,106;
  problems of, See Milk, human, insufficient,
    See Morbidity, breast;

weaning to, 23,28,51-3,65,77,80,103,104,108
Infant formula: <u>See</u> Marketing of infant formula;
   as status symbol, 19,105,177,184;
   attitudes towards, 75,105;
   companies, 50,55,80,110,161;
   cost of in Kenya, 81;
   dilution of, 51-2,61,64,81;
   effect of, on weaning, 22,28,29,39,52,53,77,80,
     87,104,108,116,117,149,150,229;
   and males, 47;
   and modesty, 75,106;
   and morbidity, 215-26;
   as supplement: <u>See</u> Infant foods
   types of, 55-59,80,105,110,170,194;
   "triple nipple," 88,89,181
Indonesia: <u>See</u> Semarang, Indonesia.

<u>Jamu</u>, 101,135,136
Japanese companies, 161

Kenya: <u>See</u> Nairobi, Kenya.

Labor force participation. <u>See</u> Maternal employment.

Marketing of infant formula: 165-86,233;
   advertising, 80,81,90,167,170,172,178,180,183;
   brand endorsement by health care professionals,
     55,83,155-57,167,173;
   company "detailers", 35,83,160-63;
   discharge package, 40,150;
   free formula samples, 32,35,39,81,114,148,150-156
     160,167,173-79,182,183,232;
   price competition, 167,169,170,175,178,179,235;
   promotion, indirect, 55,81,90,110,160,167,172;
   retailers, 80,90,110,167,170,179;
     breaking bulk, 110;
     misrepresentations, 179
Maternal Employment, 121-45,231;
   and characteristics of employed women, 1-6,56,
     96,108-09,123,132;
   and child care, 30,60,109,138;
   conditions of work, 133,140;
     and infant feeding practices, 30,36,38,56,
       61,64,80,81,109,116,125-43,178,232;
     effect on infant feeding practices, 139-
       41,184;
   female headed households, 141-42;
   history of, 126,127,131,132,134,135;
   maternity benefits, 30,31,40,41,56,91,122,123,
     136,137,235;
     and infant feeding patterns, 137,138,162;
   occupations of, 46,57,122;

About the Contributors

K. Okoth Agunda, Ph.D. has served for many years as the Director of the Central Bureau of Statistics in the Ministry of Planning of Kenya. CBS, under his leadership, has been responsible for a series of national nutrition surveys.

Mary Ann Castle, Ph.D. is Research Associate, Department of Anthropology, New York University. She is an anthropologist with research interests in health and fertility behavior, health care and social service utilization, and urban problems. Her area specializations are the Middle East and urban U.S.

Barry J. Cerf, Ph.D. is Senior Project Director at the Vanderveer Group. He is an anthropologist with interests in child malnutrition and immunological dysfunction. His area specializations are S.E. Asia and Latin America.

Terry Elliott, M.S. is a Program Officer at the Program for Appropriate Technology in Health (PATH) in Seattle, Washington. His interests include infant feeding, oral rehydration therapy, iodine deficiency disorders and water and sanitation. Currently, he is working on ORS marketing, distribution and promotion work under PATH's Project SUPPORT.

Virginia H. Laukaran, Dr. P.H. is Senior Program Officer, National Research Council of the National Academy of Sciences, Washington, D.C. Her specializations are in nutritional and reproductive epidemiology.

Michael C. Latham, O.B.E., M.B., M.P.H., D.T.M. and H., F.F.C.M. is Professor and Director of the Program in International Nutrition at Cornell University. He has worked extensively in Kenya, Tanzania, and other non-industrialized countries, conducting research on nutritional problems. For over 25 years, he has been a strong advocate of breastfeeding and has been concerned about its decline.

Lily W. Lee, Ph.D. is Manager of Techical Information and Statistics, CIBA Consumer Pharmacueticals, Edison, New Jersey. Dr. Lee's substantive research has been on lactational ammenhorea and infant feeding regimes.

Adela Morales de Look, M.A. is an anthropologist with a specialization in food, nutrition and public health. She is a consultant with UNICEF.

Moeljono S. Trastotenojo, M.D. is Profesor of Pediatrics, Diponegoro University, Semarang, Indonesia. Dr. Moeljono has been a leader in the field of child nutrition and infant feeding in Indonesia.

Fatimah Muis, M.D., M.Sc. is Lecturer and Researcher, Department of Nutrition, School of Medicine, Diponegoro University, Semarang, Indonesia. Dr. Muis, a pediatrician, is an authority on nutrition, child growth, and child health in Indonesia.

Belen Samper de Paredes, M.A. is on the faculty of Interdisciplinary Studies, Javeriana University, Bogotá, Colombia. She is a nutritionist with extensive experience in nutrition surveys.

James E. Post, J.D., Ph.D. is Professor of Management and Public Policy, Boston University School of Management. He has written extensively of the strategy and structure of the infant formula industry and has testified before United States congressional committees on the marketing of breastmilk substitutes in the U.S. and developing nations.

Maria Eugenia Romero, M.A. is an independent researcher and consultant anthropologist. Ms. Romero's professional interests are nutritional anthropology and medical anthropology.

Robert A. Smith, Ph.D. is Chief, Division of Chronic Disease Control, Center for Environmental Health and Injury Control, Centers for Disease Control, Atlanta, Georgia. Dr. Smith is involved in chronic disease epidemiology, and the implementation and evaluation of cancer control programs.

Giorgio Solimano, M.D. is Professor of Clinical Public Health and Nutrition at the Center for Population and Family Health, Columbia University, New York City. He has worked extensively on nutrition and child health programs and policies in developing countries. His area of specialization is Latin America.

Somchai Durongdej, Dr.P.H. is on the Faculty of Public Health, Mahidol University. He has worked for many years on the nutritional situation of children in Thailand.

Penny Van Esterik, Ph.D. is Associate Professor, Department of Anthropology, York University, Ontario, Canada. Dr. Van Esterik is a nutritional anthropologist with special interest in food in Thailand. Her area specialization is Southeast Asia.

Beverly Winikoff, M.D., M.P.H. is Senior Medical Associate at the Population Council, New York City. Dr. Winikoff has a special interest in breastfeeding and the institutional constraints facing mothers and health care professionals. She has written extensively on nutrition policy and issues of infant feeding as well as on family planning and the relationship of lactation to contraception.